'Theory is, or should be, the servant and facil[illegible] which cannot take place without it. In this book[illegible] Mik Meyer and [illegible]sen offer a sustained and disciplined example of that approach to theory. *Power and Welfare* is clear and accessible ... and will still be read when many fashionable theory texts have vanished from view.'

Richard Jenkins, Professor, Department of Sociological Studies, The University of Sheffield, UK

'This book is not only an examination of highly relevant and applicable theoretical approaches to power and welfare. It also shows the multiple forms and aspects of the play of power in the encounters between the citizen and the professional within the highly ambiguous context of contemporary liberalism. In both these respects, it is a leading example of what is emerging as a distinctive Copenhagen approach to public policy and governance.'

Mitchell Dean, Professor, University of Newcastle, Australia, and Copenhagen Business School, Denmark

Power and Welfare

In the welfare provision of today, power takes both the shape of juridical sanctions and of attractive offers for self-development. When state institutions punish criminals, remove children at risk, or enforce sanctions upon welfare recipients the question of power is immediately urgent. It is less readily evident that power is at stake when institutions educate, counsel or 'empower' citizens. This book offers a framework for understanding and analyzing these complex and implicit forms of power at play in the encounters between citizens and welfare institutions.

Taking as its starting point the idea that power takes many different shapes, and that different approaches to power may be necessary in the diverse contexts where citizens encounter welfare professionals, the book demonstrates how significant social theorists, spanning from Goffman to Foucault, can be used for inquiries into these encounters. Guiding the reader from their epistemological foundations to lucid 'state of the art' case examples, the book unpacks each of its six theoretical perspectives, and explains selected key concepts and explicates their potential for analysis. The final chapter discusses the usefulness of the theoretical approaches, their weaknesses and indicates some possibilities of theoretical integration.

Including case studies of patients, nursing home residents, unemployed people, homeless people, and young offenders, from the USA, Denmark, France, Sweden, Canada, and Australia, *Power and Welfare* is designed for students and researchers of social policy, sociology, anthropology, political science, education, nursing and social work.

Nanna Mik-Meyer is Professor in the Department of Organisation and the Director of Centre for Health Management at Copenhagen Business School, Denmark.

Kaspar Villadsen is Associate Professor in the Department of Management, Politics and Philosophy at Copenhagen Business School, Denmark.

Routledge Advances in Health and Social Policy

New titles

Health Care Reform and Globalisation
The US, China and Europe in Comparative Perspective
Edited by Peggy Watson

Power and Welfare
Understanding Citizens' Encounters with State Welfare
Nanna Mik-Meyer and Kaspar Villadsen

Forthcoming titles

International Perspectives on Elder Abuse
Amanda Phelan

M-Health in Developing Countries
Design and Implementation Perspectives on Using Mobiles in Healthcare
Arul Chib

Alcohol Policy in Europe
Delivering the WHO Ideal?
Shane Butler, Karen Elmeland and Betsy Thom

Mental Health Services for Vulnerable Children and Young People
Supporting children who are, or have been, in foster care
Michael Tarren-Sweeney and Arlene Vetere

Power and Welfare

Understanding Citizens' Encounters with State Welfare

Nanna Mik-Meyer and Kaspar Villadsen

Routledge
Taylor & Francis Group
LONDON AND NEW YORK

First published 2013
by Routledge
2 Park Square, Milton Park, Abingdon, Oxfordshire OX14 4RN

Simultaneously published in the USA and Canada
by Routledge
711 Third Avenue, New York, NY 10017

First issued in paperback 2014

Routledge is an imprint of the Taylor & Francis Group, an informa business

British Library Cataloguing in Publication Data
A catalogue record for this book is available from the British Library

Library of Congress Cataloging in Publication Data
Mik-Meyer, Nanna.
Power and welfare : understanding citizens' encounters with state welfare / Nanna Mik-Meyer and Kaspar Villadsen.
p. cm. -- (Routledge advances in health and social policy)
1. Human services. 2. Social service. 3. Public welfare. I. Villadsen, Kaspar.
II. Title.
HV40.M5195 2013
361--dc23
2012024760

ISBN 13: 978-0-415-53442-0 (hbk)
ISBN 13: 978-1-138-81784-5 (pbk)

Typeset in Goudy
by Taylor & Francis Books

Contents

Foreword ix

1 Introduction 1

2 Foucault: The flexible critique of welfare 10

3 Goffman: Interaction and identity negotiations 29

4 Bourdieu: Field, symbolic violence and domination 48

5 Luhmann: Welfare in communicative systems 67

6 Neo-institutional theory: Myths and legitimacy 87

7 Risk theory: Normality, deviation and neo-liberalism 107

8 Integrating the approaches 125

Notes 145
Bibliography 147
Index 156

Foreword

I first read *Magtens Former*, the Danish book of which this is in part a translation and in part a development, in 2010, three years after its publication. Its title can be loosely rendered into English as *The Forms of Power*. I had previously heard one of its authors, Nanna Mik-Meyer, speak at a conference and I had read a collection of essays on the shaping of clients in welfare systems that she had co-edited. So when I saw the book, about power, in the Athenaeum Bookshop in Copenhagen, I picked it up for a quick look at the contents.

Ten or more minutes later I was a few pages into the opening chapter and decided that I had better stop clogging up the aisles and buy it. I was immediately taken with it, and I remain so. If anything, this offspring of that original book is better than its parent: it is internationalised in its use of case material, and the discipline of writing in English has produced what is probably a leaner and clearer text. In other words, this is not just a translation; even if you already own *Magtens Former*, it is worth having *Power and Welfare* too.

I shan't attempt to summarise the book's contents or the authors' arguments, not least because that isn't my job. No, my job is to convince anyone who picks it up to put their hand in their pocket and buy it. If you have any interest in social policy, social theory (particularly with respect to power), organisation studies or comparative sociology, there are a number of good reasons why you should do so.

First, and perhaps most important, most books about power, and most theories of power, operate at levels of abstraction so rarified that they only dimly perceive the solid earth of the real world, at some great distance beneath them. This book, however, has both feet – perhaps that should be all four feet, since there are two authors – on the ground. It is undoubtedly a theory text, but it is rooted in, and derives its arguments from, the careful use of empirical case studies drawn from various public sectors and welfare regimes in modern industrial societies. In these case studies, organisations and individuals come to life as the real stuff of the human world, and how power works and is experienced by flesh and blood people comes into sharp focus.

The sub-title is 'Understanding Citizens' Encounters with State Welfare', and this book is as much about those encounters as it is about power. Citizenship in modern social democratic nation-states – and even the USA qualifies in many important respects – is intimately bound up with the relationship between individuals and the state. The encounters in which those relationships are shaped and developed are anything but abstract, and on their nature, and outcomes, depends the integration of the citizenry into the state: the social contract and the social settlement. Power – its nature and how it is exercised – is central to understanding both.

Second, Mik-Meyer and Villadsen have developed a conception of power that is usefully, and pragmatically, pitched between two extremes that bedevil discussions of this topic: it is neither so all-encompassing and universal that it is in danger of being everything and nothing, nor so rooted in individual agency that it is difficult to see any place, in a Hobbesian universe of all against all, for organisations, institutions and patterns, let alone values and culture. These two polar alternatives may be caricatures but, like all lampoonery, they have some merit. What's more, the authors are perfectly comfortable with the idea that somewhat different understandings of power may be necessary for different purposes, and that what is required is a synthesis of those different models.

Next there is a general point, which has already been hinted at, about social theory. Social theory has become a self-sufficient enterprise in its own right, an elite intellectual pursuit during which the big beasts of the social science academy go head to head in order to make their names and carve out careers. It may always have been thus, but social theory that is an end in itself – self-referential, self-regarding, self-important and undisciplined by serious attention to evidence – has moved a dangerous distance away from what I have always taken the role of theory to be, in any discipline: a means to the end of collecting and interpreting empirical data, which, in a virtuous circle, is itself shaped and tested in that process. In other words, theory is, or should be, the servant and facilitator of empirical inquiry, which cannot take place without it. In this book, Mik-Meyer and Villadsen offer a sustained and disciplined example of that approach to theory. It is most welcome.

There is also, perhaps, something to be said about the academic field of social or public policy. No doubt in exasperation at the various turns that social theory has taken in the last two or three decades, some social policy analysts have lowered their own theoretical bar, or perhaps even turned their backs on social theory altogether. This is understandable, if regrettable. If they can be persuaded to give *Power and Welfare* a chance, it may entice them back and rekindle their interest in theory.

Finally – and remarkably, given its intellectual merits – Nanna Mik-Meyer and Kaspar Villadsen have written something that, before it is anything else, is a book for students. Their teachers will profit enormously from reading it as well, for the reasons outlined above, but this is unashamedly a textbook, and it's all the better for it. It is clear, accessible and offers students as definite a vision of the uses and value of sociology as they are ever likely to come across. I dare say that C. Wright Mills would have approved. As such it is a major achievement. *Power and Welfare* will still be being read when many fashionable theory texts have vanished from view.

Richard Jenkins
September 2012

1 Introduction

Power is very much at the heart of contemporary debate about the encounter between state and citizen. Nowadays, whether you are a researcher, lecturer, practitioner or the head of an institution, you are required to reflect on the forms of power that come into play when citizens encounter the institutions of the state. On the one hand, you are required to reflect on how to place certain limits on the scope of power exercised by the state and its institutions vis-à-vis individuals and groups whose autonomy must be maintained and respected. Such reflections on the limits of power are accompanied by forms of governing that are often presented to citizens as attractive offers, using positive terms such as empowerment, coaching, self-realisation and partnership. One example of this is when social work and health care use dialogue-based initiatives designed to make clients' and patients' own words and values the basis for interventions. The aim of dialogue-based initiatives is, in this case, to avoid welfare institutions imposing goals and values on people that do not stem "from within", in other words from the individual's own free will (Karlsen & Villadsen 2008). A widely held conviction in public policy debates is that welfare institutions must avoid the conventional action plans and expert targets that too readily lead to accusations of "clientisation", "learned helplessness" and "hospitalisation". The ideal often voiced to avoid this risk is a form of power that promotes and increases the individual's capacity for self-government or taking up an "active citizenship". On the other hand, we witness, in contemporary welfare policy, trends towards an increasing use of sovereign, paternalistic power in relation to specific individuals and in specific contexts.

A number of authors have pointed out that the contemporary dominant form of governing, referred to in this book as "neo-liberal governing" or "advanced liberal governing", does not imply that sovereign power is completely abandoned, but rather that the exercise of sovereign power constitutes an inherent feature of modern Western societies. Sovereign power, in the form of coercion, incarceration and domination, can, for instance, be exercised by referring to the absence of willpower in the subject – alcohol and drug abusers, people suffering from mental illness or "uncivilised" people in the former colonies etc. (Valverde 1996, Dean 2002). However, sovereign state power is also exercised in relation to individuals and groups deemed to pose a threat to the health, integration or economic well-being of society, illustrated by the way some states treat immigrants and refugees.

The coexistence of these two forms of power creates ambiguous forms of governance. Politicians talk about the desirability of reducing the role of the state and promoting the autonomy and self-determination of institutions and citizens, while at the same time, central government tightens control and imposes sanctions in a number of spheres. Examples of this include the requirement for curricula that are formulated centrally but must be enacted locally in schools and educational institutions. Other examples include calls for local authorities and institutions to develop their own integration initiatives at the same time as the government places specific requirements on the content, objectives and sanctions of integration policy.

Critical evaluations of the recent reforms of public services, grouped under the heading New Public Management (NPM), identify a tension between political targets for imposing uniform standards (rationalising costs and ensuring compliance with legislation) and the need to allow local institutions to adapt services to local needs, develop new procedures and establish their own values. The governing paradox consists of how the state can act in an authoritarian "top-down" fashion at the same time as it guarantees local autonomy (Clarke & Newman 1997). Institutions therefore often treat people both as administrative cases to be processed by reference to sovereign state law, and as individuals with particular needs and potentials that must be given specific attention.

This ambition to treat the citizen as unique is illustrated by the current ideal in treatment facilities, schools and social work offices etc., of accepting the citizen "as he or she is" – in other words, as a whole and unique human being who must be taken into account in his/her particularity (Villadsen 2007). However, these institutions are characterised by distinct professional logics or rationalities, which guides how the staff observe and encounter the citizen (Mik-Meyer 2007, 2010a). What is considered an ailment requiring treatment, a barrier to integration, a factor motivating the individual to change or measure their capacity to work etc., is fundamentally conditioned by the professional codes applied by the social workers. In other words, particular discursive and practical frameworks shape the encounter between the citizen and the professional – and condition decisions on eligibility for benefits, for placement on job-creation schemes or education/training courses, as well as for diagnosis, treatment and so on. In this way, power, knowledge, intervention and professional logic are closely interwoven in the encounter between the citizen and the state.

Gubrium and Holstein's 2001 anthology, *Institutional Selves – Troubled Identities in a Postmodern World*, offers an excellent description of the impossibility of separating the institutional setting – and its specific forms of power, knowledge and intervention – from in-depth analyses of the encounter between the citizen and the state. These are elements that create specific "institutional identities". "Authentic selves" do not lurk deep inside the individual (Gubrium & Holstein 2001: 1). What we currently understand as our "personal self" is "increasingly deprivatized [...], our most private essence is now being constructed and interpreted under the auspices of decidedly *public* going concerns", as Gubrium and Holstein put it (2001: 2 – italics in the original).

Advanced liberalism

Extensive empirical evidence of encounters between professionals and citizens in various welfare institutions across advanced liberal societies reveals that values such as efficiency, personal responsibility, freedom, empowerment and self-help presently play a key role in professionals' encounters with the citizen (Dean 1995, Howe 1996, Mik-Meyer 2007, 2010a, Villadsen 2007, Michailakis & Schirmer 2010). We choose the terms "neo-liberalism" and "advanced liberalism" to refer to these values and new practices. Advanced liberalism is used by Rose (1996a) to point out several tendencies in contemporary Western, liberal societies. First, he observes that a new relationship between expertise and the subjects of government has emerged. Increasingly, experts must exercise a facilitating form of power that makes alliances with its citizens. Experts must seek "to align the self-governing capacities of subjects with objectives of political authorities by means of persuasion, education and seduction, rather than coercion" (Rose 1996a: 50). Second, advanced liberal forms of governing give preference to indirect mechanisms of power, or to political action that keeps the subjects of government at a distance. They use a range of techniques that can translate the objectives of welfare authorities into the choices and commitments of both professionals and their clients. Examples of this include instances when the expert adviser gives way to self-help manuals, ambulant "self-treatment", and the telephone helpline "as practices whereby each individual binds themselves to expert advice as a matter of their own freedom" (Rose 1996a: 58).

While we wish to pay attention to these "advanced liberal" forms of exercising power in the encounter between welfare institutions and citizens, we also wish to maintain that the emphases on self-help, willpower and responsibility are not exclusive, and we are thus attentive to how these new ways of exercising power coexist, intertwine or contrast with sovereign and disciplinary forms of power. Apart from taking inspiration from the diagnostics of Rose and other governmentality writers, we emphasise that the concept of neo-liberalism in this context does not refer to a coherent political programme, a distinct historical epoch or a political philosophy. Instead, the purpose of the concept of neo-liberalism is to focus on a particular way of reasoning regarding the exercise of government and the practical invention of particular technical means of governing. We thus wish to invite the researcher or student to avoid an abstract, a priori and too hasty critique ("this is simply neo-liberal domination") and to give priority to the careful study of practices.

In line with Howe (1996), we also detect changes in the more specific conditions that characterise welfare institutions' – and their professionals' – encounters with the citizen. It is a process that has been changing the nature of social work since the 1980s, succinctly described as the transformation from "diagnostic caseworker to care manager, from applied social scientist to service coordinator" (Howe 1996: 77). Howe may arguably describe this shift rather bluntly but it is relevant nevertheless to consider his key question: "What form does social work take when it no longer finds itself in a 'discourse' of discipline but rather one of radical liberalism?" (Howe 1996: 78). Commentators like Howe identify that a new context is emerging, one that increasingly places what are referred to as neo-liberal values at centre stage in current welfare provision. This is not, of course, a development that completely removes the professions and their particular codes of social work from the equation. It does, however, affect the professions' room for manoeuvre, and reconfigures the authorised assumptions about the type of individual that they are to fabricate. Research indicates that welfare recipients are assumed to be capable of developing and freeing themselves from need and dependency – a form of a self-actualising that revolves around personal responsibility, choice and autonomy (Rose 1999, Cruikshank 1999, Villadsen 2007, Mik-Meyer 2010a). There is a widely evident idea that the citizen in the role of a welfare dependent should recognise him or herself as the author of (and the potential rescuer from) his or her misfortune.

This transformation of social policies, which we are currently witnessing in advanced liberal societies, involves not only a shift in power structures (from state to market) and responsibility (from public to private domains), but also concerns who the citizen is fundamentally imagined to be and which obligations are considered legitimate in relation to citizenship. The increasingly pervasive process of individualisation allegedly experienced across modern Western societies (Giddens 1991, Bauman 1992) means that citizens are increasingly held responsible for their own situation – their health, learning, treatment or integration. The ideal citizen is one who acts responsibly, is strong-willed, and acknowledges that he or she plays the essential role in solving his or her own problems (Miller 2001, Mik-Meyer 2010a, Lessenich 2011). These normatively loaded conceptions of the ideal citizen create new conditions for the welfare institutions' encounters with him or her. As mentioned previously, it is the conditions for this encounter – and their consequences for the relationship between citizen and welfare provision – that will be studied in this book.

The changes in social work can also be related to a series of parallel trends that impact on both the professionals' encounter with the citizen and the institutional conditions for the professionals' activities more generally. We use the term social worker in a broad sense that includes integration workers, therapists, health advisers and other professionals who provide care and encourage individuals to undertake lifestyle changes. We wish to be able to study how ideals for personal development are at play both in relation to the citizen (demands for self-development) and in relation to the requirements placed on professionals to undertake a particular type of self-government. Welfare institutions are therefore required to use particular techniques that regulate practices and promote a sense of personal responsibility in the institution's users. The challenge increasingly evident in welfare provision is that the citizen is expected, voluntarily and freely, to take up politically determined development goals and obligations. As such, although services and projects that target the unemployed, the ill, immigrants and disaffected youngsters etc. are rooted in political goals stipulated centrally or by local authorities, social work now expects the targeted individuals to take up active responsibility for these goals.

Both authoritarian and facilitating

Rather than view this conflict of interests as the clash between irreconcilable demands that it appears to be, we believe mutually opposing trends such as the above-mentioned should be seen as reflecting a new kind of ambivalent or even paradoxical governance (Clarke & Newman 1997, Villadsen 2012). Contemporary welfare policies display liberal ideals of freedom by emphasising the need for the reduction of state control and expenditure, and for institutions and citizens to be made more self-responsible (Mik-Meyer & Roelsgaard Obling 2012, Villadsen 2012). At the same time, more and more governing techniques are being devised from central authorities, the purpose of which, in addition to ensuring the optimal utilisation of resources through detailed management, is to propel the institution/citizen towards the ideal state, to become: responsible, strong-willed and in complete self-control (Mik-Meyer 2010b). Howe would appear to have identified important changes in the encounter between professionals and clients when he asserts that the nature of the encounter has evolved: "From interpersonal to economic, from therapeutic to transactional, from nurturing and supportive to contractual and service-orientated" (Howe 1996: 93). These are transformations that give rise to new – and often mutually contradictory – conditions for the welfare institutions' encounter with the citizen, as the logic of economic efficiency and standardised services seeks to breach the former enclosures of welfare expertise. This means that we need to pay attention to how the goals of welfare reforms are weighed against professional discretion and specific values, including for example, holistic care.

As the analyses presented in the book will show, such conflicting trends are not only discernible in the structural conditions for the work carried out, but they also reappear in the practices that seek to define the problems and needs of the institutions' target groups. However, it should be remembered that political goals are not introduced into professional practices in a mechanical and uncontested manner. In the specific encounter between the welfare institution and the citizen, the professional staff, who have professional loyalties insofar as they refer their decisions to their professional values and guard their right to define the specific content of their work, remain a highly significant factor (see Fox 2001, Loseke 2001, Mik-Meyer 2011).

This complex, structuring aspect of the encounter between citizen and professional is the theme of the book. We engage with this theme by demonstrating how selected sociological approaches can be used to identify and analyse how power is at play in the structuring of the encounters and is actively played out in the specific encounters. A key relevance to our concerns is that traditional forms of professionalism and welfare services are affected by and intertwine with neo-liberal governance strategies in new and complex ways. Studies carried out in this contemporary terrain of conflicting political and professional rationalities that interact the demands of service-users, require, we believe, a complex concept of power.

First, this concept of power needs to be capable of encapsulating the particular rationality of government that characterises advanced liberal societies. It has to be capable of encapsulating the fact that the freedom citizens are encouraged to practice will always assume certain programmatic forms. As a consequence, government in neo-liberal societies inevitably, and always, operates with certain naturalised images of who the citizen is and what he or she is capable of (Gubrium & Holstein 2001). Since the idea is to ensure or realise what is assumed to pre-exist governmental intervention, at least latently, for example self-responsibility, the will to work, and the desire to be social (Michailakis & Schirmer 2010), neo-liberal forms of government must always keep a sceptical eye on the limits of its own power. This type of government tries to shape, facilitate and influence the actions of individuals and their self-relations, yet must avoid assuming responsibility for them or stifling the willpower assumed to reside in each individual. Neo-liberalism, then, should not be viewed as a monolithic or totalising programme that enforces its values upon society in a uniform and pre-specified manner (Gordon 1991). Rather, neo-liberalism uses forms of government that recognise that their results cannot be imposed or predetermined, but that they depend fundamentally on the activities of the governed, who are, after all, "free individuals". There is a recognition that power does not emanate from a centre, but that the exercise of power is rather about installing certain tendencies and norms into individuals' relationships with each other. These kinds of reflections on the power evident in contemporary programmes for the reform of welfare services are rather advanced, and call for analytical tools that match their complexity (Villadsen & Karlsen 2012).

Second, our concept of power must also be able to grasp the complexity in modern welfare provision. Hence, our object of analysis is a heterogeneous range of institutions, divided into distinct professional and institutional systems, each characterised by a significant degree of autonomy, a particular field of discretion, and a certain professional blindness. When different groups of professionals encounter an individual – for instance, a homeless person with a substance-abuse problem or a pain-afflicted patient – they simply do not see, in some cases, the same problem, or the same needs and potentials, for that matter (Mik-Meyer 2010b, Mik-Meyer & Obling 2012, Villadsen 2011a). In other words, the power exercised in encounters between the citizen and welfare professionals is not uniform, coherent or predetermined in a modern society with a differentiated division of labour between welfare specialisms. Modern welfare services are permeated by a range of distinct professional logics and practices, and the researcher must take into account their different rationalities, forms of co-operation, mutual support and occasional rivalries.

To that end, we need an analytical perspective that can view power as shaped in the particular institutional-professional context as well as in the specific encounter between the citizen and the institution. In brief, power must be seen as immanent to its context and should not be regarded as overarching, unidirectional or essentially repressive. In this book, different forms of power are conceptualised by terms such as discipline, government, pastoral power, dominance, symbolic violence, strategy and more. Common to these theoretical concepts is that they view power as productive, in the sense that both citizens and professionals continuously reproduce specific practices and institutions that set frameworks for the relationships that both professionals and citizens may establish with each other and with themselves. Or, in other words, power produces subjectivities, (dis)positions and relations.

Choice of analytical approaches

Common to the sociological approaches presented in this book, is that power is not reduced to a prevailing ideology that happens to have installed itself in the mentalities of professionals, nor do the approaches attribute the source of power to a single source such as the state apparatus, class relations or modes of production. Our choice of constructivist and predominantly post-structural approaches brings to the book the idea that power must be viewed as intrinsic to social relations, including the use of language, institutional practice and micro-interactions that give shape to welfare provision. This implies that there are not encounters between professionals and citizens "and then, *in addition, alongside or on top of these relations*, mechanisms of power that modify or disturb them, or make them more consistent, coherent, or stable" (Foucault 2007: 2 – our italics). Or, putting it differently, encounters between professionals and citizens inevitably involve plays of power. Moreover, we do not work with a single theory of power, but with a framework of different analytical strategies that highlight different problematics of power in relation to the encounter between welfare professionals and the citizen. We wish to demonstrate that this encounter may be explored from a variety of analytical approaches that produce different research questions, including how the encounter between the citizen and the professional plays out as micro-interaction, how the encounter is shaped by specific power technologies or organisational frameworks, how it is embedded in particular social fields or guided by certain perceptions of risk, and how certain historical forms of knowledge re-emerge in professional practice.

We have selected a number of theoretical approaches that we consider particularly relevant and effective as critical tools for analysis. These perspectives assume that the actors are woven into social structures that limit and shape the actions of both the professional and the citizen. Several of the perspectives also assume that citizens and professionals are able to exert influence on the positions reproduced and guarded by the institutional framework. In other words, we are working with structures that cannot be entirely pre-determined – discourses, rationality myths, role expectations, doxa, communicative systems and so on – insofar as they are continuously enacted, contested, negotiated and perhaps slightly modified in the institutional practices that set the conditions for encounters between citizens and professionals. Rather than fixed structures, we therefore speak in terms of "structuring", since discourses and roles etc. are constantly played out by the actors in ways that may vary greatly, and perhaps even change their meaning.

In addition, our theoretical approaches emphasise epistemology, including, first, a particular focus on the categories that turn people and forms of behaviour into objects of knowledge and intervention; and second, an awareness that the categories that we as researchers select and use have a crucial impact on how we may conduct a piece of research. We thus take as a premise that theoretical concepts fundamentally shape and condition what we are capable of observing. As the analyses in the book show, it is of crucial significance whether practices are analysed with the help of Bourdieu's concepts of "doxa" and "symbolic violence", Foucault's concept of "power technologies" or Goffman's concepts of "frame" and "interaction". These concepts are ingrained in particular analytical strategies, and one of our ambitions with this book is to show exactly what the choice of a specific sociological approach allows the researcher to see – and not see. The book fills a unique void, as it carefully follows each of the selected approaches all the way from theoretical assumptions and key analytical concepts through to real-life empirical analyses. It is intended for and designed to assist those who wish to conduct studies of citizen's encounters with welfare institutions. The book identifies and presents a range of relevant analytical options and provides inspiration for the reader's own work by presenting them with a selection of well-conducted, state-of-the-art studies.

In previous publications (see Mik-Meyer 2007, 2010b, 2011, Mik-Meyer & Obling 2012, Villadsen 2007, 2011a, 2012), we have studied the interaction between client and welfare services, the role played by philanthropy in the emergence of modern social work, and the construction of particular client categories by both public and voluntary welfare institutions. In this book, we continue to focus on the encounter between citizen and state, but the emphasis is on "unpacking" the various analytical approaches and tools that can be used to study the encounter. In order to clarify the link between the choice of a particular analytical approach and the potential results of the analysis, we present the different approaches separately. By the end of the book, however, we compare the approaches, point out their strengths and weaknesses, and propose some possible ways of combining them. An additional, and broader, goal of the book is to show the way in which the actions of professionals and citizens reflect and reproduce both particular professional discourses and, more broadly, pervasive neo-liberal values.

We have chosen to present analytical approaches advanced by four prominent critical thinkers – Foucault, Goffman, Bourdieu and Luhmann – who have, each in their own way, inspired a large number of ground-breaking studies concerning the citizen's encounter with organised welfare. In addition, two chapters are devoted to new institutional theory and risk theory, both of which are also often applied in the research of such encounters. Although we present the various analytical approaches separately, this does not mean that they cannot be fruitfully combined when designing a specific study. We have separated them mainly to highlight their various strengths as tools for analysing the play of power in the citizen's encounter with welfare institutions. In Chapter 8, we discuss the strengths and weaknesses of the various analytical perspectives and suggest possible ways to combine them.

We are aware that the analyses contained in the book could be interpreted as a wholesale critique of the real-life work of a number of welfare institutions. However, we emphasise that our concept of critique is not "absolute", i.e. it is not a fundamental critique of all that the institutions do for individuals on the margins or a complete rejection of the work done by professionals to relieve pain, detoxify the addicted or help integrate their clients. Nor do we, as social scientists "from the outside", propose a superior and universal programme for how practitioners should work. The purpose of our intellectual engagement with the forms of power in welfare services' encounters with citizens is to stimulate critical reflection about those concepts, categories, lines of division, and definitions of problems and needs that have become taken for granted or which are perhaps in the process of becoming naturalised and solidified – even though their naturalness, their objectivity, their implicit values and their appropriateness should always remain open to contestation. Hopefully, this book will encourage students, professionals, citizens and fellow researchers to reflect critically on the categories and explanations that welfare institutions take for granted, and which are, to a great extent, also much broader social "truisms".

2 Foucault: The flexible critique of welfare

Michel Foucault was born in Poitiers, France, in 1926 and died in 1984. A graduate in philosophy and psychology from the elite École Normale Supérieure, Foucault became known for his often surprising and provocative analyses of how modern man turned himself into an object of knowledge, and how this process was deeply intertwined with social conditions and relations of power. He studied how the emerging modern scientific discourses in Western Europe were interconnected with administrative and governmental practices, including strategies for governing the unproductive, the sick and the deviant, institutional reforms, and techniques for regulating towns, grain prices, contagious diseases, and more. Best known are his studies of the emergence of the modern prison (*Discipline and Punish*, 1977), the social function of sexuality through history (*The History of Sexuality vol. 1*, 1990) and his analysis of the modern human sciences and of man as a knowing subject (*The Order of Things*, 1994). Gutting's (2005) *Foucault: A Very Short Introduction* provides a solid starting foundation. *Governmentality: Power and Rule in Modern Society* (Dean 1999a) places Foucault in a sociological context, with particular focus on governmentality. The anthology by Bröckling, Krasmann and Lemke (2011), *Governmentality: Current Issues and Future Challenges*, offers an up-to-date collection of Foucauldian research, including into biopolitics.

KEY CONCEPTS: genealogy, subjectification, biopolitics, governmentality, technologies of power.

Foucault's view of power in the liberal welfare state

Nowadays, anybody conducting research into the welfare state, power and governance can hardly avoid relating to Foucault. His critical perspectives and concepts have become practically inevitable components in discussions about power and governance – not least in relation to the theme of the state and the individual, which a large number of Foucault's successors have examined under the heading of "governmentality" studies (Dean 1999a).

This chapter presents our selection of some of Foucault's key analytical concepts.

Foucault is a particularly sharp-eyed observer of the characteristic features of the exercise of power in modern liberal societies. He formulates his ideas in terms that contrast to theories which assert that the state dominates predominantly through repressive means of power that prohibit, repress and coerce. Similarly, he is sceptical of the idea that the way to restrict state power is to set limits for the state's centrally-directed exercise of power over its citizens. The form of power that characterises modern welfare states is not primarily a repressive one that sets limits and imposes sanctions. Neither, according to Foucault, does it consist primarily of ethnic, social or religious oppression, nor can it be conceived as economic exploitation – even though all of these may well take place (Foucault 1982: 212–14). The modern, liberal exercise of power is first and foremost "creative" or "inciting", since it seeks to nurture, cultivate and stimulate particular capabilities in its citizens. Foucault encapsulates this with the phrase "power is productive". Power is productive because it works by turning individuals into – or, better, it encourages individuals to turn themselves into – certain types of subjects.

According to Foucault, the modern state operates both with the citizenry as a totality and as individuals, whose individuality or self-relation may be subject to a "productive" (processing and fostering) form of government. It is in this sense that Foucault, in a late text, makes the claim that the modern state is both individualising and totalising at one and the same time (Foucault 1982: 215).

Knowledge of the citizenry is generated around two axes: one of which is overarching, quantitative and directed at the whole population; the other, analytical and directed at the individual. The modern state is totalising when it makes everybody subject to compulsory schooling and national health programmes, imposes universal taxes or divides citizens up into overarching categories such as unemployed people, students and risk groups etc. It is individualising when it pays attention to the individual citizen's personality, his/her self-image, self-esteem or psychological constitution. Foucault thus speaks about the modern state resting on a "tricky combination in the same political structures of individualization techniques and totalization procedures" (Foucault 1982: 213) that is unprecedented in history.

He argues, in a highly original manner, that these individualising techniques have an affinity with the Christian Church's methods of guiding individuals towards salvation, such as confession, self-examination and the guidance of consciousness (Foucault 2000a). The similarities lie in the way that the priest or pastor leads an individual towards salvation in the hereafter – so-called "pastoral power". The interesting aspect of this form of leadership is that it addresses the depths of the soul, that is, inner thoughts, ideas and secrets. To be able to exercise his leadership in the shape of guidance of conscience, the pastor must know each individual soul. He has to bring hidden thoughts to light – especially, of course, those that are deemed sinful or sexual and immoral. Foucault says that "a renunciation of this world and of one self" must take place in order to secure progress on the road to sanctity (Foucault 2000a: 311). In pastoral leadership, knowledge of the state of progress of each depends upon the individuals telling the truth about who they are and what they contain. The subtle aspect of this type of power is that it binds individuals by their own words – they can be kept to the truth that they have revealed about who they are. Foucault thus describes pastoral leadership as "the individualising power" (Foucault 2000a: 300).

His point is that pastoral leadership, as a form of power, has not diminished along with the decreasing importance of the Church. Rather, pastoral techniques that encourage individuals to express confessional truths have proliferated in the modern welfare state (Foucault 1982: 215). Psychologists, educators, sex therapists, social workers all use techniques that could be described as pastoral. Before modern individuals can be led, they must first tell the truth about who they are. This pastoral form of power is both intimate, as it is directed towards "the citizen's soul", and subtle, because it grants the individual submitted to government the authority to determine the nature of his/her ailments, deviations or suppressed potential. It is, however, evident that this assertion of truth usually takes place with assistance from an authority that facilitates the confessor's voice and filters his/her statements (Karlsen & Villadsen 2008).

Modern forms of power

The widespread interest in Foucault among social scientists and professions that are concerned with treating people is due, not least, to his original reformulation of conventional concepts of power. This reformulation was principally an attempt to expand our understanding of what characterises the exercise of power in modern society. Power, according to Foucault (1990: 92–103), is not something you possess in the sense that Actor A has the power to influence and control Actor B. Power emanates not from a specific point or a superior position, such as a king, government or state apparatus; nor is it simply a repressive force that prohibits, brings to heel, blocks or compels. The modern exercise of power is about exerting influence or guiding individuals who are formally free by shaping their actions and their self-perceptions. It is a productive power that aims to equip individuals with specific abilities, put them in a position to act in certain ways, process their self-relations and, in some cases, rehabilitate them. Having said this, however, in the modern welfare state, this productive and facilitating power co-exists with sovereign and disciplinary forms of power (Foucault 2007: 107). The question of how they interlink or challenge each other opens up some interesting and complex empirical studies.

Society's reaction to crime is an illustrative example of Foucault's way of describing the complex co-existence of modern forms of power (Foucault 2000b). In short, pre-modern power, emblematically represented by the

European principalities, responded to crime with corporal punishment – and, in serious cases, with torture and public executions. The aim was to force a confession out of the lawbreaker and – even more importantly – to demonstrate the sovereign's power over the people. However, along with the emergence of the modern constitutional state, modern criminology and modern behavioural sciences effect a transformation in the rationality of punishment takes place. In this process, the objectives and means of punishment are altered. It is no longer enough to determine the illegal act, identify the guilty party and mete out the appropriate punishment. Now, the legal system also has to discover and reveal the person behind the act – their motives, feelings, deviant forms of behaviour, and what influenced them. It becomes vital to make lawbreakers talk, as it is assumed that their testimony will contain deeper explanations of the criminal act (Foucault 2000b). Psychiatrists, psychologists, educators, sociologists and criminologists have been brought into the legal system to examine in more detail the lawbreaker's character flaws, the nature of their deviation, and to suggest constructive and therapeutic interventions.

As a result, a form of power emerges that aims to correct and improve the "human material" by recording and classifying forms of deviant behaviour. In pre-modern times, offenders were essentially placed outside of the community (as outlaws) by dint of their actions. Modern society, on the other hand, seeks to integrate lawbreakers and other "abnormals" by correcting deviations from what is taken to be normal behaviour. Foucault's general point is, again, that this disciplinary power is a productive, rather than a repressive, power. The objective is to foster characteristics, promote behavioural traits and improve the human material at hand. Typically, it is about encouraging the individual to conform to particular norms, i.e. standards of normality as defined by experts in modern human and social sciences.

Foucault emphasises that any exercise of modern power depends upon knowledge of the objects of government, usually derived from the human sciences. However, it is not a matter of power "exploiting science" by simply dressing itself up in scientific theories and explanations to appear legitimate – rather, it is a two-way, mutually conditioned relationship. The exercise of power finds support and justification in scientific categories, but the scientific categories, for their part, are often established from practices for the management, administration and control of people. Thus, in *Discipline and Punish*, Foucault (1977) suggests that knowledge of criminals and deviants grew out of institutions designed to rehabilitate, train, monitor or cure.

Foucault's prominence within the social sciences stems in particular from his formulation of this inseparable connection between power and knowledge. Whenever an area for intervention is established, a domain for the production of knowledge is simultaneously marked out (Foucault 1977, 1990). Grouping people together, e.g. people suffering from mental illness, offenders or pupils, thus allows for observation, comparison, categorisation and definition of "types" and standards for normality. Much of the work of Foucault and his successors indeed examines the links between government and the formation of scientific, or quasi-scientific, forms of knowledge. It problematises the modern welfare state's "naturalised" institutions, including the psychiatric institution, prison, social-work office and job centre, along with the forms of knowledge with which they are intimately connected. A stream of critical studies has thus been conducted to examine how a broad range of aspects of modern human life have become the object of power and knowledge. Foucault consistently sought to question and "destabilise" modern man's experience of himself in a number of fundamental areas such as sickness and death, madness and reason, normality and perversion. In this sense, his work can be interpreted as attempts at making contestable modern human sciences and the way in which they are deeply interwoven with institutions, administration and political strategies. By now, it is clearly evident that this critical approach has had a significant impact in professions concerned with treating, reforming and caring for people, including social work (Epstein et al. 1999), education (Besley 2002) and health counselling (Coveney 1998).

Genealogy

For Foucault, it is a basic premise that history is a necessary tool with which to shed light on the present. Taking this premise as point of departure, research into organised welfare can use genealogy to problematise contemporary institutional regimes, e.g. psychiatry or social work, by demonstrating their complex historical trajectories. Genealogical studies thus seek to make a critical impact on our present. One way to produce such critical effects is to demonstrate that what we have regarded as universal and necessary givens are in fact contingent results of past struggles, the work of governmental strategies and the re-articulation of historical elements (Villadsen 2007). Many of Foucault's works show how our modern and taken-for-granted sciences and related institutions descend from past practices and institutions that appear objectionable by today's standards. A key strategy in Foucault's work is therefore to demonstrate "inconvenient" continuities that disturb evolutionary and humanistic narratives and their claim that modern humanism entails a break with the irrationality and inhumanity of pre-modern times.

He shows how modern human sciences do not represent a clear break with pre-modern moralising. They are still involved in moralising projects – not least by rearticulating distinctions between good and evil, sinful and pure, in new forms such as the dualities of healthy and pathological, normal and deviant. The genealogical approach to historiography is not about describing constants, for example by following "the mad" over time, as if mental illness has a permanent essence. Instead of directing attention to a fixed referent – the mad, sexuality, social problems, the poor – genealogy reveals how these phenomena have been constructed as problems. It also demonstrates the way in which, for example, "abnormals" have emerged as a particular problem which has been accompanied by certain self-evident solutions. In brief, genealogy takes as its starting point the question of the construction of particular problem-objects and rationalised schemes for handling them. Its guiding questions could be: How did correctional imprisonment become the normal form of punishment? Or, how have social clients been coerced into self-development?

The scientific production of knowledge should not be interrogated in terms of whether it achieves greater congruence between our understanding of the phenomena and the phenomena per se. However, describing the historical conditions for emergence requires that we pose questions about the objectives of the welfare state's projects, such as availability for work, healthy lifestyles and suitability to be a parent. Examples of critical genealogies of the welfare state include Donzelot's (1979) analysis of the emergence of family policy, Ewald's (1991) analysis of early insurance technologies as the basis for the rationality of risk underpinning the welfare state, Dean's (1991) genealogy of liberal poverty policy and Villadsen's (2007) analysis of the historical emergence and current transformation of social work.

Finally, it should be noted that genealogy is not an exhaustive historiography that claims to establish coherency and causal mechanisms. Rather, it is a way of writing history that selects events in order to generate critical effects in the present. Typically, genealogists describe "discontinuities", when the commonly accepted histories present evolutionary and logically progressive sequences. Conversely, genealogists emphasise "continuities", recurrence and reactivation, when other historians prefer to divide history into phases, epochs or ages (Andersen 2003a: 30). As an example of this, genealogy has sought to problematise the distinction between modernity and pre-modernity by disclosing the "uncomfortable" trajectories that connect modern welfare services to pre-modern institutions like monasteries, madhouses, barracks and philanthropy etc.

Power technologies as analytical concept

One way of conducting genealogical work is to analyse the emergence of power technologies. In recent years, this approach has increasingly attracted the attention of researchers who use Foucault in areas ranging from critical management studies (Karlsen & Villadsen 2008) to international politics (Aradau & Munster 2008) and social work (Villadsen 2008c). Some commentators have even claimed that the concept of power-technology is, in fact, the recurring method that permeates Foucault's work (Raffnsøe et al. 2010).

It should be stressed that Foucault's concept of power technologies is markedly different from conventional understandings of technologies as tangible, technical tools. Rather, these are ad-hoc solutions that emerged as responses to practical concerns, and gradually, over time, became generalised as omnipresent and self-evident schemes of exercising power. In his study of the emergence of discipline as a general technology of power, Foucault thus demonstrates how mundane and dispersed techniques for correction and training at various sites (army barracks, schools and factories) gradually became linked up and systematised, eventually to take the form of a broadly applicable, or multifunctional, technology. Thus, on discipline, he says:

> "[I]t was first to be introduced [...] at the local level, in intuitive, empirical and fragmented forms, and in the restricted framework of institutions such as schools, hospitals, barracks, workshops, and so on" (Foucault 2003: 250).

One analytical advantage of the concept of power technologies is that it helps us avoid a totalising analysis of power (e.g. of discipline) in favour of a recognition of multiple co-existing forms of power, or a "topography" of different modalities of power (Collier 2010). By using power technologies as an analytical perspective, we are able to see that a phenomenon, e.g. a social problem, may be observed, analysed and managed on the basis of entirely different rationales depending on which power technology is used as the register for observation. Foucault suggests that there are three major technologies of power in the modern West – the law, discipline and security. Each offers its own distinct schematics for observing and regulating the world, and these have obvious relevance to the analyses of welfare institutions' encounters with the citizen.

In brief, the law revolves around the legal code that makes "a binary division between the permitted and the prohibited, and a coupling, comprising the code, between a type of prohibited action and a type of punishment" (Foucault 2007: 5). Within the framework of discipline, "a series of adjacent, detective, medical, and psychological techniques appear, which fall within the domain of surveillance, diagnosis, and the possible transformation of individuals" (Foucault 2007: 5). Finally, the technology of security "establishes an average considered as optimal on the one hand, and, on the other, a bandwidth of the acceptable that must not be exceeded" (Foucault 2007: 6). Taking the phenomena to be regulated as the point of departure, i.e. as a given that cannot be determined but merely coaxed towards an acceptable level, the technology of security conceives of governing as more fundamentally dependent upon the objects of regulation than the other two prototypes.

Although, in Foucault, power technologies are presented as something akin to systems, they are not to be viewed as overarching, determining or omnipotent. Rather, there is an over-determining of social space caused by the presence of several potentially conflicting power technologies. They each rely upon distinct models for observation and action, which sometimes generate friction, support each other or challenge the rationality of other technologies (Raffnsøe et al. 2010: 219). For example, we might envisage a social work office's use of a holistic approach towards its clients as presenting a challenge to the law, while conversely, the binary rigidity of the law conflicts with the objective of a holistic view.

A previous work established specific analytics for power technologies via a close reading of Deleuze's brief and somewhat obscure article "What is a

Dispositif?" (Villadsen 2008c: 179–80; see also Dean 1999a: 23). In it, Deleuze (1992) proposes four analytical dimension of or entry points to the analysis of power technologies, or "dispositifs", which we interpret as follows:

1. Domains of visibilities: Visibility is not produced by a general light source that falls on pre-existing objects. Each power technology has its own particular way of throwing light upon objects, which makes them appear before us in a particular "normative light", e.g. as disciplinary problems needing correction.
2. Regime of enunciation: Statements do not simply represent objects or subjects. A power technology activates enunciation regimes, i.e. procedures for the production of truth (developed by the modern sciences), which shape its possible objects and subject positions.
3. Strategy of power: The link between observing and enunciating, between things and words, is created by power. Power runs through all of the elements of power technology and gives it a distinct strategy. Power can, in particular, be observed in terms of practices and techniques.
4. Strategy of subjectification: The subject is not predetermined. Rather it is in the process of becoming, and this process is shaped not just by one, but by several more or less incongruent power technologies.

These analytical dimensions can be weighted in the analysis to a greater or lesser degree. For example, the focus may be on what visible entities a power technology creates or, conversely, the requirements and opportunities it provides to a subject. A further key point is that power technologies generally arise in response to "social indigestion", i.e. the precarious social conditions and problems that need to be addressed and remedied (Raffnsøe et al. 2010: 218). Finally, in relation to the analysis below, it is important that a power technology is not located spatially within a particular organisation, policy field or sector of society – rather, it belongs to a specific historical form of problematisation that would normally traverse these boundaries.

Case 1: Genealogical analysis – Philanthropy as a power technology

This example of a genealogical analysis was drawn up by Villadsen in his PhD thesis and in subsequent articles (Villadsen 2007; Villadsen 2011b). The critical ambition behind the analysis was to question the idealisation of philanthropy as a solution to welfare-policy challenges, as well as to problematise the typically sharp juxtaposition of the old days' compassion-driven philanthropy and present day neutral and reserved welfare provision. The analysis furthermore suggests that philanthropy is a technology of power in the above sense of the term.

The analysis shows that philanthropic poor relief established a fundamental dilemma – or even paradox – in the provision of assistance and that this paradox has been carried over into modern social work. The philanthropists wanted to create a space for compassion-driven care for the needy, but at the same time their practices were deeply influenced by disciplinary rehabilitation, criteria for needs assessment, sanctions and other similarities to the statutory poor relief provided by the state. Late-19th-century Christian philanthropy was one of the main wellsprings of the paradox of social work's wish to take particular care of the individual while operating with disciplinary techniques for the correction and normalization of the very same individual.

The following analysis demonstrates how the significance of late-19th-century philanthropic poor relief transcends the institutions and their immediate historical context. The analysis is rooted in a Danish context, but the development of philanthropic poor relief was greatly inspired by parallel debates elsewhere, especially in Great Britain, Germany and France. Robert T. Malthus' and Thomas Chalmers' writings became a central point of reference in the Danish debate in the early 19th century, and Danish commentators often wrote accounts of their travels to poor houses in neighbouring countries and issued advice based on these experiences (Bärens 1811). This chapter does not trace the precise way in which ideas were transferred between Denmark and other countries, but developments in Denmark were by no means an isolated trajectory.

The social predicaments of the 19th century

The industrialisation of the late 19th century could be said to be characterised by severe social predicaments, in the form of waves of immigration, unprecedented urban growth, increasing class antagonism and, in their wake, the perceived loss of social cohesion. Social revolts broke out in several European states, as well as in Copenhagen. Representatives of the propertied classes expressed growing concern over what were referred to as the "social evils" that accompanied the burgeoning population of poor workers in the fast-growing cities. These included the spread of contagious diseases from poor neighbourhoods to the rest of the population; the rise of moral decay resulting from the dangerous mixing of different sexes and ages; the disorder arising from a lack of moral authority; and, not least, the growing support for the socialist movement which, it was feared, would lead to revolt and the dissolution of the existing social order. Horrifying accounts depicted poor neighbourhoods as inhabited by "people of depraved habits" who adhered to norms and conduct that were completely alien to the majority of respectable citizens. Some newspapers even sent writers on expeditions into this "dark continent of the poor", in order to describe its strangeness to an outraged bourgeoisie (Lützen 1998: 132). A key question revolved around who was best able to instil morals in the growing number of young factory workers who had previously been subject to the moral influence and oversight of their master in the rural family or the village community.

The rise of mass urban poverty came at a time when formal civil rights were beginning to be affirmed politically and demands were growing for their realisation in practice. Procacci (1989) argues (focusing on France) that the key problem of the emerging welfare state was the co-existence of formal equality and actual economic inequality. The modern rights of citizenship entailed a kind of equality that had to be universal and could not countenance exceptions. In the face of this, the poor represented "a politically embarrassing issue: how to justify inequalities under a condition of basic equality" (Procacci 1989: 175).

As a result, 19th-century industrialisation witnessed the emergence of a set of problems related to poverty – "the social evils" – that seemed irresolvable from both a legal and economic perspective. It was partly in response to these problems that philanthropic poor relief took off in the second half of the century. The forcefulness of the philanthropic response to social evils can mainly be attributed to the movement's technical inventiveness and its characteristic reform-oriented rhetoric. During the 19th century, philanthropic societies in the larger cities invented a set of principles for poor relief that broke with the earlier alms-giving tradition and turned out to be decisive for modern social work as we know it. These principles included home visits, contractual agreements, criteria for separating the deserving from the undeserving poor, and methods for assessing the poor person's willpower (Villadsen 2007: 314).

These philanthropic associations promoted their programme for poor relief by framing it as a fundamental reform. The necessity of their endeavour rested on a series of problematisations of the former, paternalistic poor policy – in particular, questioning the practice of indiscriminate alms-giving and the use of forced labour and incarceration. Traditional assistance policies had viewed charity, in the form of alms-giving, as an act of value in itself. The benefactor represented the humanity of the privileged, while the beneficiary represented the intrinsic goodness of the poor. The deed of charity, therefore, would realise the essential humanity in both parties (Dean 1991: 229). By comparison, the focus of philanthropic work was on more pragmatic means of achieving ends (Donzelot 1979: 66). Philanthropic reformers criticised indiscriminate alms-giving as a practice that did not reflect upon its consequences. The reformers spoke of the need to develop much more pragmatic knowledge of the art of giving, which carefully considered who should receive help, what form help should take, and how to evaluate its effects. The idea that charitable giving needed to be directed and controlled was not entirely new, but had its roots in the late 18th century – in particular, in the New Poor Law of 1834 in Great Britain. In Denmark, public critique of indiscriminate alms-giving first appeared in the early 19th century, but only gradually did it become ingrained in philanthropic poor relief.

Philanthropy's domains of visibility

What kind of visibilities did philanthropic poor relief create? How could philanthropists observe the character of the poor and their degree of moral decay, which was considered crucial in determining the form of assistance? It is in relation to this question that home visits – a technique developed in the 19th century – became a key instrument in philanthropic poor relief. Home visiting provided the means to observe a number of visible signs of morality in the poor family's home, and on the basis of these, evaluate the family and their eligibility for assistance (Villadsen 2007: 315). Did the kitchen, clothes and children convey a sense of order, cleanliness and financial frugality, thereby indicating the presence of good morality and strong willpower? Or did they indicate that the family had fallen into "absolute moral decay"? Visiting became the preferred instrument for "throwing light" upon and visualising the moral qualities of the poor. The home became a space of observation because it contained a number of exterior signs that the philanthropic visitor could use to distinguish between those who might still 'be saved' and those who were permanently lost to moral decay. In particular, it was emphasised that foresight – or the lack thereof – was an indicator of the pauper's fundamental character.

The visitors sought to illuminate the inner moral constitution of the pauper, but since the poor's own statements were not thought to be a reliable source of knowledge, the visitors would instead make use of a series of indicators or symptoms. By observing these, the philanthropists could attempt to "lift up" the better members of the poor by imparting to them acceptable norms and manners.

Philanthropy's strategy of subjectification

Let us now examine the subject positions that philanthropy marked out for the recipient of poor relief, as well as for the helper. It might be argued that the philanthropic "visitor of the poor" was, in many respects, a forerunner of the modern social worker. The visitor had the task of simultaneously distributing household relief and conducting a detailed study of the character of the poor – a practice increasingly considered an absolute must for effective poor relief. The philanthropist was indeed "a figure with a great future" (Procacci 1991: 165). The philanthropic visitor constituted a figure that combined various – and, to some extent, contradictory – functions, clearly marking out the space that would later be occupied by the social worker.

These functions can be explored in greater depth by observing that the visitor combined, in one individual, two of the most significant practices for the production of subjective truth – "the confession", which incites the subject to speak the truth about his or her inner proclivities (emblematically carried out by a priest or judge), and "the clinical interview", which establishes diagnoses (carried out by various medical specialists) (Heede 2011: 117). The philanthropist utilised the confession in order to ensure the pauper's spiritual nourishment, thereby leading them to recognise their moral obligations. The confession was particularly invoked in the educative counselling of the housewife, instructing her in the art of saving, and guiding her to a "moral housekeeping". This was because the housewife was considered the pivotal governmental key for bringing the home to adequate moral, hygienic and pedagogical standards; being, as it were, "the priestess" of her own home (Schmidt & Kristensen 1986: 121). The philanthropist would give instructions on child rearing and even offer advice on persuading the husband and breadwinner to come home without opening his pay packet. The philanthropic visitor's main challenge was to establish a close alliance with the housewife regarding the proper organisation of the home and the running of domestic economics, which might often clash with the interests of the husband.

The clinical interview mainly took the form of "observations of symptoms" of the home, its visible surfaces and its inhabitants, in order to evaluate the moral state of the poor. This strategic combination of confession with diagnostics, or of therapeutic counselling with medical (or quasi-medical) categorisation, would be inherited by the modern social worker.

However, another significant aspect of the philanthropists' role was their function as a mediator between the poor, anxiety-provoking masses and the propertied classes. The philanthropists redefined "the pauper" and his or her inner qualities in contrast to earlier conceptions. Instead of containing an inner kernel of moral decay, they began to claim that even the most miserable and depraved pauper possessed an inner "essential humanity". As a mediator, the philanthropist would speak for the essential human nature presumed inherent in everyone and, in doing so, construct a less threatening picture of the poor. The philanthropists took upon themselves the discursive rights of the poor by representing them to the rest of society. As Philp (1979: 99) observed, this function was later taken up by the modern social worker, who also has to mediate, when dealing with a judge, a doctor or the local community, by alluding to a subjectivity that is not immediately visible in the client. The image of the pauper as possessing an "inner humanity" and potential for socialisation gave to the philanthropists a paradoxical double-gaze, insofar as they would conceive the recipient as at one and the same time particular and universal. Thus, on the one hand, there is a particular, "unique being", which one must "meet where he or she stands", while on the other, this "being" allegedly has a general humanity that lies behind his or her immediate appearance (Villadsen 2007: 102).

Philanthropy's strategy of power

The debates that took place in Western Europe in the 19th century on how to combat social evils involved, grossly speaking, two major, opposing political camps. On the one side, the socialists wanted to solve the problem of poverty by means of collectivisation and state regulation of the economy. On the other, liberals and conservatives argued that market forces and voluntary charity, if allowed to work freely, would ameliorate poverty and knit together the social classes (Donzelot 1979). The philanthropists adopted an intermediate position in the midst of the stand-off. Their solution was neither a state-governed nor market-based community, but a moral one – in other words, a community in which a set of collective moral standards and mutual obligations would bind individuals together. For the philanthropists, the preferred means of social integration was "spiritual nourishment" rather than state-enforced social rights or market-based exchanges.

In this way, claims for more rights, such as the right to work or a mandatory poor tax could be deemed to be of secondary importance. By this manoeuvre, or via this "strategy of power", philanthropic poor relief succeeded in diverting the demands for action from the state to poor households (Donzelot 1979). Philanthropists emphasised that, in order to improve their lives, the poor should strive to improve their moral attitudes and not make unreasonable demands upon society or succumb to the lures of revolutionary socialism. Their message to the poor was that, instead of making misplaced claims on the state and on society, they should first make sure that their own household and personal conduct were in order. Vicar Villiam Johan Hoff (1881: 16) wrote:

> "It is indeed a fundamental law in the Kingdom of God that we should never be placed higher, never be entrusted with more, before we have learnt to be faithful in relation to the smallest of things, in our everyday lives [...]. Growth always takes place by faithfulness and obedience in daily life, in relation to the minor things – and never, ever by spiritual ascensions, in one stroke, all of a sudden!"

Philanthropic societies shared with both public hygienists and representatives of the workers' movement, the idea that "the proper home" was the best remedy against social dissolution. The home was pictured as a space of sound moral standards, from which good morality would spread to the rest of society: "Cleanliness is not a private pleasure, but it is a public duty" (Johansen 1883: 196). In this way, the notion of "the proper home" became a point of support for the existing social order and a tactical invention for rejecting fundamental critiques of industrialised capitalism.

Eschewing both socialism and laissez-faire liberalism, 19th-century Danish philanthropists offered a principle for intervention in social problems that revolved around a concept of "the moral cohesion of society". This principle did not imply a formal state obligation towards the poor, since their relation to society was envisioned as a moral rather than a judicial one. Thus, "philanthropy pointed in a moral community the rationale for interpreting poverty as a concern for the whole of society" (Procacci 1989: 169). Philanthropic poor relief served as a mediating agency that would, at least temporarily, relieve both the state and private industry from the fundamental burden of solving the issue of poverty. In addition to inventing many of the principles and techniques of social work, philanthropy constituted a working compromise between state regulation and laissez-faire, which may, broadly speaking, be seen as part of the compromise of the welfare-state model.

Seen as a technology of power, philanthropy has the following key features:

- It observes the inner morals of the poor by providing a number of external indicators (or visibilities) in poor households.
- It positions philanthropy between the poor and the bourgeoisie as a mediator, to prove the existence of universal humanity in the particular pauper.
- Instead of seeing the poor as a legal subject, they are presented as possessing a broad range of behavioural dispositions that must be worked upon or corrected.
- It uses a strategy of promoting morality and moral cohesion, avoiding the need for economic and legal interventions.
- Philanthropy's strategy of power redirect demands for change away from the state to poor households and the lifestyles of their inhabitants.

The analysis presents a greater number of intricate connections between social policy, social work and philanthropy than usually admitted in literature on these themes. The analytical focus on power technology is used to help outline the ways in which philanthropy makes its object visible, manages its subjects and seeks to address social problems through a specific strategy. It also helps us to draw surprising – and apparently uncomfortable – connections between 19th-century philanthropic poor relief and modern social work. Analysing philanthropy as a general technology of power makes possible, however, more than just a simple problematisation of sharp historical distinctions between 19th-century non-state poor relief and the 20th-century welfare state. It also shows how philanthropy paved the way for the state to go beyond purely legal regulation and to progress towards a more intrusive administrative regulation of social problems. By focusing clearly on moral upbringing and the development of techniques to generate solidarity and promote responsibility, philanthropy pointed the way towards forms of regulation that far exceeded the purely legislative. It was state social workers who eventually went down that path. Philanthropy, therefore, also constitutes a key genealogical element in the history of how we ended up not with a strictly liberal form of state, but with a kind of social liberalism, which advocates that every citizen has a duty to everybody else, and a form of social work tasked with maintaining and inculcating social obligations.

Case 2: Managing the self-government of unemployed people

Our second case example unfolds a technology of power on a much smaller scale and in a contemporary welfare state context.

Mitchell Dean's study of the management of unemployed people in Australia uses many of the classical analytical components of the Foucauldian approach (Dean 1995, 1998). He describes his approach as an analytics of government. Although Dean does not explicitly refer to technologies of power as the basis for his analysis, he does mention that the reforms of the unemployment system, which he studies, could rightly be regarded as a risk technology (Dean 1995: 580, see chapter on risk in this book). This is because they permit a distinction between individuals who are able to manage their risk of long-term unemployment and those who are not, and therefore need tutelary management. The latter group can be viewed as being particularly at risk due to factors such as their English skills, indigenous ethnicity, location, age and so on. The core purpose of the reforms, which commenced in the late 1980s, is to change the nature of social security for the unemployed from reactive to activating, and change the recipient from "passive" to "active". The recipient should learn to take measures to prevent the risk of falling into long-term unemployment.

At one and the same time, this is an attempt to exert influence on the management of an administrative system and on the self-government of its clients. In this way, this case is a good illustration of Foucault's point that the exercise of modern political power often recognises its dependence on individuals' self-practices, i.e. that the people governed are committed to their own self-government. Dean states that governance initiatives should be viewed as "governmental-ethical practices". On the one hand, they aim to meet a series of politico-administrative goals, such as greater efficiency, income redistribution, alleviation of poverty, adherence to legal principles, and reducing the number of claimants for benefits. On the other hand, they also aim to shape unemployed people's abilities, orientations, foresight and moral attitudes (Dean 1995: 567). Via the concept of "ethical practices", Dean identifies that a key focus for political governance in this context is individuals' self-government – in particular, the ideals to which they subject themselves.

The starting point for Dean's analysis is a point we touched on earlier – that managing free subjects is a highly ambivalent, indeed ironic exercise (Dean 1995: 561). Partly, it is based on conceptions of what lies hidden, what is original or inherent in the governed. Partly, it seeks to maintain the status of the governed as free subjects by concentrating government on the frameworks and spaces within which they make their choices. A study of the production of persons via an analytics of government dispenses resolutely with any theory of the subject. On the contrary, it facilitates an exploration of the specific practices and techniques by which subjects seek to shape other subjects or themselves. The study includes the reflections and rationales that are involved both in this government and in self-government. Dean stresses that the study of subject formation is not simply an analysis of actual, empirically occurring forms of behaviour (Dean 1995: 566). Rather, it centres on "problematisations", which imply the ways in which people make their own existence the subject of questioning, investigation and intervention. Or, in Foucault's words, the focus point is "the problematisations through which being offers itself to be, necessarily, thought – and the practices on the basis of which these problematisations are formed" (Foucault, quoted in Dean 1995: 566). Problematisation has a practical or technical nature, since it makes use of various means to make our existence accessible to introspection, calculation and manipulation. Correspondingly, governmentality studies such as Dean's have shifted the question of the subject and its status to a question about practices for subject formation – or, more precisely, the practical techniques and intellectual models through which the subject can be made conceivable and malleable (e.g. Miller & Rose 1992).

This approach has an obvious relevance to studies of welfare institutions' encounters with citizens. It avoids classic questions about what kind of ideology is practised in the welfare apparatus, or which actor-interests and alliances lie behind a given social policy. Instead, the focus is on the specific tools and forms of knowledge that make individuals and populations conceivable as specific objects of governance. The forms of knowledge particularly relevant to the problem addressed in this book include disciplines such as pedagogy, law, medicine and psychology. Crucial "intellectual techniques" include social statistics, census-taking, motivational schemes, development contracts, graphs and charts etc. Dean stresses that the virtue of this analytic of government is that it demonstrates social policies' dependence on technical tools of various kinds:

> "[I]t directs attention to the conditions of operation of particular social security practices so that, at a minimum, such practices cannot be reduced to emanations of a particular ideology, policy perspective or even welfare-state regime. The analysis of social security measures as practices of government reveals the dependence of social policy on particular technical conditions of existence, routines and rituals of bureaucracy, forms of expertise and intellectual technologies" (Dean 1995: 571).

In his analyses, Dean investigates the reforms of the Australian unemployment insurance system as it moves from a passive principle based on the rights of "the unemployed recipient" to an active system for "the jobseeker". He shows how a new object of governance has been constructed in the form of a new subject category, "those at risk of long-term unemployment" (Dean, 1995: 568). As an analytical tool, Dean uses the four dimensions of self-government proposed by Foucault, which are almost identical to the four dimensions highlighted by Dean to analyse "regimes of practice" (Dean 1999a: 23). We also notice that they overlap with the four approaches for analysing power technologies (Villadsen 2011b: 1063). In the context of the analysis in this case, the four dimensions are used as approaches to analyse the form of self-government that targets unemployed people. These include (Dean 1995: 564–5):

1. The ethical substance: The delineation of particular objects of self-government (e.g. motivation or extroversion).
2. Working tools: The procedures and techniques used in governance and self-governance (e.g. self-examination or diary-writing).
3. The mode of subjectification: The moral principles and "truths" to which the self-governing individual subjects himself or herself (e.g. stemming from therapeutic or psychiatric knowledge).

4. Telos: The goals that subjects set for their self-government. What mode of being do we hope to create? What do we hope to produce in ourselves and others (e.g. a liberated subject or a preventive community)?

The first dimension examines which objects are made visible by certain programmes for self-government. The reform of the unemployment system makes visible several new objects of government, including a wide-ranging cluster of social and personal effects of unemployment. Dean explains that "these include the erosion of self-esteem, the effects on physical and mental health, the isolation of the unemployed from social networks, their marginalization from the labour market, their potential for criminality and lawlessness, their poor morale and motivation, their attitude to the labour market, their boredom, and their loss of social obligation" (Dean 1995: 572). It becomes clear that the unemployment system does not just concentrate on the payment of benefits and on matching up jobs with the formal qualifications of unemployed people, nor does it simply stress their financial situation and obligations. Rather, it incorporates a whole range of personal "attitudes, affects, conduct and dispositions that present a barrier to the unemployed returning to the labour market, and alienate them from social networks" (Dean 1995: 572). The catch-all category here is "job-readiness". In addition, the different phases of unemployment indicate and visualise the risk unemployed people run of finding themselves trapped in long-term unemployment. The concepts used to summarise the position of unemployed people in relation to all of these parameters are "job-readiness" and "risk of long-term unemployment".

The second dimension concerns the means with which the individual governs himself or herself (and others). It is worth mentioning in the first instance that it is not centralised state bodies that deal with unemployed people. Rather, it is a network comprising governmental, quasi-governmental and private actors. The existence of this network, in which the sovereign exercise of power is partially delegated to local and private actors, means that allegations of a colonising nanny state are difficult to substantiate. More specific tools include "the work" that aims to keep people capable of returning to the labour market during prolonged unemployment – although it was extremely difficult to find workplaces where this ability can be put to the test. There is also the "the activity test", in which the client not only has to demonstrate their active efforts to find a job, but also that they have taken part in training and job-preparation activities. Attempts are also made to set up a reciprocal obligation, based on the principle that when the state grants a citizen an allowance, it is only fair that the citizen does something in return. As such, benefits are now provided within the framework of a mutual contractual obligation. Dean notes: "Benefits are not granted, then, as a right of the citizen or taxpayer but as a part of mutual exchange or contract between the individual and the state, in which both parties accept a new pattern of obligation" (Dean 1995: 574). Finally, a case manager is charged with the task of maintaining a kind of pastoral overview of the unemployed individual, which not only consists of guiding him or her towards activities that instil job-readiness, but also encourage the recipient to adopt a certain moral self-relation.

The third dimension consists of an analysis of the truths to which the individual subscribes, as well as what kind of subject this transforms the individual into. The immediate answer is that the subject to be fostered is "the active jobseeker". This implies, in Dean's words, that "the individual is the proprietor and marketer of his or her skills, qualifications and even physical and psychological attributes" (Dean 1995: 576). The subject should not perceive him- or herself as a mere holder of rights, but as a subject with a moral obligation. Nor should the subject see his or her situation as a product of social structures, the force of tradition or simply bad luck, but perceive him- or herself and his or her own fate as the product of personal choices. It might be added to Dean's analysis that the truth to which unemployed people have to subject themselves might be described in terms of preventive knowledge. In other words, it is knowledge that specifies what the individual must do to minimise his or her current and future risks.

Naturally, the above analysis leads to the question of the telos, or ultimate goal, of these self-government programmes. It is about creating an active, responsible workforce rather than passive recipients. In this ideal world, the previous socio-political preoccupation with combating inequality and disadvantage becomes secondary to fear of the dependent, long-term unemployed individual. The way to prevent the establishment of such a dependent and passive underclass is to cultivate a constant readiness in unemployed people so that they actively, and in a responsible, forward-looking manner, seek out the opportunities available in the education and employment systems and the labour market. It should be added that the goal of this "world" is not only reflected in the Australian reforms, but was – and is – a goal advocated and championed by the OECD.

With its clear-cut focus on political governance as management via self-government, on the technical and intellectual tools for subject formation, and on the perhaps somewhat surprisingly interventionist and paternalistic aspects of liberal forms of governance, Dean's is an emblematic example of a "classic" governmentality analysis. It shows how the unemployed individual, as a formal legal entity with the right to maintenance, is fragmented into a variety of behavioural dispositions and moral attitudes that are subjected to intervention. If we were to refer to the previous typology of modern Western technologies of power, it might be said that the sovereign legal technology here is supplemented with the disciplinary technology, which makes visible a whole series of personality traits and risk factors that can be improved through minute and continuous training. The way in which disciplinary power technology relies on legal power technology – and vice versa – constitutes an area of analysis that continues to be topical in studies of citizens' encounters with modern welfare institutions.

Conclusion

In our considered opinion, Foucault provides an extremely flexible analytical conceptual apparatus. It can be used to analyse how power and knowledge are connected in many different contexts in the welfare state – the interweaving of scientific discourse into political programmes; institutions' use of various technologies of power; and how attempts are also made to govern citizens through certain technologies of the self. Foucault also provides an approach that is capable of calling into question the basic sociological categories upon which social-scientific analyses are usually based – state/civil society, public/private, autonomy/control and so on. His analytics facilitate a "versatile" critique, in which power is not viewed as originating from the state or other authoritative centre, but as something observable in a whole series of relationships and regimes that span the divide between the public and the private sectors (Miller & Rose 1992). Furthermore, Foucault's view of power as productive complicates easy and hasty assessments of some power as repressive and another as liberating.

His analytics indeed refuse to accept as a given the distinction that is often made between "evil power", where the state suppresses the citizen or "colonises civil society", and "good power", which enables the citizen through empowerment or "reaction from below" – that is, from the grassroots and dedicated activists (Cruikshank 1999). Foucault's analytics are keenly aware that it is often exactly in projects that seek to liberate and "speak out against power" that the exercise of power is at its most subtle. Foucault's analytical critique can be deployed where power is static, locked into forms of dominance, and where universalising categories that are taken for granted are in the process of stifling the openness of the discourse.

3 Goffman: Interaction and identity negotiations

Erving Goffman was born in Canada in 1922 and died, aged 60, in 1982. He was awarded his BA at the University of Toronto in 1945 and his MA and PhD at the University of Chicago in 1949 and 1953 respectively. He then spent short periods working at various universities before ending up at the University of Pennsylvania as a professor of anthropology and sociology (1968–82). He is particularly well known for his work on face-to-face interactions (e.g. *Encounters* (1972) and *Interaction Ritual* (1967)), on dramaturgy, i.e. the use of theatrical metaphors in the analysis of interaction between people in *The Presentation of Self in Everyday Life* (1990a), and on total institutions/client culture and stigma in *Asylums* (1974a) and *Stigma* (1990b). Introduction to Goffman: Lemert and Branaman (2001) *The Goffman Reader*, which gives a thorough introduction to Goffman's work while it also contains a collection of key texts from his writings. Burns (1992) *Erving Goffman* and Smith (2006) *Erving Goffman (Key Sociologists)* are two good introductions to Erving Goffman's authorship and to the key concepts in his writing.

KEY CONCEPTS: interaction, face-work, theatrical metaphors (play, performance, role and stage etc.), ritual, definition of situation, social order, strategy.

The self in interaction

The purpose of using interaction as an analytical strategy is to show that a person's actions are an interactional accomplishment that takes place in a specific situation in a particular organisational setting (for example, in a school, social-work department or workplace) and with the participation of other actors. In other words, when we interpret a person's actions – those of a client or a social worker – it is imperative that we take all of these aspects into account. The radical interpretation is that it is the actual situational and institutional setting, as well as the actions of other participating actors, that produce the actions of those being studied.

Within the sociological discipline it is the Chicago School in particular that is credited for putting the concept of interaction on the sociological agenda. The Chicago School stems from American pragmatism, which is a philosophical school that focuses on practice and the practical implications of an idea, theory, method or hypothesis. This tradition does not operate with a universalistic concept of truth, but a concept of truth that is defined by its ability to influence practice by various ideas, theories and methods. Key to this approach is its focus on the function and consequences of various theories and concepts in concrete practices, and not on whether the theories and concepts are "truth" judged in a more universalistic manner. As such, it is a philosophical school that puts truth in parentheses for studies of the social function of various theories and concepts. And, as we know, practice and concrete actions among people are also the focus of symbolic interactionism.

The term "symbolic interactionism" was coined by Blumer (1969) in his book of the same name. With it, Blumer gathers up the strands that include Mead and Goffman's work on the relationship between the individual and society. In this sociological tradition, the self is regarded as a product of social processes. In other words, the self is assumed to be created and recreated in social interaction. Symbolic interactionism therefore studies how people use and interpret symbols in order to create and maintain certain impressions of themselves and others. The interactionist perspective focuses on the real-life details of encounters between people, and explores how various symbols are drawn into the interaction that endow it with direction and meaning. Symbolic interactionism does not focus so much on what "really" happened, but instead on how different actors negotiate certain interpretations of "reality". This is what the oft-quoted Thomas theorem seeks to express: "If people define situations as real, they are real in terms of their consequences" (Thomas & Thomas 1928: 572).

The starting point is that what is real to the actors has real consequences for them, for their interaction, and even for their identity formation. A major area of discussion in symbolic interactionism is, however, how bound the actor is assumed to be by the situation. Is the focus on what structures the situation – and as a result of this, the individual's (limited) scope for action – or is the focus rather on the actors and their actions and, therefore, how they create the situation? In *Frame Analysis* (1974b: 1) Goffman points out that Thomas' theorem is often misunderstood because it is assumed, incorrectly, to mean that individuals are able to choose to create a new reality simply by redefining it. Goffman notes that the framework for social interaction is present in society before the social interaction occurs. People are only able to define themselves in accordance with statuses, roles and relationships that are consistent with the social order (Goffman 1967).

Elsewhere in his writing, Goffman slightly relaxes this structural-institutional perspective. *Strategic Interaction* (1970) focuses, for example, on the individual's ability both to manipulate and to act strategically, although these acts of manipulation and strategy are socially embedded and can therefore not be regarded as solely stemming from the individuals themselves. People orient themselves strategically and manipulatively towards other actors, but this orientation incorporates the actual situational order. Goffman works with a socially-based concept of strategy that always relates to the context (Goffman 1972). As a result, it is possible to say that it is not really the actors' "own" strategies that we see played out, but strategies that are embedded in the context. Actors must adopt these strategies – certain rituals, gestures, statements – just to be involved in the given context. Strategies can therefore be described as socially produced or embedded. In *Asylums* (1974a), Goffman shows the range of counter-strategies patients adopt when involuntarily committed to a state psychiatric institution.

On the one hand, it can be argued that the self in Goffman's work should only be viewed as a social product. On the other hand, he also writes that individuals must not be regarded as determined by society and its institutions. In other words, people are also capable of strategic manipulation (Branaman 2001: xlvii). In our cases, which shed light on social work's power and mechanisms of domination, we will provide examples of classic institutional analyses as played out in a nursing home in the USA in the 1970s and in a centre for rehabilitation in Denmark during the first decade of the new millennium. But first, we will delve more deeply into the theory that inspired Goffman, and then look at key concepts in his work.

Mead's ground-breaking book *Mind, Self and Society* (1967, first published in 1934) challenges the assumption that the individual and society are two separate entities, and focuses on how the environment affects people's understandings of themselves and their ability for self-expression. Mead divides the self into an "I" and a "me", and shows how society's norms and values shape a person's self-perception. Via these two components, he seeks to capture the processes that mean that a person's identity cannot – or ought not to – be confused with a private, personal, unchanging self. We are part of a social community (in Mead's terminology, "the other") that affects our self-perception. Put very simply, Mead uses the term "me" to refer to a specific and/or generalised "other", whose function can be viewed as a kind of "censor". The "me" determines (and reflects) the nature of the social interaction that, in conjunction with the "I" of the present, defines the self. The point is that the social community ("the generalized other") necessarily exerts an influence on the individual's self-perception. There is, therefore, an ongoing mental process of "role play", in which individuals incorporate ideas about how others will react to their actions, with the consequence that the individual's self-presentation incorporates "the other".

If we, in our capacity as researchers, students or social workers, are to analyse an encounter between a client and a social worker, for instance, it will be necessary to study how "the generalized other" – for example, in the shape of norms such as the idea that citizens today are supposed to demonstrate responsibility and the desire to be self-supporting – affects the ecounter between the two parties. We must also study how distinct and separate "others" affect the interaction. For example, what expectations do the social worker and the client have of the interaction's outcome? The social worker may have been appointed because of a special interest in conversational therapy or group-dynamic methods, and will seek to adapt the problem to these methods in the interaction with the client. The client may have expectations of a work placement that will enhance his or her job skills, and will try to turn the conversation towards themes that underpin this desire. The point is that in the interaction they will try to decode "the other's" expectations and adjust their own actions so that each supports their own objective for the encounter as best they can. Central to Mead's work is that a kind of "role play" always takes place, in which the interacting parties try to incorporate "the other's" expectations into their own self-representation.

This is the part of Mead's research on which Goffman builds. In his words (Goffman 1990a: 26), "An interaction may be defined as all the interaction which occurs throughout any one occasion when a given set of individuals are in one another's continuous presence". In relation to the self, Goffman (1990a) shows, however, that communication between two or more parties is not just about making the other person's expectations your own, but just as much about "impression management", i.e. the impression we give of ourselves to both the specific and the generalised other. Goffman (1990b) operates with a virtual and an actual social identity. Socially excluded people experience a discrepancy between these two, i.e. between the category in which a person is placed and their own self-assessment.

This takes us to the concept of stigma. For Goffman (1990b: 51), "stigma management is an offshoot of something basic in society, the stereotyping or 'profiling' of our normative expectations regarding conduct and character". The significant aspect here is that a stigma or a deviation is not something absolute, i.e. it does not relate to the specific characteristics of a person, but rather provides information about the relationship between social norms and an individual's self-presentation. As a consequence of this, the relationship between the normal and the deviant is viewed as socially constructed. Stigma is not an inherent property of specific individuals, who can be divided up between the stigmatised and the normal. For Goffman, stigma is exclusively a relational role-marker that is ascribed to all individuals, at least in certain situations and at certain stages of life. Goffman identifies three general types of stigma: first, abominable features of the body, including physical deformities and disfiguring blemishes; second, defects in a person's character, such as weak willpower and overpowering or abnormal passions; and third, "tribe" stigma related to race, nation and religion. These types of stigma make it clear that what is considered normal is always only perceived as such in relation to the stigmatised. It is also obvious that, in many cases, welfare institutions in particular treat stigmatised individuals and reproduce their stigma in a variety of ways.

This relational perspective on what creates a person also explains why it is irrelevant to look "into" and conduct an in-depth interpretation of the people the researcher is studying, something that Goffman indeed also refrains from doing. In *Asylums* (1974a), for example, in which he analyses the interaction between doctors and patients in a US state psychiatric institution, there are no descriptions of what the different parties "feel" or "experience". Instead he gives detailed descriptions of how the interaction between the two parties appears from a distance.

Working within an institutional framework, Goffman focuses both on client culture, which to a high degree relates to the institution's bureaucratic structures, and on how the clients survive by acting strategically in relation to the opportunities offered, despite everything, by the institution (Goffman 1974a: 23ff). Regardless of the long descriptions of institutional rules and routines, the institutional perspective always focuses on the clients' carefully developed systems of privileges (ibid. 51ff), options for adjustments (ibid. 171ff) and the fact that every world develops its own "underlife" (ibid. 267). This analytical approach provides a good example of how it is possible to consider the self as socially created and at the same time operate with a self that is capable of manipulation and strategic action. This duality is also shown in the case about everyday life in a nursing home, where the elderly both assume the role of the institution's (passive) patients and simultaneously manage to act strategically in this rule-driven institutional setting.

In *Asylums*, Goffman (1974a: 61–3) presents four "modes of adaptation" that reveal the various stages of patients' moral career:

1. The patients withdraw into themselves, i.e. refrain from participating in the interaction ("situational withdrawal");
2. The patients adopt an obstinate attitude and refuse to co-operate with the staff;
3. The patients allow themselves to be colonised by the institution, in other words begin to co-operate with the staff and, as a result of this, the tension between the inside and outside worlds is reduced substantially;
4. The patients are converted, they adopt the official verdict on themselves and try to act out the role of the perfect patient.

The main point to notice in relation to these four stages of the patients' moral career is that Goffman is describing a process in which an identity is developed and adjusted in relation to a range of institutional and organisational conditions, which underlines the important focus on the frameworks for any interaction between individuals.

However, Goffman does not only deal with socially-excluded people. Let us look at the other concepts in his sociology that may be relevant to the analysis of the state's encounter with the citizen, and the actual practices in which this encounter unfolds. Goffman is known for using a series of metaphors to analyse everyday life. Best known are his theatre, game and ritual metaphors.[1] He uses the theatre as a metaphor for society, and shows how people act in different roles, which are rehearsed "backstage" with various props (Goffman 1990a: 109ff). Front stage and backstage are relational and flexible analytic categories that refer to each other. Something that is backstage in one situation may be front stage in certain other situations (as exemplified in Case 2).

The theatrical metaphors – just like the game metaphors – serve to emphasise that people are strategic actors, i.e. they are not exclusively determined by the structures of social interaction. We manipulate, put up façades and play roles, the purpose of which is to control the impression we give of ourselves. Goffman's focus on the rituals of everyday life demonstrates the interdependence between the self and the many roles that the individual plays in everyday life, with its order and embedded morality. "[I]n oscillating between three metaphors for describing social life – the drama, ritual and game metaphors – Goffman demonstrates the inherent interplay between manipulation and morality in social life, challenging us to recognize the everyday techniques upon which morality is based" (Branaman 2001: lxxxii). It is precisely when individuals act strategically in order to achieve a credible "I" and a scope for action that they inevitably end up adopting a moral code of behaviour and thus partake in reproducing society's moral values. In other words, Goffman's metaphors help make visible the morality that guides every society and every organisation and institution, and which is circulated and reproduced at the individual level.

Let us look more closely at the concept of the role (nowadays the concept of "identity/identification"), which is central to many interactionist analyses. The role concept is regularly criticised for suggesting a stability that does not directly harmonise with the processual concept of identity that we have described above with reference to Mead. However, stability is not a key property of the role concept used by interactionist-inspired researchers. Rather, in an interactionist analysis, it is the ambiguity in the theatrical metaphor that is stressed. Attempts are made to show that different actors step into and out of different roles, sometimes even within the same conversation. As far as social work is concerned, the focus is on the social worker's and the client's ability to operate with a series of identities/identifications (and roles). What all of these identities (and roles) have in common is that they express and interact with the actual social situation that forms the framework for the interaction in which they are involved. In other words, people cannot play anywhere near all of the potential roles and identities in all of the conceivable situations. It is precisely the situation, organisation and other actors' limitations on our potential for expression that are often at the centre of interactionist-inspired analyses. What is fruitful in Goffman's theatre and game metaphors is that they make it possible to regard a person's acts as both strategic and controlled by the social interaction. In brief, during the "play" the individuals concerned are given a role – with or without their consent.

Goffman's ritual metaphor draws attention to the fact that people follow very specific procedures in their interaction with each other. He cites numerous examples of micro-sociological processes in which people follow quite definitive rituals in their encounters. He shows, for example, how a phone conversation usually ends, how two people avoid colliding when they pass each other on a narrow path, etc. Goffman is also at pains to show that people do not always follow the given rituals, which results in equally ritualistic attempts by the actors to repair the damage. The point in this context is that Goffman's sociology suggests that we, as researchers, should study micro-sociological processes with great care, since these processes reveal the series of rituals that hold together the society or the culture that is the object of study. By looking at very small, everyday occurrences, it is possible to obtain useful knowledge of the micro-social patterns with which we work.

Other key Goffman concepts are "interaction order"/"social order" and "definition of the situation", which pop up frequently in his work. "Interaction order" refers to the fact that people's face-to-face encounters are not random and unpredictable, but rather relate to a particular social order's structure and rules. What interests Goffman is the micro-order that affects – indeed, actually regulates – individuals' encounters with each other. It is this relationship that he refers to with his concept of "face-work", which draws attention to the ritual aspects of interaction – that we seek to avoid losing face and control the impression we give of ourselves (see the terms "impression management", "in face", "wrong face" (Goffman 1967, 1990a)). "Definition of the situation" refers to the fact that people relate actively to their current situation, i.e. when we meet, our definition of the situation is embedded in our orientation towards each other. In other words, the participants in any situation must agree upon the nature of situation in which they are interacting (Goffman 1990a). Sometimes the parties will disagree about the definition of the situation, for instance about whether the interaction is related to an economic rationality or to psychological explanations. Which of the "definitions of the situation" will assert itself is not necessarily a given. The struggle to define situations therefore has a crucial role in interactionist-inspired research.

Power and control in the institutions of the welfare state

How can Goffman's analytics be applied to the theme of the citizen's encounter with the representatives of the welfare state? Can Goffman be seen as a theorist of power? And if so, what do we understand by the term "power"? And what about the state? Does Goffman shed any light on it? Let us start with the final question. As our introduction suggests, the emphasis in symbolic interactionism is predominantly on looking at local, intensely practical interaction between people. However, some researchers have paid attention to the principles of how structural features influence the interaction. Järvinen and Mik-Meyer (2005: 100) distinguish between studies of how institutional features affect practice and studies of practice in its own right, specifically to maintain this difference. "Institutional studies" explicitly focus on the conditions that structure the interaction, whereas "practice studies" take a more ethno-methodological approach and, in the relationship between practice and institution, focus primarily on the former. "Practice studies" such as conversational analysis, for example, only incorporate structural features if the participants in the observed interaction explicitly activate them.

Even if the researcher stresses the conditions that structure the interaction between, for example, clients and social workers, this is not the same as focusing on the state's role in a sociological perspective. And although the concept of state is typically absent from institutional studies, this does not mean that it is not possible to read into these micro-sociological studies an indirect criticism of the way in which the state operates. For instance, when Goffman (1974a) reported back on his experiences of a state psychiatric institution in the USA (cf. *Asylums*), his writings were of great importance to the contemporary design of treatment facilities for mentally ill people. His study enabled the reader, by an indirect route, to obtain knowledge of this type of institution and also of the state model underpinning it. It should be added that a typical criticism of symbolic interactionism is precisely that this branch of sociology does not, in its exploration of people's interactions, explicitly relate to a state concept or a social model (see the discussion in Maines (2003) of whether symbolic interactionism can be considered a (too) narrow current in sociology).

As to the questions of whether Goffman can be considered a theorist of power and what, in that case, we understand by the concept of power, our answer will be "yes" to the first question under the condition that the concept of power is not, as is so often the case in sociology, linked to an overarching theory of the state. If, however, power is instead understood as a designation for a number of concepts that are particularly suited to encapsulating the struggles for status, recognition, domination and resources, then Goffman can be considered a theorist of power (see also Jenkins 2008).

Goffman's work revolves around defined concepts such as situation, framework, social order, intentionality and strategy. As previously mentioned, the first three of these concepts draw attention to the structuring (and often limiting) conditions to which people are subject in their encounters with each other. The next two – intentionality and strategy – draw attention to an individual's ability to act with intent and in a strategic manner in a range of situations.

Goffman does focus on power, albeit in different ways. He has a strong focus on the situational power that restrains individuals and which is embedded in the situation and equally a strong focus on how an individual is able to think and act intentionally in relation to the situation he is part of.[2] In analysis of how institutions work, we typically see both forms of power. The power of the institution can be studied and analysed by looking at the series of invasive mechanisms that an institution utilises (Goffman 1974a), by looking at the categories forced upon the inmates and by looking at the rules and norms that structure encounters between, for example, social workers and clients, and which both parties have difficulty changing. An individual's power – the ability to act strategically and intentionally within a framework not established by ourselves – can be observed in a number of the contexts in which citizens encounter the state. Here, too, Goffman's (1974a) *Asylums* is a prime example of how patients act strategically within a highly constrictive framework.

Goffman's (e.g. 1970) point is that an individual possesses an ability to act strategically and intentionally, so even though the interaction between a social worker and a client may seem very unequal with regard to status, and – at first glance – the ability to define the situation etc., an interaction may still reflect a powerful client's choice of the role of the victim, if this role enables the client to achieve what he or she wants. However, another key point is that it is a "strategic interaction" – each participant's (strategic) actions have consequences for the other participants' (strategic) actions. One dimension of the situation concept in symbolic interactionism that is particularly crucial when one studies power and control is the degree of formality. A situation may be more or less formal (see Goffman's (1990a) concepts of "front region/stage" and "back region/stage"). Very formal encounters, such as an encounter between a social worker and a client to determine a client's status under the law, typically have a clear plot. The participants – both the client and the social worker – will try to adapt to the expectations placed on them by the situation. In this type of encounter, it will typically be the prevailing definition of the situation – in turn underpinned by the overall institutional organisation of the encounter – that produces the rules and routines of the situation. However, in more informal encounters – such as clients and social workers chatting over coffee at a rehabilitation centre – it will to a greater extent be the participants who produce the rules and routines in such "cosy" and "informal" meetings (see Mik-Meyer 2004).

Goffman (1990a) also introduces the concept of "presentation of self" in order to clarify the series of selves which it is possible to draw upon in different social situations. The ability to be cynical, inferior or superior in a given situation – irrespective of whether this role is played out at an informal meeting in a rehabilitation centre or at a formal meeting in a nursing home – is not something inherent in the individual. Rather, these roles should be interpreted as actions regulated by the setting (the other participants or the situation). A number of rituals serve to reaffirm society's moral values regarding what might be considered "natural" superiority in the relationship between social workers and clients, doctors and nurses, or professors and students, which causes the inferior – in this case clients, nurses and students – to "play down", i.e. accept their position as subordinates, and in doing so help to maintain and reproduce their relation of inequality.

Goffman (1990a) uses the term "misrepresentation" to draw attention to the fact that we sometimes encounter "wrong faces" or "wrong representations" in relation to the context. This may occur when a client rebukes a social worker, for example, or when patients adopt a know-it-all attitude when discussing illness with a doctor. This type of situation does occur, of course, but by dint of the very fact that we acknowledge that they are atypical, and that every society has its "institutional authorities" – defined as people who, by virtue of their position, are empowered to present an official version of reality (Goffman 1983: 17) – the misrepresentation concept serves to highlight where the power lies in any given situation. This power is a power that often reflects society's authority structures, despite the fact that power in symbolic interactionism is understood as continuously being renegotiated in the local, situational order.

In cases where a participant breaks with the expected pattern of behaviour, the concept "wrong face" is applicable, signifying the opposite of being "in face", which is a positive social value, to which an individual has laid claim and which is accepted by the other participants in the situation (Goffman 1967: 5). If participants are in "wrong face" or otherwise violate the "line" established by the situation, they are normally swiftly ushered back on track by the other participants. With the "line" concept, Goffman (ibid.) focuses on the patterns in the verbal and non-verbal actions used by participants to express their views on the situation – and hence also their evaluation of the other participants. Again, we are dealing with a concept that, like "face" and "wrong face", sheds light on the setting for our actions – in other words, the fact that people are always part of a social order that we have to decode and in relation to which we must seek to regulate the way we act. This creates and recreates both the social order and the participating actors' selves.

The point, in this context of interactionist studies, is that the social order is powerful because we, as interacting participants, will always try to maintain it so that neither our fellow participants nor we display a "wrong face". Maintaining not only our own "line" but also those of the situation's other participants is a prerequisite for interaction (and, as such, is not the purpose of the interaction). More generally, Goffman's work demonstrates how interaction among individuals in society is comparable to staged acts in a theatrical performance that "requires a thorough scripting" and "stage directions" (Goffman 1990a: 79). In other words, individuals continuously adapt and adjust their behaviour so that they, along with the situation's other participants, are able to sustain their roles in the specific social order in which society's norms are embedded. These norms can be seen as having a structuring effect, all the way down to the details of the various situational moments. As Goffman (1967: 3) writes in the foreword to *Interactional Ritual*, we are not dealing with "men and their moments, but moments and their men".

We will now turn our attention to how roles and identities can be studied and analysed on the basis of social work's "moments". The first analysis is taken from Gubrium's (1997) classic monograph, *Living and Dying at Murray Manor*, in which he analyses the encounter between nursing home staff and senior citizens. Gubrium's monograph is in many ways similar to Goffman's seminal work *Asylums*, in that the focus is largely on the different "worlds" in which the "top staff", "front-line workers" and "clientele" operate. The second analysis is derived from Mik-Meyer's (2004) analysis of clients' encounters with staff in a rehabilitation centre in Denmark in 2000. This case has been chosen to show a more structural-institutional approach, in the sense that the analysis also incorporates circumstances outside of the interaction. In this context, we should also mention the anthology *Institutional Selves* (2001), edited by Gubrium and Holstein, because it contains a number of illustrative chapters showing how identities are created and negotiated in specific institutional contexts. The anthology includes examples from a number of key welfare areas, such as prison (Fox), women's shelters (Loseke), social agencies for homeless people (Spencer) and therapy work (Miller).

Case 1: Everyday life in a nursing home

In this case, we will show the strength of an ethnographic institutional analysis of everyday life in an American nursing home. The study stems from Jaber Gubrium's fieldwork in 1973. It uses the same analytical strategy as Goffman's *Asylums* (1974a), in that both studies are based on extensive empirical data, primarily collated during fieldwork, both studies include detailed descriptions of the sites studied (a nursing home and a psychiatric hospital, respectively), and both study the different worlds in which the employees and patients find themselves in the two organisations (Goffman 1974a, Gubrium 1997).

In his introduction, Gubrium outlines the book's central concept of "worlds": "I used the concept of 'worlds' to emphasize how the nursing home, while a single organization, consisted of virtually different worlds for the administrative staff ('top staff'), front-line workers ('floor staff') and the clientele" (Gubrium 1997: xiii). He uses the concept of worlds to focus attention on the fact that both staff and patients can be said to live in their own worlds, i.e. "they organize their lives in relation to each other, not outsiders, and define their individual identities in terms of being group members" (Gubrium 1997: xx). Whenever there are multiple coexisting worlds within an organisation, multiple logics will also exist or, as Gubrium writes, several forms of "taken-for-grantedness". This often means that "little or no attention at all is paid to what is or isn't reasonable, life is simply going on for members as if nothing else mattered" (Gubrium 1997: xxi). Later, he writes: "Each world provides its participants with a way of looking at and understanding daily life at the Manor, and each has its own logic: Its own ideals, sense of justice and fair treatment, method of experience, prescribed duties, rhetorical style, and proper mode of making decisions" (Gubrium 1997: 37).

Fieldwork is the most obvious method for a researcher when seeking insight into everyday life in an organisation and how participants generate their own meaning in the local situation. Gubrium cites Goffman's book *Asylums* as an illustration of the strength of fieldwork:

> "My immediate objective in doing fieldwork at St. Elizabeth's was to try to learn about the world of the hospital inmate, as this world is

> subjectively experienced by him [...] It was then and still is my belief that any group of persons – prisoners, primitives, pilots, or patients – develop a life of their own that becomes meaningful, reasonable, and normal once you get close to it, and that a good way to learn about any of these worlds is to submit oneself in the company of the members to the daily round of petty contingencies to which they are subject" (Goffman in Gubrium 1997: xxi).

Inspired by Goffman, Gubrium was interested in the concept of the meaningful, as seen from the different actors' perspectives. He looked at how administrative staff, care staff and clientele understood "care" and "care-giving" in the nursing home concerned (Gubrium 1997: xxii). He discovered, among other things, that "what the top staff saw as good and efficient care-giving, floor staff could consider 'just getting the work done' [...] [and] what a resident felt was time well spent chatting with a friendly nurse's aide could, from the aide's point of view, be time away from other duties. The aide, after all, was not only providing care but also doing a job" (Gubrium 1997: xxii–xxiii).

Again, the symbolic interactionist perspective, with its attentiveness to everyday practices, is used to show how – in this case – different perceptions of "care" are able to coexist in an institution, precisely because the institution serves as the framework for multiple worlds, each with its own distinctive logic.

Through his fieldwork, it became more and more obvious to Gubrium that the physical location (cf. his concept of "place") should play a key role in the analysis: "Top staff conducted their daily affairs in their offices and in meetings [...] Floor staff, especially nurse's aides, spent most of their work lives on patient and resident floors, caring for and mingling with the clientele and each other [...] The clientele, too, carried on life in their own places, in their own rooms, the dining areas, lounges, and other locations on their floors" (Gubrium 1997: xxii–xxiii). This focus on location (place) helped Gubrium to understand areas of conflict and the lack thereof between the groups that (partially) shared the location, which gave rise to clashes between their respective "worlds" and embedded logics (e.g. between care-givers and clientele). On the other hand, the various "worlds", with their routines and rituals, found it easy to co-exist within the institution, as long as they did not share a place. "Places allow their varied participants to operate in seemingly contradictory worlds that look and sound quite reasonable from a position within each world" (Gubrium 1997: 38). As such, the fieldwork directed the attention of the researcher towards the impact of the physical place on the different "worlds". This was therefore an important relationship to examine as part of the work of analysing what "nursing homes were like as settings for living, working, and dying" (Gubrium 1997: xxiii).

Another central tenet of Goffman-inspired studies is that an official interpretation of an organisation's activities and objectives often does not coincide with the practice observed by the researcher. Gubrium notes that "the logic of the official view of the world is one thing; how it is expressed in practice from place to place is often quite another [...] The logic of an official view of the home is used by top staff to present the Manor to themselves and to relevant publics in certain places. The same logic is unwittingly ignored, for the most part, in other places" (Gubrium 1997: 82).

The focus on place naturally directs attention towards the many rituals and routines that make up everyday life. Unsurprisingly, therefore, place is particularly significant in institutions that have a large number of scheduled tasks, e.g. nursing homes. Inspired by Goffman, Gubrium (1997: 123–57) devotes a chapter to what he calls "bed-and-body work", in which he minutely examines the floor staff's bed-making duties and their work with the residents' bodies (washing, going to the toilet, etc.). This includes detailed descriptions of routines associated with, among other things, "awakening", "body-work", "dining", "treatments", "bed-making", "toileting", "bathing", etc. (Gubrium 1997: 125–40). He aims to show how breaking with routines creates major problems for the care staff and for their reproduction of the logic of their "world", and in this situation it is far less important whether the logic definitively counteracts what constitutes "good care" (for example) for those on the receiving end. As he puts it:

> "When top staff deals with floor nurses and aides, the official business at hand is patient care. When floor nurses and aides deal with their superiors, what stands first in their minds is bed-and-body work. And when clientele deal with floor staff, it is their desire to live as proper human beings despite the constraints of institutional living at Manor that is at stake" (Gubrium 1997: 158).

As in other analyses in the book, it is in the meticulous descriptions and quotes from residents, or conversations between staff and patients, that we detect a power imbalance that can lead, for example to much "waiting", which patients often find frustrating. Gubrium quotes a patient who says: "They come around to wake us up around five-thirty or six [...] Breakfast is supposed to be at seven-thirty, but it gets to be 8 o'clock once in a while. We wait all the time. They get us down there at quarter to seven. We wait for breakfast for 45 minutes" (Gubrium 1997: 164). The power imbalance is also clear when Gubrium reproduces a "staged" therapy session (Gubrium 1997: 191), showing therapy as a kind of institutionalised life training. Inspired by Goffman's theatrical metaphors and eye for detail, Gubrium introduces a "reality-oriented" (RO) therapy session at the nursing home:

> "When the scene is set so that all participants have taken their proper places and have at least tacitly decided to play their respective roles as therapist and disoriented patients, RO begins. RO sessions involve an aide as instructor and usually five patients as students. Instructional materials, which are provided by top staff nurses, consist of a chart

(reality board) that lists the name of the nursing home, its location, the date, the day of the week and the state of the weather, and a cardboard clock to teach timekeeping [...] Patients are asked to read the items on the chart, one by one, and then are quizzed on the content [...] Correct (board-oriented) answers to questions presumably mean that patients are 'oriented' and 'accepting reality'. At least, this is what top staff believe. The following exchange between an aide conducting RO and a patient being asked about the state of the weather shows how critical 'place' is in defining reality.

AIDE: [Pointing to the weather on the RO board, which reads 'raining'] What's the weather like today, Emma? Emma turns her head slightly and quickly looks out the window.
EMMA: Well, it looks like the sun is shining kinda bright.

The sun happens to be shining at the moment.

AIDE: Are you sure? It says it's raining? Doesn't it? [Finger still pointing to board]
EMMA: Well, it doesn't look like it from here
AIDE: What does it say here, Emma? [Directing Emma's attention to the board]
EMMA: It says it's raining.
AIDE: [Warmly] That's correct. Very good".

(Gubrium 1997: 191–2, emphasis and punctuation as in original text)

Later, Gubrium (1997: 195) explains that rituals like these often have the (unintended) effect that staff perceive patients as "disoriented" or "confused". Just as in Goffman's work, Gubrium studies and analyses power relations via the meticulous reproduction of practice, unleashing the full potential of Goffman-inspired studies. The critical potential of detailed, ethnographic studies in institutions lies in this approach's descriptive nature, which reveals how people live their lives in treatment institutions. A key point of this type of research is that its documentary nature means the results can be difficult to reject.

Case 2: Client roles and institutional identities

In this case, which draws on Mik-Meyer's research of Danish rehabilitation centres (Mik-Meyer 2004, 2006, 2007), we will briefly outline how external factors can be traced in a concrete interaction between a client and staff at a Danish rehabilitation centre. The purpose of the encounter between Diana (the client) and a series of professionals is to clarify what will happen to her in future – should she be given a light job or an early retirement? Is further assessment required of her capacity to work, or is she perhaps capable, in the long term, of doing an ordinary job? In this case, we are dealing with an individual whose actions and self-representation correspond to the expectations associated with the role of the client within a rehabilitation centre. We are dealing with a client who acts strategically and uses the role of client, i.e. to be a person in need (Loseke 1999: 160) to create a situation (early retirement) that is desirable for her. The negotiation of the client's identity is a strategic exercise played out in various settings. The following text is quoted from Mik-Meyer (2004: 110ff):

> "On an overarching level we can look at the rehabilitation centre's activities as ones that are played out 'back stage' in relation to the client's visit to and contact with the local-authority social services ('on stage'). Many of the activities in rehabilitation centres are designed precisely to feel informal (morning sessions, excursions, hobbies in workshops, informal group chats about personal issues, etc.), the intention being that clients 'throw away the mask' and credible pictures of their potential emerge. This description is later passed on to the client's local-authority caseworker at a number of formal meetings. Ideally, the clients' participation in rehabilitation-centre activities should be limited only by their abilities, whereas the evaluation conducted under local authority auspices is to a great extent based on the options provided by legislation and local political conditions [...]
>
> In cases where the views of the rehabilitation centre and of the local authority about a client differ, the social workers in the centre will automatically assume a key role, as they are not only actors in a 'play' staged by the local authority, but essential co-ordinating actors in the rehabilitation centres [...] The diffuse position of the social workers is caused because they operate in a 'backstage' environment (cf. the informal activities in the centres) and are also active 'on stage' (cf. the formalised activities involved in contact with the local authority). This means that the social workers at the rehabilitation centre have to establish an informal and natural relationship with the client to a greater extent than the local authority caseworkers. This may explain the routine (informal) pre-meeting with the client preceding the meeting with the local authority caseworker. At this pre-meeting, the rehabilitation centre social worker has the opportunity to anticipate potential reactions to the 'surprises' that they may present during the formal meeting. They can also, as we shall see in Diana's case below, reassure the client prior to the meeting [...] At the pre-meeting 'back stage', Diana is told not to be nervous about the coming meeting 'front stage' with the local authority caseworker. The following dialogue is from this pre-meeting:
>
> CONTACT PERSON: There isn't the slightest disagreement about your case, so you can take it easy [...]

SOCIAL WORKER: We won't literally write 'early retirement'. We'll put it some other way. As far as the meeting is concerned, what we usually do is get the person in question to talk about their situation.

DIANA: [Slightly worried] You mean me?

SOCIAL WORKER: Yes, no need for big words. Just say how you feel. Where is it you're from?

DIANA: X council.

SOCIAL WORKER: That's a very good council to apply for early-retirement pension. They're fast. [Laughs] You're lucky. Did you know that? [Serious tone] I can't imagine them needing more [...] Our doctor will also write about you. We tell him the situation and his statement usually conforms with our view of things [...]

It is during this meeting 'back stage' that the next 'performance' is planned, rehearsed and reviewed. Diana is made aware of a number of issues that it would undoubtedly be problematic to discuss openly in front of the local-authority caseworker – for instance, that she lives in a place where the council is 'good' as far as her desire for early retirement is concerned [...] The pre-meeting illustrates that the negotiation about Diana's identity is a process in which the staff are strategically working toward a particular (and, for Diana, constructive) identity. In Goffman's terminology, during this meeting the roles will be allocated and the script rehearsed. The objective is to write Diana's local-authority caseworker into the centre's production in the role of 'saviour', who will do the work that leads to the desired outcome for Diana [...]

However, at the actual meeting (not reproduced here), the local authority caseworker rejects the role of saviour, and instead adopts the role of a critical questioner in order to evaluate the bombastic description of her weak condition presented by Diana, her husband and the staff at the centre. For instance, the local authority caseworker notes that it is not possible to 'prove' that Diana actually suffers from all of the conditions that the staff at the rehabilitation centre, and Diana herself, claim she does. This critical questioning of Diana leads to her 'learning' to focus on one of her many problems – an allergy – as this would appear to be a productive approach conducive to her getting what she wants, an early-retirement pension. The local authority caseworker is, in fact, acting in a different play as well, one that is about minimising the number of applications for early-retirement pensions. Her saviour role is defined by an entirely different situation, and it is these two contrasting definitions of the situation (Goffman 1990a) that collide during the meeting, at which the local authority caseworker repeatedly tries to discredit both the centre's and Diana's own assessment of Diana's situation."

A third aspect the researcher has learned about through participant observation, and which is key to the analysis of the negotiation about Diana's situation, is the staff's general view of Diana as expressed in a number of different contexts. The staff at the rehabilitation centre explain to the researcher on different occasions that Diana really wants to be self-supporting, even though they also deem her incapable of holding down a regular job. The will to support herself, and to generally lead a more responsible lifestyle, reflects the dominant norms of our society, as identified in a great deal of recent research into social work in Scandinavia, see for example Mik-Meyer (2010a), Villadsen (2008b) and Michailakis and Schirmer (2010).

This case analysis provides examples of several institutional factors, i.e. conditions that are not necessarily verbalised in the interaction, but which it may nevertheless be useful to include in the analysis. It is proposed, for example, that the analysis incorporates the various professionals' assessment criteria and institutional placing (contact person = employed in the rehabilitation centre and the client's "advocate"; social worker at the rehabilitation centre = co-ordinating actor between the rehabilitation centre and the local authority; and local authority caseworker = employed by the council and therefore subject to local political conditions), as well as the social norm that citizens today are supposed to want to be self-supporting. Both the staff and the client herself have, in a number of contexts, pointed out that Diana has the will to support herself, even though they think she lacks all of the requisite skills.

The specific analysis of the encounter between Diana and the various staff also takes into account the organisational level (i.e. the difference between the rehabilitation centre and the local authority), which can be presumed to affect the interaction between the different staff and the client, as well as observation notes and interviews that, for example, deal with the assessment of the extent to which Diana wants to be self-supporting. The meeting with the local authority caseworker (which is not reproduced here for reasons of space) illustrates how two institutional cultures and their views of the client (that of the rehabilitation centre and of the local authority) impose different conditions on the encounter, since they have different definitions of what constitutes the "normal" applicant for early retirement. In the pre-meeting, we see how the rehabilitation centre staff and the client act strategically in relation to the prevailing definition of the situation, which reflects the practice in the caseworker's local authority. This is, therefore, an empirical example of how a person's self must be viewed both as socially created (framed) and as strategic (acts in relation to a changing setting).

Conclusion

In this chapter we have presented Goffman's work on social interaction as a particular approach with which to analyse the encounter between professionals in state institutions and the citizen. We have focused, in particular, on how roles and identities in symbolic interactionism must be seen as inextricably linked with a situational order, which to a greater (Case 2) or lesser (Case 1) extent is linked to norms at organisational and societal level.

Central to symbolic interactionism is the idea that a person's self "is not an organic thing that has a specific location, whose fundamental fate is to be born, to mature and to die; it is a dramatic effect arising diffusely from a scene that is presented, and the characteristic issue, the crucial concern, is whether it will be credited or discredited" (Goffman 1990a: 245). In both cases, we saw how different client roles were produced (and, situationally at least, accepted) in a nursing home and a rehabilitation centre.

The first case focused on the major role played by the concrete physical location (place) in relation to the possibility that the social worlds of different groups (administrative staff, care workers and clientele), each adhering to particular logics, are capable of coexisting in the same organisation. This case illustrated how symbolic-interactionist studies look at power in the encounter between staff and clientele by conducting in-depth analyses and reproducing people's interaction. The critical potential of this type of ethnographic approach is in the meticulous reproduction, as shown by Goffman's study of the conditions faced by patients in a US psychiatric hospital in the 1950s. Our case illustrated how a Goffman-inspired study such as Gubrium's makes analytical use of theatrical metaphors and therefore views interaction between staff and clientele as a drama that follows certain pre-determined plots and is supported and structured by certain props, stages, etc. It is therefore in the detailed analysis of a "play", for example a "reality-oriented therapy session" for nursing-home residents, and through the researcher's documentation of how a session like this is prepared and carried out, that researchers gain insight into factors that may lead to criticism – in this case, the treatment work in the nursing home. In this context, power is conceived as embedded in the treatment sessions in a nursing home, which both staff and clients continually help to reproduce, despite the fact that this kind of ritual ascribes to the clients the roll of "confused" or "disoriented".

Our second case also focused on a form of client conditioning, in as far as we saw how the staff encouraged a client to adopt the appropriate behaviour for a subsequent meeting with a local authority caseworker. In particular, this case highlights the fact that people relate actively to the setting they are part of, which is also a key tenet of Goffman's work (and of symbolic interactionism).

The second case also exposed counter-strategies in relation to a system which takes it for granted that it is the system itself – represented by the local authority caseworker – that ultimately determines a client's situation: the client plays her role in the situation, indirectly influencing her future in a positive direction (seen from her perspective). Her counter-strategy to focus only on allergy can be seen as an orientation that shows her capability to adapt to an organisational, institutional role (it might be argued that her adaptation to this particular role corresponds to Goffman's category of "conversion", as she actively tries to adopt the right role – to be converted into an accepted player in the interaction). In this way, Case 2 showed a client that actively helped to reproduce a system that, from a different perspective, can be seen as oppressing her – exactly as postulated by Foucault's productive understanding of power (see Chapter 1).

When the focus is on power – and therefore, in relation to the theme of this book, on clients' counter-strategies – symbolic interactionism does not operate with a top-down understanding of the exercise of power. As our cases illustrate, both patients/clients and staff actively reproduce the prevailing definition of the situation – although, viewed from the patient's/client's position, the outcome might look somewhat different.

Finally, we have also underlined that, when conducting an interactionist analysis of work with senior citizens, clients or others seeking help, it is possible to choose exclusively to base the analysis on ethnographic data (Case 1), or incorporate social norms and other institutional conditions in order to show how these more external factors are embedded and reproduced in encounters between people (Case 2). Regardless of the weighting of institutional conditions for the analysis of the encounter between patients/clients and welfare professionals, we must examine how the self-perceptions of care-home residents and clients (for example) are adapted and reproduced in the social order in the actual encounter between the two parties. For the symbolic interactionist, therefore, local, situation-specific actions will always be the starting point for the analysis. It is then up to the observer to decide to what extent he or she wishes to incorporate institutional and more general social norms and dominant discourses.

4 Bourdieu: Field, symbolic violence and domination

Pierre Bourdieu was born in south-west France in 1930 and died in 2002. He studied at the elite École Normale Supérieure and worked as a professor at the École Pratique des Hautes Études and Collège de France. He is particularly well known for his anthropological study of the Kabyle people in North Africa, which inspired his theory of practice (*Outline of a Theory of Practice* (2000a), *The Logic of Practice* (1999) and *Pascalian Meditations* (2000b)). He is known for his cultural studies (*Distinction* (1987)) and his critical studies of the relationship between the education system and power (*Reproduction in Education, Society and Culture* (Bourdieu & Passeron 1990), *Homo Academicus* (1988), and *The State Nobility* (1998a)). Short and precise introductions to Bourdieu: Jenkins (2002) *Pierre Bourdieu (Key Sociologists)*, in which Richard Jenkins, with clarity and insight, gives a critical introduction to Pierre Bourdieu's work; and Grenfell (2008) *Pierre Bourdieu: Key Concepts*, which examines in detail the concepts of field, habitus, capital and symbolic violence/doxa.

KEY CONCEPTS: field, habitus, capital, symbolic violence, doxa.

Since the mid-1970s, Pierre Bourdieu's sociological work on various classification processes has had a prominent role in analyses of the state's role in exercising power and contributing to the reproduction of social inequality.[1] Throughout his extensive research output, Bourdieu was particularly interested in power and reproduction in a number of contexts. He paid special attention to the types of reproduction processes that most statistical studies, including contemporary ones, confirm. How come the children of lawyers become lawyers, and working-class children rarely go on to higher education? Or how do studies of family patterns – categorised into groups like married, cohabiting, single, etc. – have a reproducing effect on the very identity construction of people in those categories, and hence the population's self-perception? In other words, Bourdieu's sociology on classification processes is well suited to the study of a wide variety of reproduction processes.

He is particularly interested in the education system, as the study of dominance largely seems to reflect its structures. The longer the period of education, and the more status a given educational institution has, the more capital it bestows upon the agent, and the more power he or she wields in a variety of contexts. Individual educational institutions should not only be analysed in their own terms – focusing on the processes at play in the individual school programme – but must be seen in a wider context, both in terms of peer ranking, and in terms of the institutions' close ties to the state. Bourdieu himself studied critically the elite of the French education system in *The State Nobility* (1998a).

As well as the education system, other – in Bourdieu's terminology – objective structures such as the economy and social class, are also central to the study of dominance and subordination processes. The very idea of the existence of objective structures, like education and economics, differentiates Bourdieu from other constructivist-oriented sociologists such as Goffman, whose analyses remain at a micro level, or Foucault, who does not wish to attribute prominence to explanatory social factors like education or economic conditions. Bourdieu develops an analytical apparatus that stresses the importance of real-life studies of practice (just like Goffman), while at the same time continually showing how practice relates to objective, recordable and structural conditions outside the individual's consciousness (and, in relation to interaction studies, also outside the researcher's observations).

His ambition of transcending conventional sociological dichotomies, such as micro–macro and agency–structure, is also characteristic of Bourdieu's sociology. Micro-processes – for example, analysis of the interaction between individuals – require, for Bourdieu, the researcher to analyse the objective structures that play a conditioning role in the field being studied (and which also have macro-characters). The same applies to the agency-structure dichotomy, which is also a problematic dichotomy for Bourdieu because he wishes to show that what agents do is subject to structural conditions that the agents continuously contribute to, reproducing through their actions (see the concept of habitus). In brief, Bourdieu seeks to solve the following (classic) sociological problem: How do we establish a research strategy that makes it possible to view each element as part of a conditioning social system that is objective (as in Durkheim and Marx), while maintaining that what constitutes a system are the actions of individuals, and not a theoretical construct?

In this chapter, we will draw on the part of Bourdieu's work that explicitly focuses on power and control in the welfare state – which is, of course, the theme of this book. We do so by discussing key concepts in Bourdieu's sociology and by including his discussion of the state in differentiated societies (e.g. Bourdieu 1998b).

Power and governance in the institutions of the welfare state

Bourdieu is critical towards the ambition to sum up dominance and power by means of a classic Marxist analysis, in which the two social classes – workers and owners of capital – struggle against each other. Nor does he countenance the concept of "the ideology", i.e. the ideology that is installed in individuals via the institutions of bourgeois society, as Althusser does. Bourdieu similarly takes a conflict perspective, but sees modern, differentiated society as fragmented into a number of areas in which the battle for recognition and resources takes very specific forms (cf. the term differentiated societies).

He agrees with Foucault that power is not a substance people acquire, but has to be viewed as an effect of certain social relations in certain fields. It is here that Bourdieu identifies the state and the education system as two key – and mutually interdependent – fields:

> "It follows that the construction of the state proceed apace with the construction of a field of power, defined as the space of play within which the holders of capital (of different species) struggle *in particular* for power over the state, that is, over the statist capital granting power over the different species of capital and over their reproduction (particularly through the school system)" (Bourdieu 1998b: 42 – italics in original).

As a consequence of this, analyses of power and dominance place the state and school institution in a quite central position. For Bourdieu (1998b: 97), one of the most potent means of power exercised by the state is when we take over "the thought of the state, i.e. of applying to the state categories of thought produced and guaranteed by the state and hence misrecognize its most profound truth" (Bourdieu 1998b: 35).

Much of Bourdieu's work is dedicated to showing how closely the school system is linked to the state and its categorisation processes, and consequently how deeply the state is involved in giving shape to the individual's perception. We can only understand and interpret the world around us by using the concepts with which the state – qua the school institution – has endowed us. In differentiated societies, the state:

> "Has the ability to impose and inculcate in a universal manner, within a given territorial expanse, a *nomos*, a shared principle of vision and division, identical or similar cognitive and evaluative structures. And the state is therefore the foundation of a 'logical conformism' and of a 'moral conformism' (these are Durkheim's expressions), of a tacit prereflexive agreement over the meaning of the world which itself lies at the basis of the experience of the world as 'commonsense world'" (Bourdieu 1998b: 53 – italics in original).

This means that in Bourdieu's sociology, the state is not just another agent, it constitutes a centre of power by virtue of its monopoly on the key instruments of domination. It is thus under state auspices that we find the legislative, judicial and executive power.

In this context it is also crucial to emphasise that the state does not only exercise power over low-status individuals in society, e.g. the ill, the criminal or the so-called maladjusted. In Wacquant's foreword to *The State Nobility*, he sums up Bourdieu's work on the state's role in differentiated societies by this quote: "*It [the state] bears upon us all,* in myriad minute and invisible ways, every time we perceive and construct the social world through categories instilled in us via our education" (Wacquant 1998: xviii – italics in original). Under state auspices, the educational system is regulated by bodies such as a Ministry of Education and a Ministry of Research, which set the legislative framework for school programmes and exams etc. In doing so, these state institutions directly influence which social order is presented as being the natural one. However, the question of the state's legitimacy and of the order it institutes most of the time remains unasked because we are all socialised in the same schooling system (Bourdieu 1998b: 56).

Bordieu introduces the concept of symbolic violence to focus sharply on the control of mental perceptions that the state – via social services, schools, cultural institutions, and the church etc. – uses to reproduce the social order in its own image. The point is that the individual agent is not aware of this process, so he or she rarely questions the fundamental, self-evident conditions that are the base for his or her actions: "Being born in a social world, we accept a whole range of postulates, axioms, which go without saying and require no inculcating" (Bourdieu & Wacquant 1996: 168). In brief, then, the state introduces an arbitrary (cultural) order that is considered the natural one. Or, to put it another way, there is a tendency for conformity between the agent's mental structures and a given society's objective structures (Bourdieu 2000a: 164). For example, through schooling, pupils learn how society institutions work, and later apply this knowledge to analyse and understand their own society. The state has a dual method of operation – objectively, in the form of specific structures, and subjectively, in the form of mental structures. It regulates how the world should be perceived and understood. The state in this way constructs "the national identity" or "the national character" (Bourdieu 1998b: 46).

We are not only socialised in our families, we are also socialised at school institutions and in all other social contexts. According to Bourdieu, this socialisation results in a particular habitus that is both individual and collective (Bourdieu & Passeron 1990: 60). It is individual because it involves a physical internalisation of a number of structural factors that incite us to view the world in a very particular way. The individual aspect is that we, as agents, each have our own experience(s) that combine with (external) structural conditions to provide us with our specific viewpoint. It is collective because we, as social agents, are also socialised collectively, for example in residential areas, at school, and at work.

Another important agent in the collective socialisation process that contributes to the formation of national character or national identity is the media, which is an important player in the production of culture according to Bourdieu. The media, including mass media like television, national newspapers and weekly magazines, plays a significant role in setting the agenda. In common with sociologists, historians and politicians, journalists seek to impose their worldview and their principles of categorisation (Bourdieu 2005).

In a study of the relationship between citizen and state in modern, differentiated societies from a power and domination perspective, a Bourdieu-inspired analysis will have at least three obvious areas of focus: the state (including the education system, other forms of disciplining and care institutions), the mass media and the economy. The researcher or student who wishes to undertake an analysis in this vein will become acquainted with a number of key concepts. These include the concepts of field, capital and habitus, which Bourdieu discusses throughout his writings, regardless of the specific empirical material with which he is working. In analyses that focus explicitly on power, control and domination processes – as in this book – it is also appropriate to look more closely at the concepts of symbolic violence and doxa.

Analytical concepts

Field

For Bourdieu, fields are the true object of social science (Bourdieu & Wacquant 1996: 107). In highly differentiated societies, the fields would include politics, journalism, art and education, and perhaps sub-fields such as social work and health science etc. Fields are relatively autonomous in that they operate according to "a logic and a necessity that are *specific and irreducible* to those that regulate other fields" (Bourdieu & Wacquant 1996: 97). A field is constituted by a set of positions in which a conflict is played out between newcomers and the dominant players – these conflicts are about the fundamental interests that bind together the field's agents. Bourdieu writes that "the limits of the field are situated at the point where the effects of the field cease" (ibid.: 100), and also compares it with a magnetic field (it is assumed to affect the objects and agents that pass through it, precisely to highlight the relative and empirically defined character of the concept of the field).

Analytically, we operate with networks of relationships that create particular frameworks for the agents in a particular field. These agents will typically compete for the rewards available in that field, and will naturally sometimes disagree and struggle about the rules, norms and values that constitute the field.

In his understanding of how meaning and status-bearing signs evolve in social fields, Bourdieu is inspired by a structuralist concept of meaning, i.e. it is created relationally. For example, imported beer is now considered "classier" than local beer and wine as "classier" than imported beer, but there is nothing in these beverages *per se* that justifies such culturally generated differences in status (see Bourdieu's analysis in *Distinction* (1987)). A field analysis works with a structuralist concept of relational oppositions: the social is to be understood as a field of meaningful signs that only derive meaning through their relation to other signs (Saussure 1974). This way, a field analysis is positioned against naturalisation or substantialism in relation to social phenomena such as taste, class, gender or ethnicity. Field-specific differences are not rooted in the things themselves. Bourdieu's ambition of exposing and analysing the dominating, but hidden, structures that determine the agents' scope for action in the social fields is also inspired by structuralism.

There are three phases in a field analysis: 1) the researcher situates the given field relative to the field of power; 2) the researcher maps out the objective structures of the relations between the participating agents, which bind them to each other; and 3) the researcher analyses the agents' habitus and their varying impact in the given field (Bourdieu & Wacquant 1996: 104–5). He uses the metaphor of trumps in a card game to shed light on the processes whereby agents struggle over resources that are or may be activated (Bourdieu & Wacquant 1996: 98). With this metaphor, he emphasises that fields can be compared with card games, which of course have different rules and trump cards (forms of capital). It is precisely concepts such as rules and logic that separate fields from more periodic networks, since fields have a structure (the objective relations) that actualise certain forms of power and capital. In other words, fields are far more stable than networks, which, according to Bourdieu, overlook underlying structures (e.g. history) in favour of studies of specific and transient couplings between agents and institutions (ibid.: 113–4).

Capital

The concept of capital is designed to encapsulate the values and resources to which the agents have access (qua their habitus and the field in which they interact), as well as the fact that any field is characterised precisely by its specific forms of capital. Just like the field concept, the capital concept is defined relatively. This means that any given capital provides agents with a variety of options, depending on the field in which they seek to invest it. More specifically, Bourdieu lists three key forms of capital – economic, cultural, and social – and also adds symbolic capital, which is distinguished by the fact that it stems from collective recognition.

Symbolic capital requires collective recognition, and can be described as one of three forms of capital (or combinations of them) onto which symbolic value is added. The requirement for collective recognition actualises perception categories that are dominant in society. As mentioned previously, Bourdieu asserts that these cannot be detached from the state. Put simply, the state can be viewed as an agent that reproduces itself by trading in symbolic capital: the purpose of the state is to solidify a particular, culturally generated order as the natural one. To understand how the social world becomes natural to its agents, one has to view the social world as "a *point of view*, the principle of a view adopted from a point located in social space, a *perspective* which is defined, in its form and contents, by its objective position from which it is adopted" (Bourdieu 1998b: 13 – italics in original). The state plays a significant role in connection with the culturally and economically embedded perception categories by which we are characterised in institutions such as the education system, the legal system and social-work institutions. These reflect the state's dual mode of operation: objectively, by establishing and maintaining specific institutional structures; and subjectively, by installing mental structures that regulate the way in which the world is perceived and understood (Bourdieu 1998b: 40). Bourdieu designates the state's capital as a form of meta-capital that "enables the state to exercise power over the different fields and over the different particular species of capital and especially over the rates of conversion between them" (ibid.: 41). In this context, social work, for example, is seen as a field, as the work conducted in this field is characterised by a certain degree of autonomy and by the fact that specific forms of capital are brought into play.

Habitus

According to Bourdieu, if we want to understand what agents do, we need to analyse how society's objective structures are internalised physically. In other words, it makes no sense to operate with a deterministic concept of structure, which is assumed to condition the agents' actions, nor does it make sense to assume that the individual acts freely. Habitus designates a practice-oriented process, "a practical construction, even of practical reflection, that ordinary notions of thought, consciousness, and knowledge prevent us from adequately thinking" (Bourdieu & Wacquant 1996: 121). Social practices and representations are, Bourdieu explains, born out of a:

> "Double and obscure relation between habitus, i.e., the durable and transposable systems of schemata of perception, appreciation, and action that result from the institution of the social in the body [...] and fields, i.e., systems of objective relations [...] and, of course, of everything that is born of this relation" (Bourdieu & Wacquant 1996: 126–7).

The concept of habitus designates the fact that objective structures are internalised and shape the agent's opportunities for action, yet the process should not be viewed as mechanical (Bourdieu & Wacquant 1996: 121). Different upbringings create different conditions for the internalisation of objective structures, and provide the agents with various forms of capital that establish unequal resources for asserting themselves in various fields. Habitus refers to dispositions for action in social space that are pervasive, but not immutable (Bourdieu 1999: 53). An agent's habitus reflects an acquired system of action schemas, preferences and principles for their conception of the world. Bourdieu (1999: 56) writes that habitus can be considered "embodied history", in other words, experiences that have been internalised, but which, as a result of the same process, it is possible for us to forget that they are historical conditions, i.e. "the active presence of the whole past of which it is the product" (ibid.: 56).

Habitus in this way links structure and agent. Since agents – by virtue of upbringing in a particular neighbourhood, schooling system and so on – have different habituses due to different class affiliation, economic conditions, and morals etc. and their individual perceptions are therefore limited by these conditions. Habitus is a theoretical construct designed to mediate between position (objective social position), and the individual's positioning ("choice" because of habitus). The concept is an attempt to explain the interrelationship between inert, objective structures and what actively involved people choose to do (which mostly, but not always, reproduces the structures). Habitus can be seen as a form of "spontaneity without consciousness or will", a counter-argument against both theories of mechanical action as well as theories of the reflexive, subject making free choices (Bourdieu 1999: 56).

Doxa and symbolic violence

Doxa is the tacit knowledge that forms the basis for the "natural" categorisation process that the agent continuously reproduces throughout his or her life in many different arenas. A field's doxa – i.e. its truisms – determines the difference between good and bad arguments, for example. Doxa reproduces the mental structures, and as such it is a particular viewpoint – the dominant view, or as Bourdieu (1998b: 57) also writes, "the universal point of view". Often, there is a battle between newcomers, who wish to make the truisms visible and challenge them, and the dominant, who wish to preserve them. In other words, they struggle about the field's truth, "the universe of possible discourse" (Bourdieu 2000a: 169), or one could also say all of that which in a given culture or field has achieved the status of being taken for granted (ibid.: 164).

As previously mentioned, Bourdieu seeks to illustrate the fact that a struggle is carried on between people who dominate in a given field and those who are dominated by the field's "truths". In many cases, the field's truths are so "natural" that agents submit to them quite voluntarily, exposing themselves to symbolic violence. Precisely because the universal view is upheld by state institutions – e.g. by schools, the health service, and social work institutions etc. – the agents will allow themselves to be regulated and subject themselves to it. Since they have internalised the state's (educational) perception categories, i.e. the principles of categorisation, the domination tends to be perceived as natural and correct (Bourdieu 1998a: 30f). This means that the actions of those who are dominated will support and contribute to their own submission. In other words, symbolic violence is a "gentle, invisible form of violence" that is not recognised as such (Bourdieu 2000a: 192). Using the concept of "misrecognition", Bourdieu points out that the agent fails to recognise "a violence which is wielded precisely inasmuch as he does not perceive it as such" (Bourdieu & Wacquant 1996: 168). Symbolic violence can only be exercised as long as the oppressed actively co-operate with those who oppress them (however, according to Bourdieu, this does not mean that the oppressed are conscious of the process). Here, Bourdieu is inspired by one of Max Weber's key points, i.e. that a hierarchical order is only sustainable if it is supported by the individual's perception that it is legitimate.

Case 1: Health policy as a tool of state ideology in Denmark

Our first case will show how a powerful health field in a differentiated society as Denmark results in subjection practices aimed at unhealthy, overweight citizens. There is no doubt that modern, differentiated societies are today being swamped by a wave of all-pervasive health concerns. Many private and public organisations in Denmark have launched health initiatives for example, many of them focusing on the rising numbers of overweight people. Smoking policies have likewise been introduced, pedometers handed out and health consultations offered. Some Danish companies use the fact that they offer health insurance to employees as part of their recruitment strategy. In the media we see a corresponding exponential increase in articles with "health" or health-related issues in the title. For example, a search of the Infomedia database in Denmark for newspaper articles containing the terms "obesity" and/or "overweight" revealed 405 articles in 1995, 1,342 articles in 2000 and 3,757 in 2005. In five years – from 2000 to 2005 – the number of articles on obesity and/or weight problems has almost tripled. Over 10 years – from 1995 to 2005 – the number of articles on these same topics has multiplied by a factor of nine. The same heightened interest is reflected in Danish TV shows about weight, health websites and slimming books targeting the overweight. TV series also depict the struggle with obesity and the often difficult living conditions of the overweight. This type of reality TV typically adopts the stance that weight is a problem for the individual and now we, as viewers, will see how big the problem actually is. Viewers are typically shown interviews with people who are overweight, in which the many problems associated with weight are explored – ranging from bullying to physical difficulties and worries about the future (linking social, aesthetic, medical and economic-based arguments).

Inspired by Bourdieu, one can argue that we are witnessing the sedimentation of a strong health field in society that in turn activates the overall economic and social capital in society. Various agents in the health field often do not question whether this quest for health is good. This tenet, along with supportive health data, can therefore be seen as an objective structure in the health field, one that codifies the discussions within it and excludes those who think that the requirements of a healthy lifestyle could be synonymous with a decrease in their quality of life – as, theoretically, might be an obvious attitude among overweight people who enjoy fatty foods.

We see a health field that is apparently gaining more and more ground and is, as a result, becoming more and more powerful. Based on extensive qualitative data by one of the authors (Mik-Meyer 2009, 2010a) – which for

Bourdieu is the starting point for any field study – as well as other research that points in the same direction (e.g. Novas & Rose 2000; Greco 2004), we can place the health field high up in the general field of state power. Health is very much a politically motivated phenomenon that has been given attention politically because of population statistics on health issues etc. (cf. Bourdieu's "objective structural conditions"). When you read national reports on health in Denmark, it also becomes clear that health is apparently a "meta-value" (Greco 2004). What is up for discussion is not whether we should be healthy, but exclusively how we can most effectively make people – in this case, the Danes – healthy.

This can be viewed as a doxic assumption: it is taken for granted that healthy is good and that health promotion is a matter for the public sector, and one for which the state can legitimately impose responsibility on its citizens. This tacit knowledge has, as we will see later, consequences for health initiatives that are offered to unhealthy, overweight people (and to which they normally "voluntarily" submit themselves). The health field's doxic tenets – and the positions outlined by this field – are about minimising unhealthy citizens' risk of falling ill, because lifestyle diseases are not only assumed to impair the quality of individual's lives, but are also presented as expensive for the state, and ultimately the general public. Several national reports in Denmark point out that unhealthy lifestyles are a multisectoral problem, which therefore "logically" have to be resolved by a multi-sectoral approach. Logically is in quotes to remind the reader that the logic concept in Bourdieudian approach is an "oxymoron", i.e. a logic that is not based on logical principles, as any logic is limited and defined by the field in which the action is claimed to be logical (Bourdieu 2000a: 109; Bourdieu & Wacquant 1996: 120). This is not, therefore, a logic that is absolute, i.e. applicable at any time. Rather, the statements/actions are only logical in relation to the character of the field in question – in this case, the health field.

How then does one map the logic of the health field? How do we study and analyse the field's "objective structures" and the forms of capital that influence it? Can it be argued that the range of health measures mentioned in the introduction – such as pedometers and health consultations etc. – is an expression of the state exercising symbolic violence? And is it significant that the target audience for the initiatives being offered mostly belong to society's lowest economic layer, i.e. persons with a particular habitus?

The logic of the health field, its objective structures and forms of capital

Depending on the agents in question – e.g. politicians or managers at workplaces – there is a distinct difference in how health, weight and obesity are discussed. This difference characterises the breadth of the debate in the health field. Economic arguments dominate the political discourse on health, in which the unhealthy body is often equated with high costs, which legitimises state intervention even in areas that would otherwise have belonged to the citizen's private sphere, and thus would in the past have been outside the remit of state intervention.

However, the health field also reproduces social arguments that link the unhealthy body with social problems, such as a higher risk of bullying and the assumption that unhealthy people have a generally diminished quality of life (see Mik-Meyer 2009). This type of argument is found in interviews with managers at workplaces, who stress that health initiatives are merely offered to employees who should be able to benefit from them and enjoy a better life (ibid.).

A wide-ranging analysis of the health field will shed light on the battles between powerful and less powerful agents in the field. It will identify the different agents' habitus, both collective and individual. In a field analysis, it will be important to study the different agents' (politicians, managers, overweight persons etc.) education, background and training and look at how their position relates to the health field's objective structures. In this context, it would be expected that individuals with a background in professional health education will be able to utilise the forms of capital that are embedded in the health field in a more powerful manner than, for example, people who do not have such a background – or any training at all – but suffer from a "lifestyle disease" such as being overweight.

The purpose of studying the different agents' habitus, possibly at an individual level – for example, through analysis of a conversation between a health consultant with experience or training in this area and an overweight person with no training in health, is to examine how different habituses result in hierarchically subordinate arguments and discussions, which means that some statements attain the status of "obvious knowledge" (i.e. they support and reproduce the field's logic) and therefore gain ground. The analysis of the agents' habitus is placed in relation to the field's forms of capital and its objective structures. The below analysis of an encounter between an overweight woman and a health consultant outlines the contours of such an analysis, and how a Bourdieuian analysis can demonstrate the way in which encouraging people to lose weight voluntarily can be viewed as a state-initiated domination process, i.e. symbolic violence. The upcoming analysis will also outline how these types of initiatives make the overweight person an active participant in her own "habituation" as an inferior person.

Health and symbolic violence

As previously described, Bourdieu uses the concept of symbolic violence to describe the process whereby the agents collaborate in maintaining an unequal social order. This process is characterised by the agents internalising the state's principles for categorisation – in this case, in relation to the conceptual dichotomies healthy/unhealthy, happy/unhappy, good lifestyle/bad lifestyle –, so they understand that their situations and actions are problematic, and thus ripe for change. Empirically speaking, it is possible to argue in general that the participation of overweight people in current health projects reflects their subjugation. This subjugation can be viewed as the result of powerful objective structures in society actualising a health discourse which presents the slim body as a universal human ideal.

In the upcoming dialogue, we see how a health consultant and an overweight woman, Karen, jointly make the lifestyle of the latter an objective problem that needs to be addressed. Note that, in terms of argumentation, it is almost impossible to distinguish between the health consultant's narrative and Karen's, since they both accept and reproduce the doxic assumptions entrenched in the health field (see also Mik-Meyer 2010a).

Karen turns up for her third consultation. She is weighed, her body fat is measured and she talks about how she is getting on with her plan to lose weight. At the end of the consultation – together with the health consultant – she signs a revised contract containing the areas on which she needs to work. Karen's first words follow immediately on from them recording how much weight she has lost.

KAREN: It's really exciting to put numbers to it. It made a huge impression on my family when I showed them.

HEALTH CONSULTANT: In what way?

KAREN: Yes, well, uhm, I suppose it was a bit like I was pretty bowled over when I saw how much fat my body actually contains and the effects that has – and the same with the other data – it made a huge impression on them when we talked about it. And maybe that's why they're taking me seriously at home [...] I know that I haven't lost the three pounds in a month that I wanted to, so I'm a bit ashamed of that, because – and somewhere or other it's a question of me not being good to myself because each time I ram something into my mouth that's bad for me, I am in fact being bad to myself. I'm punishing myself. Even when I'm comfort eating. So I consider it as a punishment. I don't know how to be good to myself. [Last sentence tearfully] [...] It's unbelievable that you can be so disgusted with yourself, because – when you're as fat as I am – I'm harming myself every time I ram something into my mouth that's bad for me. And that's also one of the things I need to work on, it's something you have to work on, like when you quit smoking, you need to know within yourself whether you really want to stop smoking [...] And the worst thing is, sometimes I've thought: 'You weren't even hungry.'

HEALTH CONSULTANT: But it's all about something else...

KAREN: That's the problem. And, of course, I'm punishing myself every time I cram a piece of shitty bread into my mouth. But that's what I mean – I should work more on myself and on my own head...

> [The consultant suggests that Karen's husband should help her say no to white bread, and asks how Karen thinks she will react to her husband's intervention.]

KAREN: I would probably be pissed off sometimes [...] but the fact is that I lie to myself every time I eat [...] and people like me, we can't afford to eat an extra slice of bread every day. [But] it is a great help to tell me things. I might not take it as well every time, but it is helpful to remind me when I'm being weak and forgetting what's good for me. At times like that it's helpful for me to say, 'I'll just find myself an apple'. So yes, it is helpful.

HEALTH CONSULTANT: So it's an act of love and care.

KAREN: Yes, it is actually love...

HEALTH CONSULTANT: Maybe that's what will help you fight the bread monster. That's the way it is sometimes with monsters, they need a lot of care.

KAREN: 'Cos it's misunderstood love if you just let things slide. And love does hurt sometimes [...] So he has to do me a favour and show me he cares enough to tell me it's not good for me. But it hurts just to be alive sometimes, and it isn't always fun to have the truth battered into you, but never mind.

[After some small talk, the meeting is brought to an end. Karen signs the revised contract].

From a Bourdieuian perspective, the health consultant's work can be viewed as orchestrated by the state to create a better match between the objective structures in society (including in the health field, in which obesity and being overweight are presented as problems) and Karen's mental structures. The aim is that by the end of the talk she will have internalised the state's knowledge, which turns her lifestyle into a problem. In this context, the state-authorised ideology produces an individual who perceives being overweight as an indisputable problem to be addressed.

The conversation shows that we are dealing with someone who quite willingly co-operates in maintaining a stigmatising social order. Karen thinks it's "exciting to look at the data" – numbers that demonstrate that her life situation is highly problematic. The data have made an "impression" on her family, who are also learning that Karen's lifestyle is a serious problem that needs to be addressed. This first brief exchange of words shows that Karen and her family had not previously internalised the state's – including the health field's – principles for categorisation that make Karen's lifestyle into a problem. Karen then assures the health consultant that the fact that she has not lost enough weight makes her "ashamed", illustrating that she actually has adopted, or at least is in the process of adopting, the correct view of her lifestyle, despite the fact that her body weight does not "prove" this. Thereafter, she is engaged in a fairly comprehensive submission process – not only is she ashamed of not losing enough weight, she also says she is "disgusted" by herself, and she assures the consultant that it is something she must "work on".

This is a case of turning a social conflict – which, in a Bourdieuian perspective, can be viewed as being generated by unequal social conditions that produce systematically poor nutrition standards in certain population groups – into an individual, internal conflict.

The health consultant then tries to set her off down a new path, which apparently consists of more learning generated by the logic of the health field, on which the consultant wants to "test" Karen. In passages omitted at this point, the health consultant tries to get Karen to speak about the struggle between what she wants (white bread in the evening) and what she, rightly, knows that she should want (to not eat white bread, but to lose weight and be healthy). This inner struggle, as the health consultant puts it, can be viewed as a struggle between Karen's old, problematic self-perception and her new, correct self-perception, created by the health field's logic.

In the latter part of the excerpt, we see how Karen is put to the ultimate test. She is asked to consider a hypothetical situation in which her husband intervenes in the problematic situation by discouraging her from eating white bread. The consultant wants to know how Karen would react if her husband intervened which can be seen as an attempt to test whether she has actually internalised the health field's logic that makes her eating habits and lifestyle problematic. Karen explains that she probably will be "pissed off" (i.e. at her husband) sometimes, but she also knows that he would be doing it to help her. The consultant helps the conversation along and suggests terms such as "care" and "love" to describe the husband's interference. Karen promptly gets the concepts, revealing yet again the extent to which the health field's logic steers their conversation. She admits that her husband's intervention would, of course, be "actually love", and that "the truth" is not always something that it is "fun to have [...] battered into you". Her own concept of "truth" confirms once and for all that we are not dealing with two agents who are struggling to define what constitutes a good life (which is what this conversation is basically about), but two agents who both reproduce a health logic that continuously postulates one of the agents' lifestyles and desires as problematic. Here we see, in all its simplicity, how symbolic violence works: Karen co-operates in her own subjugation process, precisely because it feels "natural" (it refers to the state's principles for observation and division). She is unaware that she is helping to confirm the position as a problematic personality, one that makes her inferior in relation to the health consultant.

The meeting ends with Karen having to embrace the health consultant's advice and sign a contract. The very fact that she has to sign a contract can be seen as yet another reproduction of the unequal power relations that characterise her encounter with the health system. The contract can be viewed as a tool that is used to create a better match between the logic that reigns in the health field and Karen's mental structures. The template for the contract, and its purpose, were certainly not conceived by a person in Karen's situation (despite the fact that it is she who is assumed to benefit). Rather, its logic and demands are a direct product of the health field. Karen gradually accepts the logic during a series of meetings at which she is forced to reassess her personal situation due to the requirements for information placed by the contract.

Case 2: Poverty in the USA and France

Our second case further illustrates the range of potential in Bourdieu-inspired analyses, in that it consists of a comparative analysis of poverty in the USA and France, conducted on much bigger scale than the first case. Its author, Loïc Wacquant, makes use of a wide-ranging and varied set of data, collected over many years and using different methodological tools – very much in the spirit of Bourdieu. The case is exemplary in terms of demonstrating how researchers can overcome the usual micro–macro, agent–structure dichotomy found in a great deal of sociological research, from which Bourdieu's sociology seeks to dislodge itself.

Wacquant commenced his study of "urban outcasts" in the 1980s in Chicago and Paris, and has spent many years collecting an expansive data set with which to analyse poverty in major urban cities. His analysis shows how history, state structure, economics and politics are crucial to the way in which social class and race are articulated in the USA and France – or to put it even more clearly, in Bourdieuian terms, how the agents' habitus should be seen as an embodiment of history and other structural factors (Bourdieu 1999: 56). Wacquant's study focuses on how poverty is constructed differently depending on the role of the state and its features across different societies. A key point is, again, that poverty cannot be detached from the objective, recordable structural conditions present in society, of which the agents are often unaware.

Wacquant (2001, 2010) employs the term "advanced marginality" to depict how marginalised citizens (the so-called urban outcasts) are the result of particular conditions of life in "advanced capitalist societies". His analysis is based on quantitative surveys, in-depth qualitative interviews with residents and local employees in vulnerable neighbourhoods, statistics, analyses of policy documents and ethnographic observational studies (Wacquant 2010: 136–7). By comparing poor neighbourhoods in the USA and France, the respective "class logics" are revealed. As Wacquant puts it, the comparison "uncovers the principles of social outlook and division that pattern the consciousness and practices of their residents, anchored by the pervasive opposition between blacks and whites on the American side and the vivid dualism of 'housing estate youths' against the rest of the world on the French side" (Wacquant 2010: 5).

His studies show that the American ghetto is an ethnically and socially homogeneous universe that operates with little state interference, while the French urban periphery (les banlieues) is characterised by a more heterogeneous population in terms of ethnicity and class. In contrast to the ghetto of Chicago, the Parisian banlieue is also the object of considerable public and institutional attention. An important discovery in Wacquant's empirically anchored analyses is his claim that a European welfare state like the French one is not becoming Americanised and ghettoised in the American sense of the term, and that this is precisely due to the fact that the American and

French states differ significantly from each other in several key areas. In relation to both the state model and the market: "They are heirs to different urban legacies, produced by different logics of segregation and aggregation" (Wacquant 2001: 39).

In line with a Bourdieuian approach, Wacquant wants to show and problematise how "folk concepts" like "race" and "ghetto" – which are also often used in research – have an effect on the agents they claim to describe. As a researcher and political decision-maker, it is important not only to be aware of the different meanings associated with the concepts, but to be mindful of the fact that these concepts, under the guise of describing marginality and poverty, also help to organise the collective perception of what marginality and poverty actually are (Wacquant 2010: 8). Ghettos "operate as mere metaphors, calling forth an emotive imagery that hides fundamental structural and functional differences, thereby stopping inquiry elsewhere, just where it should get going" (Wacquant 2010). The categories therefore appear to have a reproducing effect on the elements that comprise the phenomenon they describe. As per Bourdieu, it is precisely for this reason that it is crucial that the researcher examines empirically what a ghetto/banlieue is, and what kind of social order it reproduces (and is reproduced by) in the specific geographic area that is the object of the analysis. In Wacquant's analyses, a series of key concepts are often placed in quotation marks in order to emphasise that they are charged with meaning in a way that may not comply with the actual practice that the concepts claim to describe (see, e.g. the "race" concept, Wacquant 2010: 17).

In a Bourdieu-inspired analysis, the analytical work is based on tangible empirical reality, so fieldwork is an obvious method to adopt. Fieldwork facilitates insight into "the lived relations and meanings that are constitutive of the everyday reality" (Wacquant 2010: 9). The objective is to explore what a "rebellion" consists of for different groups, so that a riot by young people in a poor residential area is not automatically seen as a race issue simply because its participants share the same ethnic background. A more in-depth analysis – which as well as seeking to uncover and interpret "lived relations and meanings", also includes quantitative data (such as statistics etc.) – will show how a revolt relates to "a massive *structural violence* unleashed upon them by a set of mutually reinforcing economic and socio-political changes" (Wacquant 2010: 24 – italics in original). As structural factors, Wacquant mentions mass unemployment, reduced funds for housing schemes and increased stigmatisation because of social class, ethnicity and where you live (see his concept of "territorial stigma", Wacquant 2010: 169f). A thorough empirical analysis such as Wacquant's, can document whether there has been increased economic polarisation in differentiated societies such as the USA and France. This can be interpreted as structural violence, because exacerbated economic polarisation has affected the living conditions (and hence mental structures) of poor people, without them necessarily being aware of the significance to their situation of this important structural determinant.

Economic polarisation can therefore be assumed to cause greater discontent and anger among poor people who live in an increasingly wealthy society (Wacquant 2010: 30) but without the frustrated relating their dissatisfaction explicitly to this structural relationship.

Like Bourdieu, Wacquant recommends that "field observations, structural analysis and theoretical constructions advance in unison and mutually reinforce each other" (Wacquant 2010: 10). In other words, fieldwork cannot stand alone, but always has to relate to analyses that focus on structural factors, since the agents' perceptions and actions are embedded in structural conditions. Wacquant's prioritisation of how structural factors (such as economics and history) influence a specific empirical phenomenon (a riot by young people), highlights an important point in Bourdieu-inspired analyses – namely that the agents' actions must always be interpreted in the light of structural conditions that not only set the conditions for the actions, but which can also be seen as entrenched in the actions and the agents' self-perception. The agent is therefore not only limited by – but helps to reproduce – the field in which he or she is positioned. We recall, again, that the field shapes the agents' habitus.

While African-Americans direct their anger against their neighbours rather than the "system" or "the state", the French underclass target a more omnipresent state that, because of its proximity, is held responsible for the poverty experienced by both groups. Wacquant quotes an African-American who outlines why he believes there is so much crime and violence in his ghetto:

> "Cause, see, the Man downtown who pullin' the string, they cain't get to him. So they take they frustrations on the guy next door to them, the guy across the street from them. Instead of bein' *wise* and goin' to see Mayor Daley or Governor Edwards or somethin'. Go take out your frustration on *them: go see Bush* [the father], *go see Ronald Reagan!* Don't bother me, '*cuz I ain't did nuttin' to you.* A lotta guys, it's the frustration: *they frustrated, man, with they lives*" (Wacquant 2010: 225 – italics in original).

The isolation of American ghettos from the rest of society is due to the specific historical circumstances of American ethnic segregation into black and white (Wacquant 2010: 161), as well as economic and political conditions. As Wacquant puts it, "The isolation of America's urban outcasts is the *product of an active process of institutional detachment* and segregation (in the etymological sense of 'setting apart') fostered by the decomposition of the public sector" (Wacquant 2010: 224 – italics in original). His point is that if an analysis of why the American ghetto (as opposed to poor areas in European countries) has developed "a climate of terror" (Wacquant 2010: 205) does not take into account its specific American social context, then the analysis will remain superficial and perhaps even be misleading. The French banlieue not only differs from the American ghetto in terms of ethnic composition (it consists of more than 25 nationalities), but most of the inhabitants of the French banlieues in the 1990s were in work (Wacquant 2010: 204).

Wacquant's Bourdieu-inspired approach shows how comparisons allow a deeper understanding of a common problem in the relationship between state and citizen, which he calls "advanced marginality". He also employs this concept to focus sharply on the features that are shared by advanced capitalist societies. He shows, for example, how today's increasing deregulation of the financial markets, individual orientation among wage-earners and the modernisation of work so that it becomes more flexible, affects poor people in Western, capitalist societies. These developments can be seen as structural power that has a negative effect on poor citizens' everyday lives – although, as outlined above, the impact varies. These trends are often invisible to the agent, regardless of whether the agent is the poor resident of the ghetto/banlieue, a local politician or a bureaucrat in the (welfare) state. A major potential in a Bourdieu-inspired analysis such as Wacquant's is therefore that it aspires to link the structural social conditions to an analysis of the particular individual's actions and self-perception in order to show how the conditioning but hidden structures predispose agents to do what they do in two different national locations.

Conclusion

In this chapter, we have adopted a field-analytical approach to study two important areas of welfare policy – health and poverty – to show how a Bourdieuian analysis, with its focus on the state, power and especially the hidden exercise of power, is able to describe the suppression mechanisms that are embedded in state-driven initiatives (or the lack thereof).

The first case provided an example of how Bourdieu's concept of symbolic violence enables the researcher to focus on and explore particular aspects in the data material. Despite the fact that our overweight person, Karen, shows great willingness to co-operate with the health consultant, the conversation can be analysed as a process of submission, in which she actively contributes to her own objectification and subjugation. Bourdieu's sociology is particularly well suited to studying exactly this kind of hidden power mechanism.

In this health case, in which we marked up the embedded truths (doxa) that are continuously reproduced by the health field, we also suggested other areas that researchers might include in order to conduct a more comprehensive Bourdieu-inspired analysis of the health discourse. The researcher might also integrate into the analysis the statistically documented inequality that is evident in relation to being overweight. Globally, it is predominantly the underclass, i.e. typically people with low or no education, who are categorised as overweight. In terms of Bourdieuian concepts, these are agents with low economic and cultural capital, the two dominant forms of capital in differentiated societies. Since organisations like the WHO and most Western states present obesity and being overweight as fundamental threats to health (and implicitly also to the economy, especially in welfare states), and since these countries have "declared war on fat" as it is sometimes described, it is important for a Bourdieuian analysis to look more closely at the problem structure as a whole – because, of course, it appears to follow the objective power structures in society. Men and women in powerful positions – agents with great cultural and economic capital – are not generally overweight, whereas the powerless, i.e. people with low cultural and economic capital (the unemployed in Denmark, African-Americans in certain parts of the USA etc.), are over-represented in the obesity statistics.

As a result, while the state – qua disciplinary institutions and economic sanctions (for example, against people who are unable to support themselves financially) – devises programmes targeting precisely these groups, who primarily belong to the underclass, evidence suggests that the submission process upon which we focused sharply in our case also takes place at macro level in Western societies. From a Bourdieuian perspective, it is thus relevant to study whether current health initiatives help reproduce the uneven (objective) power structures that characterise differentiated societies.

Our second case was selected to show how a Bourdieu-inspired analysis focusing on the role of the state in relation to domination mechanisms can also be studied via a large amount of diverse empirical material. This case was chosen because it is an excellent illustration of how specific, practice-based studies of poverty and domination processes relate to the objective, recordable structural conditions that often exert an unacknowledged or "misrecognised" influence upon the agents. This second analysis is included to show the range of both empirical data and analytical problems to which Bourdieu's sociology may be addressed.

In this case, we also shed light on another key aspect of Bourdieu's sociology, namely that categories – both "folk concepts" and the researcher's own concepts – are not neutral, but have a reproducing effect on the very constitution of the people/phenomenon that they describe. In other words, concepts such as "ghetto" and "race" create a social order that associates deprived neighbourhoods with violence, insecurity and racial issues, which in turn affects the local residents' expectations of their everyday lives, as well as how the local politicians devise and provide specific social services.

Both cases have hopefully made it clear that the state is a key field in a Bourdieu-inspired analysis. Bourdieu's concept of symbolic violence directs attention to the fact that the state continually shapes the agents' perceptions, and in this way tend to reproduce the prevailing social order, irrespective of whether the agents involved in this reproduction would approve of this particular social order.

5 Luhmann: Welfare in communicative systems

Niklas Luhmann was born in 1927 in Lüneburg, Germany, and died in 1998. Originally a law graduate, he studied administration science and sociology at Harvard University from 1960–61, where Talcott Parsons, his sounding board and major source of inspiration, was a professor at the time. In 1968, Luhmann was appointed Professor of Sociology at the University of Bielefeld, where he remained until 1993. He is known for his theory of society as consisting of systems of communication, as presented in *Social Systems* (1995). The theory is based on a unique combination of biology, mathematics, philosophy and more. Luhmann has written a series of books about the different function systems of modern society: law, economics, politics, education and mass-media etc. In their *Luhmann's Theory of Social Systems: An Introduction* (1993) Kneer and Nassehi provide a very well-explained and comprehensive introduction to Luhmann; Borch's (2011) *Niklas Luhmann: Key Sociologists* focuses on key concepts in Luhmann and positions his work in relation to other social theories; and Seidl and Becker's *Niklas Luhmann and Organization Studies* (2005) offers a good starting point for studying organisations via systems theory.

KEY CONCEPTS: communication, social systems, observation, binary codes, structural coupling.

Niklas Luhmann's systems theory has only recently begun to be applied to analyses of power and governing in welfare services. It is a highly complex theory that contains many counter-intuitive concepts. Acclimatising to Luhmann's systems theory requires effort but, in return, it offers surprising and often provocative perspectives on otherwise familiar problems. His work has yet to make a real global breakthrough – so far, his adherents are mostly found in Northern Europe and Scandinavia (particularly in Luhmann's homeland, Germany). As far as analyses of welfare are concerned, systems theory is used by two main camps. One is theoretically focused, primarily based in Germany, and is mainly concerned with social work's contribution to modern society (Scherr 1999), and whether social work is an autonomous function system (Baecker 1994, Wirth 2009). The second group is based in

Scandinavia, primarily Denmark, and has produced several empirical studies into the encounter between welfare institutions and citizens. These studies have, for instance, focused on the use of contracts between the social services and the individual client (Andersen, 2008); inclusion criteria in health care (Højlund 2009); and how homeless shelters construct their users (Villadsen 2008a).

As the list shows, systems theory has been applied to a wide variety of objects of study. Despite the fact that the theory is often described as the last "grand theory" in social science, and the fact that systems theorists typically work on an abstract level, we will show that it is actually possible to use systems theory to conduct very specific empirical studies. Indeed, it has even been argued that Luhmann's systems theory can be combined with grounded theory to generate a "grounded observer" capable of making theoretical observations about everyday institutionalised communication (Gibson et al. 2005). We choose to emphasise this point at this early stage because, at first glance, systems theory may appear rather abstract and not very empirically "grounded". It is presented by Luhmann as a "general" theory that aims to be sophisticated enough to describe the complexity of modern society. The aim is to develop a programme of observation that is both complex and general enough to describe a society that already produces complex self-descriptions (Luhmann 1982b: 76). The premise is that modern society (as opposed to its pre-modern predecessor) consists of a series of distinct social systems that reproduce themselves in an autonomous and self-referential fashion.

The following section develops further this theory of the differentiated modern society. Next, we focus sharply on the parts of Luhmann's universe that are particularly relevant to analyses of citizens' encounters with welfare institutions. Here, we present systems theory's concepts of organisations, membership criteria and the relationship of the organisation to its environment. We then offer a real-life example of an analysis in which systems theory is deployed to study the citizen's encounter with welfare institutions, in this case services for the homeless. Finally, we discuss the functional perspective that a group of predominantly German systems theorists apply to modern social work.

Basic tenets of systems theory

To illustrate what the concept of "the differentiated society" means, we can posit a schematic distinction between the modern secularised society and pre-modern society, in which religion was a universal explanatory reference. With the transition to modern society, human reason, rather than divine intervention, became the crucial explanatory category. This transition started in the Renaissance in the 15th century, but made its major breakthrough in the 18th and 19th centuries. In this process, for instance, art ceased to represent God and instead began speaking on behalf of mankind. In the same way, a shift was observable in the domain of science, away from religious ideas and justifications as the ultimate foundation and towards internally defined criteria for truth and falsehood.

In other words, a plurality of systems emerged with the advent of modern society, each of which refers to its own internal logic and values, including economics, law, education and art. Modern society, then, implies a differentiation into a series of systems that are foreign to each other's rationality. It makes immediate sense, for instance, that an offence cannot be adjudged to be more or less "artistic" by the legal system, but that the art system is perfectly capable of assessing actions in this manner. The fact that the systems are fundamentally incapable of understanding each other's assessment criteria and values is an important point in systems theory, to which we shall return later.

Luhmann builds his theory of society on sociological theory of modern society as differentiated into various functions (as did Durkheim and later Parsons), as well as more implicitly on Weber's diagnosis that modern society is characterised by the existence of incommensurable and competing value spheres, and that modern man no longer has access to ultimate justifications for choosing one value over another. Luhmann combines this sociological perspective in surprising ways with a number of other theoretical elements, including the biologist Maturana's (1981) concept of life as autopoietic and the mathematician Spencer-Brown's (1969) idea of observations as operations that draw distinctions.

We will now explain the basic elements of Luhmann's systems theory in more detail. This involves understanding modern society as "polycontextual", that is, it consists of a series of self-referential social systems that it is unfeasible to govern in conventional political fashion, via a hierarchical, top-down steering. This is because the political system can no longer claim to represent society as a unified whole. Rather, the political logic runs parallel to, and competes with, other logics such as economics, law and health in the modern welfare state (Willke 1997). Luhmann formulates the point about the impossibility of a unifying centre in modern society as follows:

> "Modern society, through its change to functional differentiation, has become so increasingly complex, that a representation of it as a unity in itself has become impossible. Society has neither a top nor a center, there is no place where its unity can find expression" (Luhmann, quoted in Merten 2000: 181).

The theory is also capable of undertaking analysis at the level of organisation. In a section below, we therefore focus on the theory's ability to analyse organisations in which the citizen encounters welfare professionals. The aim is to study how modern welfare agencies construct themselves through self-description and descriptions of their environment, or how they structure their communication by coupling to function systems and their particular communicative logic. The idea is that welfare institutions are (like all organisation systems) at one and the same time, closed around their own operations, and yet they receive and process "irritations" from the environment. In relation to welfare institutions, irritations may take the shape of citizens who present complex demands, desires, problems and needs. Furthermore, the theory strictly refutes the focus on individuals and their intentions in favour of an observation of how welfare institutions construct roles and role-expectations. The general point is that all social systems communicatively construct their own particular "actor-fictions", for instance, the economic system's "rational agent" (Teubner & Hutter 2000).

The modern, differentiated society

To understand Luhmann's systems theory, it is helpful to look closer at his basic historical postulate of the modern, differentiated society. It is in this regard that systems theory, as mentioned previously, may be understood as an elaboration of Durkheim, Weber and Parsons' theories of society's differentiation. Luhmann reformulates them by instead considering society as consisting of communication (Schimank 1996, Luhmann 1995). Luhmann shares the classical sociologists' perception that modern society breaks with the traditional by becoming increasingly complex and functionally separated or differentiated. Modern society becomes "functionally differentiated" with the emergence of more and more specialised, but mutually dependent, work functions. At the same time, a process of differentiation occurs in relation to values, partly due to the religious understanding of the world diminishing in significance and being replaced by a series of conflicting world views. Modern society is dominated by a plurality of competing values, so it is no longer possible to invoke ultimate and indisputable justifications.

Max Weber's well-known thesis about the differentiation of modern society serves as a useful point of entry to Luhmann's theory of communicative differentiation. Weber's starting point is that religion ceases to provide universal and ultimate reasons for modern man's choices and values. Instead, a series of self-referential secular systems emerge – economy, politics, science, religion, aesthetics, and eroticism – which are, according to Weber, engaged in an irreconcilable conflict with one another. Hence, these systems, or "value spheres", are incapable of reaching into each other's spheres of validity. For example, science is incapable of providing meaningful answers to ethical or political questions. Weber says:

> "The impossibility of 'scientifically' pleading for practical and interested stands – except in discussing the means for a firmly given and presupposed end – rests upon reasons that lie far deeper. 'Scientific' pleading is meaningless in principle because the various value spheres of the world stand in irreconcilable conflict with each other" (Weber 1946: 147).

The more that individual value spheres are developed and systematised, the more they appear to be irreconcilable, with each propelled by its own internal logic. Specialised, profit-oriented market organisations, bureaucratic apparatuses governed by legislation, and scientific institutions that strive for true knowledge all constitute tangible manifestations of the differentiation of modern society.

Like Weber, Luhmann sees modern society as differentiated into a range of systems, each of which operates in accordance with its own peculiar logic. As in Weber's diagnosis of modernity, society is characterised by the lack of a centre that determines how the world should be viewed. Instead, a number of different sub-systems – so-called function systems – operate with their own specific criteria for the creation of meaning (Luhmann 1982a, 1995, 1997).

The crucial point is that these systems consist of communication, through which they reproduce themselves "autopoietically", i.e. they reproduce by means of internal processes and elements. Or, in other words, the systems are closed and self-referential. They themselves continually create the elements of which they consist, and according to their own internal rules. Luhmann's general point in using the concept of autopoesis is to introduce a perspective capable of viewing society and its systems as independent realities that cannot be explained by reference to various external conditions such as consciousness, aggregated actions or underlying structures. In brief, systems theory can be described as a programme for observing how social systems make their observations (Andersen 2003c: 310).

More precisely, social systems use binary distinctions that allow for redundancy in their communicative operations. Based on Spencer-Brown's (1969) calculus of distinctions, Luhmann argues that communication is to be understood as consisting of distinction-generating operations. The basic premise is that to observe is to indicate inside the framework of a distinction that divides the world into two parts (e.g. legal/illegal). Such observation-guiding distinctions may be described as contingent modes of observation that, over time, achieve stability and bind elements of communication together by creating expectations for subsequent communication. At this juncture, it is worth emphasising Luhmann's dispassionate "anti-humanism" where it is the communicative systems that have expectations, not the human subjects. Binary codes such as "legal/illegal" represent neither the world nor the subjects' thoughts. Rather, they are a product of communications that refer back to previous communications and, over time, form redundant and more pervasive distinctions (Gibson et al. 2005).

When the act of observation indicates something, it creates a distinction between a positive, indicated inner side and a negative, unmarked outer side. In other words, it installs into the communication a basic binary preference between a positive and a negative value. In the judicial system, for example, the distinction is between what is indicated ("the legal") and what it is now distinguished from ("the illegal"). Judicial communication transforms everything that it observes into judicial problems that can be determined as legal or illegal. The distinction instils an unequivocal preference without, however, specifying the content of this preference. Thus, in judicial communication, it is better to be positioned at the inner ("legal") rather than the outer ("illegal") side of this distinction (Luhmann 1992).

According to Luhmann, in modern, differentiated society there can be given no overarching point of determination or meta-value. In other words, there is no place from which it can be determined whether a legal observation is fundamentally better than an economic one, whether scientific is superior to political, and so on. Modern society can be described as polycontextual and hyper-complex (Qvortrup 2003).

It should be stressed that the function systems are abstract systems of communication logic. We must not visualise them as fixed and spatially localisable entities. Function systems, with their specific codes and forms of logic, are potentially "available" everywhere in society and are not tied to specific locations. In principle, communication recurring around these codes can take place across diverse settings. The concept of function systems is thus a theoretical starting point that allows us to examine how specific communication (in organisations or interaction systems) links up with the distinct forms of communication logic that have developed in modern society.

Welfare organisations

According to systems theory, organisations also constitute communicative systems, but they differ from function systems by reproducing themselves through decisions about who is a member and who is not, i.e. by communicating specific criteria for membership (Luhmann 1982b). Organisations are closed in terms of who is eligible for membership, but are open in relation to society's function systems and their reservoirs of communicative forms

When an organisation decides to connect to a particular function system, this colours the organisation's communications – both its self-description and its description of its environment. Changes in coding have radical consequences for an organisation's communicative operations: "It does not only cause a shift in code, but also a change in self-description; the environment is observed anew, the players change, and the chains of argument are replaced" (Andersen 2003b: 163). For example, if communications about a client in a social services office change from a pedagogical coding about learning potential to a financial codification concerning lack of resources, this will change the entire content of the dialogue and any potential continuation of it.

In systems theory, organisations do not receive "input" in the traditional sense. In line with other social systems, organisations generate information by taking "irritations" from their environment and transforming them according to the organisation's own particular rationality. Thus, the communications triggered by external perturbations are dependent on the organisation's self-description, on its internal, retroactive communications.

To this end, Luhmann offers the concept of "structural coupling", which seeks to explain how two systems can be "disturbed" by each other, despite the fact that their operations are closed off from each other. In general terms, the two systems are structurally coupled when their structures permit mutual irritations. Such irritation occurs when "an autopoietic system is contingent upon another autopoietic system's complex services, when it can treat them as if they are parts of its own system" (Luhmann, in Seidl & Becker 2006: 21). Analysing structural couplings consists of exploring how a specific form of irritation is allowed to occur at the same time as the systems' differentiation and closed nature are maintained. Any media that allows this occurence may serve as structural coupling in social work for instance, a contract, program or plan.

An organisation needs to stabilise its self-description and the way in which it observes its environment around certain regular operations. This is also the case for welfare organisations, which have developed programmes that entail particular observations of how help can be given, who should give it and what kind of problems can be addressed. "Client problems", "needs" or "welfare" are simply what are defined as such by organisational programmes that can only observe what they can observe according to their particular logic. Thus, one might say that welfare organisations reduce complexity by turning the indeterminate, unmanipulatable complexity of the world into a determinate, manipulatable complexity, i.e. by constructing "needs"and "diagnoses" etc. Or, to put it differently, all irritations from the world outside the system must be converted into a system-logical form, in order to be defined and processed (Moe 1998: 34).

The general point is that the organisation cannot observe its surroundings in any direct and all-encompassing way, and is forced to construct its own picture of reality – with all the simplicity and risk that entails. This means that in principle a welfare organisation is only able to make observations based on its own specific communications logic and programmes. For example, a hospital uses medical programmes that observe by means of diagnosis and treatment and thus cannot observe, for instance, a suicide attempt as a product of existential loneliness or societal conditions. Organisations can communicate on common themes such as "education and training", "health", "social help" or "integration", but they do so according to their own particular horizon and self-description.

It should be noted that all help programmes operate with reference to concepts of intervention, development and change. Seen from the perspective of systems theory, help programmes communicate "fictions" about their capacity to transform the elements that they deal with. If we consider the distinctions that operate in modern help programmes, we notice that they all share a conception of "moving" or transforming the client, the child or the patient. Childcare operates by the distinction progress/no progress, healthcare operates by the distinction sick/healthy, and the social services departments operate by the distinction powerless/empowered. Thus, all of these programmes are based upon what might be called "an interventionist distinction" (Moe 1998: 11) – if the programme is to be effective, the child, the patient and the client must all be observed to traverse the distinction.

Specifying the object of analyses

One of the basic premises of systems theory is that an observer always has to specify, extremely carefully, exactly what is being observed and the means by which it is rendered observable. Or in Luhmann's terms: we must always specify our own programme of observation and our guiding distinctions. Systems theory offers a range of different and distinct options for conducting organisational analysis, and it is a fundamental tenet that our choice of categories of observation determines how the world appears to the observer. Let us briefly present some of the most important analytical strategies in systems theory that are applicable for organisational analysis. Andersen (2003c) highlights systems analysis, form analysis and semantic analysis.

In systems analysis, the guiding distinction is "system/environment". The idea is to observe how an organisational system creates itself at the same time as it constructs its environment. The way in which an organisation creates itself depends on whether it describes its environment as consisting of, for instance, consumers or citizens with legal rights to its services, as a political landscape of alliances and power struggles, or as a market for products.

However, modern organisations should normally not be conceived as a single system and a single environment. They tend to operate with multiple system/environment constructions, and we thus need to observe how organisations communicate a plurality of system/environment differentiations. Envisage, for instance, that an organisation constructs itself as both a bureaucratic implementer of political decisions and as a market agent in competition with other "companies". This type of thinking allows us to abandon the idea of an organisation as a stable entity with a coherent self-image, in favour of analysing how organisations create themselves through a range of system/environment distinctions (Andersen 2003c: 315).

The objective of "forming analysis" is to examine how organisations link up with society's function systems (Andersen 2003c: 316–17). Organisations do this by forming one of the so-called symbolically generalised media that every function system has at its disposal: money (the economic system), law (the legal system), power (the political system), or "the child" (the pedagogic system). When an organisation turns a specific problem into a question of payment or non-payment (with a view to prioritising resources), it forms the medium "money", which has important implications for future communications, and for how the organisation emerges in general. As we shall see below, it certainly makes a difference whether welfare organisations couple with the legal or the pedagogic system in their communication about the client. When an organisation decides to communicate in terms of money, rights or power, it becomes a "container" for the abstract communication logics made available by the different function systems. However, the specific effects of this "activation", or act of connecting, on the organisation's communication must, in each individual case, be examined empirically (Villadsen 2008a).

Semantic analysis is about how organisations create themselves communicatively by drawing upon a reservoir of concepts and symbols (Andersen 2003c: 317–19). Semantic analysis considers concepts to be a way to condense meaning, which is achieved by coupling the concepts to counter-concepts such as us/them, now/before, inside/outside and up/down etc. In semantic analysis, an organisation is simply a conglomerate of concepts that provide and make possible certain forms of self-description (Andersen 2003c: 318). The process includes describing the staff, placing the organisation in a time sequence, and defining its relevant surroundings etc. Semantic analysis involves examining the historical emergence of particular conceptual and symbolic reserves. For example, we could imagine a study of how social services have developed their own self-description from a "case-worker semantic" (consisting of concepts of impartiality, objective needs and equality before the law), through a more pedagogical semantic with notions of learning, development and realisation of inner personal resources, and onwards towards forms of communication that resemble religious semantics, with concepts of personal support, "meeting people, not cases", and giving unconditional care. Semantic analysis examines the conceptual constructions upon which organisations base their communication and self-construction.

Welfare organisations and roles

In modern society, organisations have developed that are not dependent on specific individuals' actual presence. Organisations are differentiated from each other and from the rest of society, and this allows a high organisational specification of behaviour. They can be indifferent to the other social roles of their members, e.g. religious belief, political affiliation or family relations, and their personal conditions or motivations (Luhmann 1982b: 79). Luhmann argued that by employing "impersonal membership rules", organisations do not have to depend on the creation of personal motives, moral commitment or consensus for every required action (1982b: 75).

Contra intuitively, individuals as thinking and living beings were relegated to a position of "environment" for communicative systems, including organisations. Thus, Luhmann states categorically: "Persons as concrete psycho-organic units belong to the environment of systems of social communication. Only communication variables belong to the internal processes of social systems" (Luhmann 1982a: 247). For present purposes, the analytical problem, therefore, is not one of analysing how helpers and clients interact but rather one of analysing how specific aspects of individuals are made relevant by the communicative operations of welfare organisations. We must make the question of how the helper and the client are formed as specific "actor-fictions" an empirical one, to which certain competences and expectations can be ascribed.

People may be ascribed a role in the communication, but only as something to which the communication refers. Social systems, including welfare organisations, work with their own distinctions between that which is "relevant to communication" about individuals, and that which is not. Major and obvious differences arise from communication that treats people as legal entities, patients, "learning pupils" or investment objects respectively. A welfare organisation will, through its construction of the patient, user or citizen, decide which aspects of the person are pertinent to the organisation and which ones are irrelevant. Welfare organisations work on the basis of their own image of what constitutes an expression of motivation, dynamism or idleness. Again, we underline systems theory's idea of organisations as closed systems that process the environments' irritations, e.g. clients, in relation to a particular internal logic.

Again, social systems consist exclusively of communication. People only appear in this context as "roles", which are generalised points of identification and exist independently of concrete individuals. They may include brother, doctor, patient, therapist and, as in this case, client. Welfare organisations operate with a gallery of roles that serve as a kind of filter that assigns specific, defined places for citizens and professionals and thus stabilise communication. This means that professionalism and the professional are essentially products of the internal communicative operations of the system. It should be noted that understanding roles in terms of how they stabilise organisational communication constitutes a departure from most sociological theory in the strict priority that systems theory gives to communication (excluding explanations by actors' "motives", "interpretations" or "particular life world").

In general, the organisation reduces complexity by deciding who is allowed to participate (by formulating criteria for membership), in what way (by creating defined roles) and for what purpose (by using action-oriented programmes). A crucial point is that organisations themselves cannot see the distinctions that they use as the basis for their observations, and this includes their criteria for inclusion and exclusion. We must presume that even welfare organisations involved in integration work have their own exclusionary dynamics – simply because of the fact that it will never be possible to include and help everyone.

Case 1: Organisations that work with homeless people

We will now present a case analysis that uses systems theory to describe social work with homeless people in two regions of Denmark, Odense region and Copenhagen city (published in Villadsen 2008a, 2011a).[1] More precisely, it deals with how homeless people are observed by the organisations that seek to help them. These organisations construct a particular image of who the homeless are, what kind of assistance they need, and, not least, the role the organisation itself plays in relation to them. The analysis shows how homeless clients, as an "irritation", are processed very differently by the organisations involved and how these organisations construct widely differing criteria for inclusion and what is viewed as potential and progress. This places homeless people in a vulnerable position, and gives rise to problems in relation to co-operation between the organisations.

The analysis uses three different perspectives on organisations derived from Luhmann's systems theory. First, a system analysis shows how organisations that work with the same homeless people create a self-identity through an internal construction of their environment. Or, put more simply: it is by creating an image of the external "others" – clients, other organisations – that organisations make their own self-description. Furthermore, the study involves an analysis of the roles that organisations define for social workers and clients. This analysis shows that who or what a homeless client is, and how he or she ought to be integrated, depends very much on the organisation doing the observing. Finally, the analysis suggests that contracts and action plans serve as means of coupling between the organisational systems involved. The analysis observes the social work in an "unsentimental" manner, claiming merely to describe how homeless clients are observed by certain welfare agencies, not to provide a truer observation of what the clients "really" are, feel, or need.

The focus of the case is on social work that aims to prepare the homeless clients for "re-housing" and re-integration into society and permanent accommodation – a process termed "re-absorption". This transition work involves several different organisations – typically, an emergency shelter or simply a homeless shelter (either under the auspices of the regional authority or a voluntary organisation), a municipal social services office (in the form of a case-worker), and a municipal unit for supporting the homeless in new accommodation. The homeless shelter and municipal support units are the two most important actors in the practical work with the homeless individual, while the municipal caseworker typically plays a more remote, administrative role.

Observation of the environment and self-construction

An interesting observation in this study is that the homeless shelters (some of which are run by voluntary organisations) and the municipal support unit, formulate almost diametrically opposite pictures of what constitutes a "good client" and a good transition towards permanent housing. They have a largely negative construction of each other and the work done by the other part (Villadsen 2008a). The representatives of the shelters generally consider themselves to be a "care institution", in contrast to the other organisations, which allegedly are driven by the requirement to change the client. The head of the municipal shelter in the Odense region identifies care as its primary purpose. The shelter's position is that the training of its social workers is very much focused on thoroughly thinking through what it means to them to work in a care institution, including weeding out old ideas about "change through treatment". The head of the shelter makes a clear distinction between care and treatment:

> "Shelter [for the homeless] is a place of care. It's about providing care in relation to the users' actual conditions, unlike all the other organisations, which try to treat things [...] The challenge has been to remain a caring institution, where treatment is not a prerequisite" (Head of homeless shelter, Odense Region).

The shelters generally observe the homeless as being in need of care and describe themselves as places that provide care. In interviews, the staff emphasise that it is close, "trust-based relationships" between social worker and client, between client and client, and between the client and everyone else that make the necessary changes in the clients possible. One example of this emphasis on close relationships comes from a description of best practices at *The Shelter*, run by the municipality in the city of Odense

> "There has to be a trusting relationship before you dare divest yourself of [...] your former undesirable habits or lifestyle. You need something to lean on and relate to while you make the change" (Shelter worker, Odense region).

It is worth noting that the homeless shelters spend little time thinking about "keeping their distance" from the client. They presume that it is only through close relationships that clients' deep-seated problems are unveiled and that the homeless become aware of their own wishes and opportunities, which helps them undergo a successful process of development towards living in their own homes.

If we turn now to the municipal housing support units, the self-descriptions of these organisations are noticeably different. They observe homeless people as individuals who are in constant danger of being "clientised" and pacified. They are constructed as individuals whose self-will and problem-solving abilities have been stifled by various types of alcohol and drug abuse, psychiatric issues, a negative subculture and by the welfare system's excessive measures designed to help them. As one housing-support worker puts it, they have become "specialists at getting others to do things for them". In contrast to the shelters' self-description, in which care, trust and close interrelationships constitute the basis for facilitating change in clients, the municipal housing-support worker emphasises what might be termed as "the impersonal relationship".

The municipal housing-support units are important actors, since they come into contact with clients at a transitional stage, when the remit of staff at the homeless shelter ceases. An emblematic concept in the housing-support units' self-description is "help for self-help", which several members of staff stress as the core principle underpinning their work. Counter-concepts to the self-help concept include "clinging", "pacifying help" and "robbing of responsibility". When asked about the pedagogical doctrine that underpins their work, the principle of self-help is the very one that a housing-support worker chooses to stress:

> "All the housing support workers are veterans, each with a background they draw on. If there is a dogma, it's 'help for self-help' – I mustn't do things for them that they can do themselves. Maybe it's ultimately a question of being patient enough to let clients proceed at their own pace. To let them be slow, for example in their contacts with the system. And that can be difficult, because some of the shelters' residents are adept at getting others to do things for them" (Social worker, Housing support unit, Odense region).

This quote expresses a need for self-restraint in social work – the social worker must maintain composure, be patient and avoid taking control away from clients, even when they are extremely slow and passive. The housing-support unit constructs itself by means of a negative construction of the environment – in particular, the homeless shelters and their tendency to provide excessive care and guidance. In several interviews, municipal workers state that the type of care exercised in the shelters can seem "clingy" and pacifying. For example, one front-line municipal worker said of the workers at the shelters:

> "They make a safe environment that retains people and has a staff that forges bonds – you hold Christmas and Easter together, go to the beach together, do stuff together, and so on. Maybe it's too much. I think sometimes it gets a bit nursemaidy – a bit nauseatingly caring" (Social worker, Housing support unit, Odense region).

The housing-support workers highlight, as illustrative of good social work, efforts that are rooted in a "professional relationship" with the client – efforts that "maintain distance". Many housing-support units have a principle that professionals should not form close relationships and develop friendships.

It appears that the two organisational systems base their self-descriptions on constructing particular images of their environments. One crucial element in the homeless shelter's self-description is that the efforts of the municipal staff are "inadequate" and "distanced". One facility indicates that it is problematic that municipal housing-support workers possess insufficient knowledge of the typical needs of clients who return to the community. The homeless shelters claim that municipal staff give up too quickly, while they work according to the motto "27th time lucky". They argue that, although municipal workers "respect a closed door", the problem is that the client's closed door "may be a cry for help". The municipal staff give up too quickly and fail to actively seek out the clients.

The homeless shelters also argue that the housing-support workers' methods are not at all geared towards the often extremely vulnerable clients whom they encounter – which may lead to the client being let down. Staff from the St. Dannesbo shelter facility in Odense say that when they find out about such cases, they opt, informally, to provide the necessary help:

> "When they [municipal workers] go into a flat, and it smells of puke, and the clients have shat their pants or pissed on the sofa or whatever, they just leave again. They call somebody in to clean up. What shelter workers do when they provide unofficial support, when they come in and record things like that, is call me and say: 'You know what? This will take a bit longer. There are a few things that need done'" (Front-line worker, Homeless shelter, Odense region).

We keep in mind that systems-theoretical analysis does not reveal the inner motives or worldviews of the social workers involved. The analysis has no access to people's thought systems, to the way their psychological systems operate. However, the analysis does show how the organisational systems' retroactive communication creates certain observational "views" that, inter alia, construct both the client and the social worker in completely different ways. In fact, the analysis shows that the organisations construct diametrically opposing roles for the client. To be seen positively, the client must, in one organisational system, be viewed as somebody who forms close and trusting relationships; in the other system, the client has to be viewed as someone who is autonomous and self-determined.

Making clients recognisable

For the staff at the homeless shelters to assist their clients in achieving help from the municipal social services office in securing permanent accommodation, the description of the homeless is decisive. In this context, action plans or case descriptions can be identified as instruments that couple organisations, which is confirmed by many shelter workers, who state that in-depth client descriptions are a crucial element in achieving a positive working relationship with the local social services office. They also argue that it is important to "write the right things in the right way" when working with the social counsellors. In systems-theory terms, we can say that the homeless shelters employ a "strategy of a second order", as they observe how other organisations observe the client and then seek to codify the client accordingly (Andersen 2003b: 178). The organisation observes and describes the client, aware that it could have observed and described the client differently. This allows it to adopt a strategic attitude in relation to the particular themes of the communication. A leader from one homeless shelter clearly articulates this problem:

> "But there's still a catch – on the form, you have to evaluate the client based on certain criteria and make this recommendation. But you also have to remember what it is they want you to write, what kind of form it is" (Leader, Homeless Shelter, Copenhagen City).

The client has to fit into the appropriate "form" and its related requirements to gain access to various services, as assigned by the municipal social counsellor. To access the prospective benefits and types of treatment available in the Danish welfare system, the client must appear to be both "good" and "bad" at one and the same time. The crucial thing here is that the homeless person is described or codified as "dysfunctional" and unable to fend for themselves on the one hand, but as "developing" and potentially able to cope in their own homes on the other hand. In terms of the action plan, the client must be codified with so many social, psychological or substance-related problems that they are clearly unable to solve their own housing problem. However, they must not appear incapable of fending for themselves in homes of their own. A precise balance needs to be struck, as expressed by this front-line worker at the emergency shelter in Hillerødgade, Copenhagen:

> "It's best if you are not too capable, but not too bad either. Referring them to homes of their own is a very difficult thing to do. Of course, you have to tell the truth, but when drawing up an action plan you must use the correct language to articulate what the real problem actually is. It sometimes comes down to a few words being weighed wrongly or correctly to make a difference one way or the other" (Front-line worker, Shelter, Copenhagen City).

Municipal advisory centres are also aware that a detailed action plan is a crucial factor in ensuring that the client receives the quickest and most positive treatment from the local council. This is underlined by the head of a shelter in Copenhagen:

> "As far as I understand it, it isn't done on a first come, first served basis. There's no queue as such. The client is evaluated according to professional statements on how ready he is to move and things like that. It's important to prove that there is development going on in the case. And it is for this reason that I ask for continuous assessments, so that the people in charge can see that there is progress in the case" (Head of homeless shelter, Copenhagen city).

This quotation illustrates several interesting details. First, the City of Copenhagen does not adhere to a queuing principle when allocating housing – rather, it is apparently of decisive significance how the client is described. Second, the crucial factor in ensuring the most positive decision from the local social services office is that the case file appears to describe a client who is making progress. This means, third, that the individual volunteer or shelter leader's input, contact network and perseverance, as well as letters of support from other agencies, will determine the outcome of the individual case. The individual shelter worker's willingness and ability to codify the homeless in a way that is recognisable to the local social services office becomes crucial for the client's inclusion in the "re-absorption" process.

In summary, the analysis shows how different welfare organisations such as homeless shelters and housing support units create self-descriptions via internal – and negative – constructions of each other. This establishes and maintains organisational systems that operate on the basis of incompatible ideas of what a homeless person is, what a good transition process consists of, what form acts of help should take etc. The analysis suggests that the two main forms of organisation are linked to different function systems which colour their communications via, respectively, a religious coding revolving around concepts of giving unconditional care and embracing the particular person, and a legal and educational codification implying norms of eligibility, impartiality and progress.

The analysis, therefore, shows how welfare organisations reduce the complexity of the environment in contingent ways, and how this reduction places the client in a precarious position. The client is always in danger of being observed by the organisations as inadequate, that is, as either "too shut off, isolated and asocial" or "too dependent, clinging and pacified". The existence of self-referential, but mutually coupled, welfare organisations challenges the political ideal of equal treatment for all citizens. At least in this case, the two conflicting criteria for the client who is suitable for social re-integration leave considerable room for the individual social worker's subjective assessments and strategic efforts on behalf of the particular client.

Case 2: The role of social work in modern society

As mentioned by way of introduction, much of the systems theory research into welfare institutions, social policy and social work follows an abstract, theorising approach. In fact, it is extremely difficult to find empirical studies of these areas outside of a narrow, Nordic – particularly Danish – context. In Germany, the homeland of systems theory, the vast majority of research has focused on theorising about social work's function in modern society and whether it is reasonable to identify social work as an independent system with its own logic and functionality. Although this book aims to pave the way for empirical analyses, rather than remain abstract or oriented towards internal theoretical considerations (although this may also generate fruitful output), we have chosen to devote some space to the research into systems theory. In order to give an impression of this quite widespread use of

Luhmann's work, we must briefly look at two illustrative studies in this tradition.

The first concerns the characteristics that define social work as an independent function system, and includes some observations on its historical emergence. The second is about what social work can contribute in a situation of growing social segregation and exclusion. Jan Wirth (2009) represents the camp who argues that social work is an independent function system. Wirth stresses that systems theory offers an alternative, more plausible and non-normative approach to social work. This is a functional reading, which stresses that any contingent social system "may be seen simply as an answer to a specific, concrete problem, above all as an attempt to reduce the complexity of the environment" (Wirth 2009: 406). Where systems theory was used above in a critical analysis of the power implicit in welfare organisations' inclusion criteria, Wirth's approach seeks to demonstrate the particular qualities of social work that place it on a par with other modern function systems. The systems-theory approach to social work is used here to defend its uniqueness and to refute "the widespread fallacy that other (mostly unpaid) forms of social help, such as 'civil society', voluntarism, and neighbourly help, can take the place of professional social work" (Wirth 2009: 408).

By means of a quick historical overview of the development from segmented society to stratified society to modern society, Wirth questions the form of this help and asks to which problem it is the solution (2009: 408–12). Briefly, in segmented society, help took the form of gifts, the exchange of which was systematised between two equal parties. Help was, therefore, largely horizontal and reciprocal. In stratified societies, the differentiation between groups resides in hierarchical differences – between nobility and commoners, bourgeoisie and proletariat, or high and low caste. In this context, the emblematic form of help is the good deed, which was religiously based and involved a unidirectional transfer from higher to lower. However, in the modern, functionally differentiated society, the hierarchical model came under pressure. In this new context, there is no common perspective accessible to the different function systems, and problems – including the question of whether overall political intervention is required – are conditional upon the individual systems. The complete integration of individuals into "society" is an impossibility, since society is fragmented into a multiplicity of social systems. The best that can be hoped for is a partial inclusion, in which the system allows individuals to be included for certain periods and only in relation to specific aspects, e.g. customers in a market or the plaintiff in court.

Modern society's function systems are in principle blind to exclusion problems. According to Wirth (2009: 414), it is imperative that social work takes on the job of facilitating the re-inclusion of individuals in the most crucial function systems, including the family, the economy, justice, education, the health system and the political system. The social worker cannot guarantee the inclusion of individuals in these systems, but can increase their degree of "addressability" in relation to the function systems. This attributes to the social worker a mediator function, in other words they represent the client in relation to key agencies identified in other social-work theories, the court, the policy, the family or the local community (Philp 1979). Wirth (2009: 416) adds two further aspects. First, that social workers must keep an eye on both sides of the basic distinction help/not help – that is, they must recognise when not helping is actually helpful. Second, social workers ought to adopt a functional, constructivist approach that creates new possible solutions by ascertaining the "functional equivalent solutions" to a specific problem. For Wirth, systems theory is therefore a heuristic tool, which facilitates reflections that extend beyond conventional and self-evident solutions.

A somewhat more sceptical view of the role of social work is provided by Albert Scherr (1999). He does not think that social work has differentiated itself as an independent function system, since it is subject to decisions – taken in the political system or determined by legislation – about whether help should be given. Rather, the social worker is a "secondary safeguard" that supplements welfare benefits defined politically and legally, with person-related services such as counselling, training and therapy etc. (Scherr 1999: 22). Scherr's view of social work's function runs parallel to Wirth's in one respect, however – for both, the main function of social work is to seek to enable individuals' integration into society's function systems. Scherr thinks that this function should be split into three sub-dimensions: "exclusion prevention", "inclusion mediation" and "exclusion management", which he describes as follows:

> "Linked to the social systems (especially job markets, school and family), social work attempts to prevent exclusion, to encourage inclusion, and to manage exclusion in cases where inclusion (or re-inclusion) proves impossible" (Scherr 1999: 22).

The last function, "exclusion management", is particularly relevant in a time of increasing social segregation and permanent exclusion of large groups, especially from the labour market in Western countries such as France and Britain. Scherr stresses that those who are forced into an existential struggle for material necessities need not be formally excluded in order to find themselves prevented from participating meaningfully in politics, education and culture (Scherr 1999: 16). Exclusion is at its most glaring when applied to refugees who do not enjoy formal status as citizens, but in the context of the current economic crisis it also applies to people who possess few, or the wrong, qualifications. As a result of globalisation and the diminishing importance of national governments, as well as the lack of compensation via social policy, social exclusion is expected to be exacerbated (Scherr 1999: 18).

While other systems theorists have suggested that social work is, or may become, an independent function system that operates completely on a par with other systems, Scherr has an alternative interpretation. Assigned the impossible mission of helping marginalised people in ghettoised urban areas, social work should rather be designated "exclusion management". The principal task of social work is to take care of the residual group whose problems are not covered by the general welfare schemes such as unemployment insurance, health insurance and pensions. However, according to Scherr, the function ascribed to social work is not just to work with excluded individuals' psycho-social problems, but also to protect society against the risks posed to it by individuals who are unemployed and have minimal income and poor health (1999: 21–2). The critical interest in Scherr's analysis is that he poses a functional question about the role of social work, which can be applied to an analysis of the current situation in crisis-hit Western nations: "Exclusion management is accorded greater importance at a time when the growing discrepancy in supply and demand for manpower is accompanied by a dismantling of welfare state services" (Scherr 1999: 23). If social work's basic function switches from enabling inclusion to tackling exclusion, this will have a crucial impact on the entire social-work paradigm, its role and self-identity. In this way, Scherr's analysis shows that the functional question about social work can be posed both in relation to thematic discussions about social models and in the light of the problems faced in the contemporary social context, such as fragmentation, inequality and the increasing number of people rendered superfluous by the current situation of economic crises.

Conclusion

In this chapter, we have shown how systems theory offers a range of opportunities to analyse how welfare organisations' encounters with the citizen are staged communicatively in specific services. Let us summarise the key points. The system/environment analysis allows us to study how welfare organisations generate self-descriptions by internally constructing their environments. Instead of seeing organisations as stable units with a given environment, we can study how they constantly generate and communicate their own self-identity. Welfare organisations can, for example, construct their environments as allies and partners, people with rights or "whole people" with a need for self-development. The analysis above documented how incongruent system/environment constructions generated not only scepticism between the two types of organisations, but also that they adopted different criteria for clients' inclusion and exclusion in social work with homeless people.

The analyses of forming allow us to analyse how the citizen is constructed differently depending on whether the organisation connects to the legal system (and thus observes a citizen with rights), the health system (observes a patient), the educational system (observes a "learning child") or the economic system (observes an investment decision based on the scarcity of resources). It is then possible to study which specific communications emerge from the codification used in the organisations when the communication must link to one particular side of a distinction.

With its concepts of organisational criteria for membership and roles, systems theory affords the opportunity to describe how the professional and the service user are constructed in welfare organisations' communications. The question is how certain role expectations are established and reproduced communicatively, independently of specific individuals' motives, attitudes or convictions. This analytical perspective also enables critical analyses of how citizens may be forced to enter into certain codified roles in order to gain access to welfare provision. Similarly, it is possible to study how specific categories of persons are excluded from welfare organisations because they do not meet the complexity-reducing – but contingent – membership criteria and role expectations. The various analytical perspectives make it possible to study how welfare organisations process the elements with which they come into contact, with the help of observations and programmes that in principle have the reproduction of the organisational systems as their fundamental function. Based on moral, political or ethical criteria, they may be judged as neither necessary nor desirable. Assessments of desirability and necessity are, however, beyond the remit of systems theory and its dispassionate analytical gaze.

Finally, we discussed two theoretical studies of social work, both of which are based on systems theory. These illustrate that the question of social work's function (including welfare institutions in a general sense) can be discussed from a classical functionalist perspective and from a more contemporary critical perspective. Systems theory does not provide a direct socially-critical approach, but the analytical tools that it provides can, quite easily, be mobilised and brought into play for critical purposes.

6 Neo-institutional theory: Myths and legitimacy

Neo-institutional organisation theory is not the result of the work of a single main author but was developed by a number of researchers, primarily from the USA, in the latter half of the 1970s. It is a current within organisation theory that emphasises the centrality of culture and socially constructed norms to the way in which organisations function. As such, it contrasts with a number of other perspectives on organisations, for example, theories that view organisations as rational production units, as functional responses to social needs, or as products of the strategic actions of elites. Prominent neo-institutional theorists include John Meyer (1938–), Richard Scott (1932–) and Paul DiMaggio (1951–). The theory is particularly relevant to the study of organisations providing products and services that are difficult to measure and quantify, such as education, culture or other forms of "soft" (typically public-sector) services. Good introductions are available in: John Meyer and Richard Scott's classic work *Organizational Environments: Ritual and Rationality* (1983), Paul DiMaggio and Walter Powell's important anthology *The Neo-institutionalism in Organizational Analysis* (1991a), which contains a selection of key articles, and Richard Scott's updated introduction *Institutions and Organizations* (2001).

KEY CONCEPTS: rationality myths, institutions, legitimacy, isomorphism, decoupling.

Neo-institutional theory can, with some justification, be viewed as dominant in contemporary organisation studies. As a theoretical current, it is particularly well suited to the study of public-sector institutions, which makes it especially relevant to this book. In relation to welfare organisations, neo-institutional organisation theory has been applied in a variety of studies spanning different sectors, including health, education and social work (Scott 2000, Cooney 2007, Sosin 2009, Contandriopoulos & Brousselle 2010). In common with the other perspectives covered in the book, it takes a deconstructivist approach. In this case, the theory seeks to problematise practices, organisational models, technologies and values that are taken for granted and are difficult to question. These are grouped under the heading "rationality myths". One of the main tasks of neo-institutional theory has been to show

how such "mythical" elements are maintained and disseminated without increasing organisational performance or fulfilling an organisation's stated objectives. Herein lies its key critical potential.

Neo-institutional organisation theory was developed around two main questions. First: why do we often see a striking similarity in organisational forms and practices? And, second: how do we explain the widespread adoption of "organisational elements", for example, management practices, for which there is little empirical evidence of their contribution to substantive performance? Neo-institutional organisation theory poses a particular challenge to two explanations in its response to these questions. It rejects evolutionary and functional explanations, which assert that certain forms of organisation survive and proliferate as a product of natural selection – in other words, organisational structures, practices and modes of production are supposedly weeded out over time if they fail to adapt to the needs of the environment in which they operate. Also rejected are explanations that see organisation as the product of deliberate actions by certain actors, whether in the form of attempts to maximise self-interest (rational choice theory) or elites who design organisations in accordance with a particular ideology (Marxist theory). None of these, according to the neo-institutional perspective, provides a satisfactory explanation of modern organisations' paradoxical use of ineffective structures and instruments.

Advocates of neo-institutional organisation theory start from the assumption that modern organisations exist in institutional environments, in which socially defined and sanctioned norms prevail for how an "up-to-date", rational and efficient organisation ought to look. Over time, such norms become *institutionalised* and taken for granted – they are incorporated into consultants' organisational charts, disseminated through reform programmes, written into legislation, and promoted by advisory bodies, parent companies, trade unions, employers, higher education institutions and state agencies. It is presumed that, in order to survive, an organisation not only has to deliver good products or services, it must also appear legitimate to the environment with which it interacts. The organisation has to be able to sell its services, obtain capital input or government grants, find partners, attract talented staff, etc.

Every organisation is therefore exposed to environmental pressures to appear legitimate. Neo-institutional organisation theory posits that whatever an organisation assimilates from its surroundings in order to achieve legitimacy is not always directly compatible with, or beneficial to, the specific practices of the organisation. The models and instruments that we take for granted for the rational organisation's operations are not necessarily conducive to the actual activity of the organisation, not least because they are general, rather than tailored to a specific context. According to the theory, they constitute powerful "myths" about what constitutes an effective, good, democratic and rational organisation.

Neo-institutional organisation theory is often described as "middle-range" or focused on the "meso-level". The theory's attempts to explain the development and behaviour of organisations are not based on objective, social reasons (society's increasing complexity and functional divisions) or on actors' strategic actions and micro-interactions. As such, neo-institutional organisation theory does not focus on macro- or micro-explanations, but instead aims to focus on the institutions, myths and logics that organisations help to create, reproduce and disseminate within their area of work. In other words, this approach wants to establish an area of research that is exclusively on the organisational level, as it focuses on intra-organisational and internal organisational processes.

Next follows a general presentation of the key concepts of neo-institutional organisation theory, and then we shall go on to discuss the concepts in relation to the analysis of welfare organisations and citizens' encounters with them.

Various sources of theoretical inspiration

Unlike most of the perspectives covered in this book, neo-institutional organisation theory cannot be attributed to a single main author. Rather, it derives inspiration from a variety of sociological, political-science, anthropological and ethnographic theories, including the historical sociologist Max Weber, the ethnologists Harold Garfinkel and Erving Goffman, the anthropologist Mary Douglas, the political scientist Herbert Simon, the sociologists Peter Berger and Thomas Luckman, and Pierre Bourdieu. Although the approach is inspired by several of the theorists covered in this book, we think that it offers its own particular way of observing citizens' encounters with welfare services, as well as the organisational frameworks for those encounters (a good presentation of some of the sources of inspiration for neo-institutional organisation theory is found in DiMaggio & Powell, 1991b).

What is "new" about neo-institutional theory is its claim that an organisation exists in an institutional environment in which adaptation to the norms and expectations of their environments is crucial to the organisation's ability to survive (Levin 1998: 25). The neo-institutionalists reformulate the concept of the organisation and the idea of organisations' relations to their environments in a number of ways. They stress that organisations are completely dependent on their environment's resources, and thus have to deal with and adapt to their environments in a continuous and strategic manner. They stress that legitimacy in their environments is critical to organisations' survival, and emphasise that organisations that fail to deploy institutionalised myths and organisational elements lack legitimate narratives. According to the theory, organisations consist of loosely-coupled entities that are connected to various networks through which values, models and technologies are diffused. Proponents underline that the relationship between means and ends is often unclear in organisational fields, so organisations tend to make use of popular, apparently successful and previously-tested models and technologies. Rather than being seen as distinct, defined entities that conduct exchanges with their environments, organisations are viewed as imbued with the norms and values of their environments. In its most radical version, the neo-institutional perspective sees organisations as "theatrical displays of the rationality myths that permeate modern society" (Meyer & Rowan 1977: 346).

In what is now considered a classic article, the importance of which is difficult to overstate, John W. Meyer and Brian Rowan formulated a number of key assumptions and concepts for neo-institutional theory. The article, with the apposite title *Institutionalized Organizations: Formal Structure as Myth and Ceremony*, argues precisely that organisational structures are often used "ceremonially" in order to attain legitimacy. The existing organisational theories have, to a large extent, assumed that organisations operate in accordance with formal organisational charts, hierarchies and official procedures (Meyer & Rowan 1977: 342). However, this assumption contradicts empirical studies, which show that a large gap often exists between the formal structure of organisations and their actual activities and processes. A theory is needed that explains the prevalence of formal types of organisations without basing the explanation on an assessment of whether they manage and co-ordinate their work processes in the most effective manner.

The elements that make up part of the formal structures of organisations act as myths – in other words, as a kind of narrative that organisations reproduce and use to describe themselves in order to appear efficient, useful, modern and rational. This applies to the use of specific expertise, to programmes and to the use of certain technologies. Formal structures thus include a range of elements such as organisational charts, covering the various departments, offices, job titles, lines of command and process descriptions, as well as stated targets, values and programmes that guide the organisation's activities. The radical contribution of the neo-institutional perspective is that even widespread technical instruments are afforded mythical status. Heavy caveats are thus placed on the effects and efficiency of these technologies. They are viewed as examples of types of rites that must be practised and reproduced for symbolic reasons. About technologies, Meyer and Rowan write:

> "Technologies are institutionalised and become myths that bind organisations. Technical procedures for production, accounting, recruitment of staff or data processing become obvious means of achieving organisational goals. Irrespective of their potential efficiency, such institutionalised techniques present an organisation as appropriate, rational and modern. Their use shows responsibility and counters accusations of neglect" (Meyer & Rowan 1977: 344).

The concept of institutionalisation also indicates a process of normalisation that ignores the myths' historical origins and original context. Meyer and Rowan define institutionalisation as the process whereby certain classifications of the world are endowed with an objective status for the actors – a definition they take from Berger and Luckmann (1966). Classifications are established in social practice as mutually-confirmed typifications and interpretations that have become indisputable and are sanctioned socially or supported by legislation (Meyer & Rowan 1977: 341). Institutions are described as "codes of appropriate behaviour" (March & Olsen 1989: 160). Institutions work regulatively (non-compliance can be sanctioned socially, or even prosecuted), normatively (they have a moralising effect and stipulate how things ought to be done) and cognitively (they filter perceptions of the world via classifications that naturalise phenomena). By creating order, assigning roles and reducing uncertainty, institutions constitute regulatory agencies in society.

Organisations that fail to incorporate institutional elements, or which create unique structures, will not only lack legitimate descriptions of their activities, but may also find themselves facing legal sanctions. A notable example of this was the *Tvind* schools, an alternative school movement, inspired by socialist principles, which originated in Denmark in the early 1970s. The schools attracted fierce public criticism – not only because of their dubious accounting and tax practices. The target of the criticism was not so much what the schools actually did – which included teaching maladjusted youngsters. Rather, the indignation was due to *Tvind's* unique and, in the eyes of the public, illegitimate, structures and processes – e.g. "collective time", "collective money" and its "cult-like" organisational culture. From a theoretical perspective, a significant cause of the schools' problems was its conspicuous lack of legitimate institutional elements. For an analysis of the *Tvind* schools' socio-educational approach, see Chamberlin and Chamberlin (1993).

However, not all organisations are required to demonstrate the same degree of conformity with their institutional environment. In neo-institutional organisation theory, it is commonplace to distinguish between what are referred to as "technical environments" and "institutional environments". Whenever output is relatively easy to evaluate, a market usually emerges in which efficiency is crucial to success (Meyer & Rowan 1977: 354). However, modern society – and especially societies organised as welfare states – has developed a series of domains characterised by complex interrelationships that do not mainly function according to market-based conditions. Organisations that work in areas such as teaching, care, culture and social security use non-transparent technologies to produce "products" that are difficult to quantify. Such organisations tend to be evaluated on the basis of whether they use legitimate institutionalised elements.

As a result, a general distinction is made between technical environments, in which organisations are evaluated on the basis of output, and institutional environments, in which evaluations are based on an organisation's processes and structures. As shown below, a distinction can also be made between output-based evaluation on the one hand, and structural and process-based evaluation on the other.

Neo-institutional organisation theory talks about a tendency for organisations to shift their criteria for evaluation of their own activities. In cases where it is difficult to conduct output-based evaluations of efficiency, process- and structure-based criteria are often used instead. In other words, evaluations are made of how production is organised and works, and this provides an indication of the extent to which products or services of high quality may be expected to be effectively produced. The crucial point in this context is that organisations that supply "soft products" – such as culture, education, social security or consultancy services to public-sector management – are typically rooted in strong institutional environments.

From this perspective, welfare organisations are assumed to be under particularly strong pressure to present institutionalised myths to their environments. We must assume that welfare organisations constantly decode their environments to identify existing institutional myths and monitor the changes that occur in them, in order to maintain their own legitimacy and survival prospects. We can also assume that welfare organisations will be particularly prone to assimilating organisational elements that are vaguely tested – or even undocumented – in terms of their effects and efficiency. This applies to organisations such as social services, welfare-to-work projects, treatment for addicts, institutions for homeless people, hospitals, prisons, children's homes, integration units, etc.

A critical theoretical point is, therefore, that welfare organisations are often oriented more towards assimilating and presenting institutional myths than examining how specific structures, processes or technologies work in relation to the users – in other words, whether the citizens actually do receive the most efficient social services, job training, treatment, integration, health services and so on.

Organisational isomorphism and decoupling

Neo-institutional organisation theory argues that modern society is characterised by increased structuring of "organisational fields", namely, areas in which organisations have a high degree of interaction, dependence and exchanges of information. This is the starting point for Paul DiMaggio and Walter Powell, authors of the influential article that introduced the concept of organisational isomorphism (1983). Isomorphism is described as "a constraining process that forces one unit in a population to resemble other units that face the same set of environmental conditions. At the population level, such an approach suggests that organizational characteristics are modified in the direction of increasing comparability with environmental characteristics" (Dimaggio and Powell 1983: 149). DiMaggio and Powell offer a definition of the processes that work toward isomorphism within an organisational field by describing three types of isomorphism (ibid.: 150–2).

Coercive isomorphism: direct and indirect pressure is exerted on the organisation by other organisations upon which it depends – for example, public-sector funding bodies or by parent companies on subsidiaries. Pressure is exerted through expectations, legal requirements, offers of partnership, etc. Legislation can, for example, force government agencies or non-government social organisations to introduce specific treatment technologies, budget submissions, formal management structures, etc.

Mimetic isomorphism: in situations characterised by uncertainty about the relationship between means and ends, and in which the objectives are unclear, it may be easiest and least expensive to choose a "success model" rather than conduct complex surveys. In other words, imitate "successful organisations" and introduce certain innovations, new working practices, etc., that demonstrate that the organisation is "taking care of the problems". Models and technologies can be popularised by particular professions or consultants.

Normative isomorphism: isomorphic pressure is also exerted through professional networks that transcend organisations, and through which values, organisational models, working practices, etc. are difuse. Particular educational establishments, consultancy companies, continuing-education institutions, etc. generate specialists who share approaches, solutions, and so on. In many cases, staff are recruited from the same educational institutions or from organisations in the same field.

As is evident from the above, DiMaggio and Powell seek to capture the mechanisms by which organisations are led to conform to standards of professionalism and to adopt systems and techniques that are considered legitimate in their environment. The concept of "normative isomorphism" highlights how organisational norms are conveyed through the education and training of professionals and through the processes of certification and accreditation by professional bodies. It is therefore noteworthy that DiMaggio and Powell identify the nation state and the professions as key shapers of contemporary institutionalised norms: "the great rationalizers of the second half of the twentieth century" (DiMaggio & Powell 1983: 148).

Nevertheless, neo-institutional theorists contend that rationality is difficult to study and criticise in a general sense. They emphasise that rationalised myths are enshrined in the rules, categories and concepts that have taken root in specific social domains (Meyer & Rowan 1977: 344). Institutionalisation and isomorphism should thus be examined specifically by marking out and focusing on an "organisational field", that is, "those organisations that, in aggregate, constitute a recognized area of institutional life" (DiMaggio & Powell 1983: 148). Several points in Bourdieu's theory of "social fields" explicitly or implicitly inspire DiMaggio and Powell's concept of organisational fields. The institutional myths must be viewed as relatively independent or specific to each field. Or, to put it in Bourdieuian terms: the symbolic capital is specific to the individual field, and cannot be directly converted. The actors in a field have difficulty seeing the socially constructed nature of the myths. They are acting within what Bourdieu terms the "illusio", i.e. they are too engaged by the game itself to recognise their roles as players. Within a social field, symbols of recognition are diluted over time, and new ones are invented in their place. Actors or organisations are forced to distinguish themselves in their fields to gain recognition, and thus "good taste" is always sought after, even at the risk of losing its status.

Acknowledging that the assimilation of new technologies and models by organisations is often due to pressure from their environment is important to our understanding of politics, including the political governance of welfare organisations. If thoroughly institutionalised organisations, such as public-sector welfare agencies, are highly responsive to field-specific myths, there will be fewer opportunities than conventionally assumed to manage them in a "top-down" manner, via traditional political control. According to neo-institutional organisation theory, the relationships between organisations within a field are critical to the processes of change that we can observe in welfare organisations. To illustrate the point, we briefly refer to a study of organisational change processes in Danish local authorities (Gregersen 1996). One of the central questions in this analysis is why, over a number of years, a large number of social services set up similar job-creation units. The analysis challenges two explanations: a) that local authorities act as the final link in the parliamentary chain of government, and thus can be viewed as entities that merely implement policy; and b) that local authorities act as rational actors with clear objectives – for example, seeking to maximise state subsidies and minimise municipal expenditure. Based on neo-institutional theory, Gregersen focuses instead on the relationships between the local authorities, which he sees as key to processes of organisational change.

His point is that local authorities imitated each other because of "ambiguity in terms of production". Considerable uncertainty reigns about the relationship between means and ends in job-creation programmes, so local authorities were subject to severe institutional pressure to display legitimising structures and processes, as a result of which many chose to assimilate tried and apparently tested models. It is only later, once the changes had already been made in the organisation that a political decision was made that stipulated an obligation to establish job-creation secretariats in local authorities. In this way, the analysis explains how a particular organisational element (in this case, the job-creation department) was able to spread throughout local government without a decision having been made at a central political level. As a result, the neo-institutional perspective has implications for our way of thinking about policy. If important organisational changes happen through, for example, a process of imitation between local authorities (rather than them implementing policy decisions), we can speak of "policy-making administrations". This approach focuses on the fact that the organisational design and technologies are pursued for both political and technical reasons, and that public-sector managers seek formal legitimacy as well as substantive results. This is probably even more the case in times where "greater efficiency", "increased user-responsiveness" and "high-performance management" are requested from managers of welfare services (Ashworth et al. 2009: 172). Naturally, micro-political organisational changes of this kind affect the citizen's encounters with welfare organisations.

The problem with assimilating institutionalised models and technologies is, as mentioned previously, that they are normally general and standardised. They originate from a specific context, but have since been generalised, and so they are not adapted to the individual organisation's specific activities and production processes. In addition, organisations are often subjected to pressure from various parts of their environments, which means that institutional myths may be conflicting with each other. For example, a young offenders' institution is expected to simultaneously punish, care for and train the inmates (Levin 1998, 2002). This requires a combination of legal, care-related and pedagogical institutional myths, which can be difficult to negotiate. As a result, inconsistencies and paradoxes might occur.

Organisations that need to negotiate legitimising elements with actual activities, and balance conflicting institutional myths against each other, tend to use the strategy known as decoupling (Meyer & Rowan 1977: 356). The concept of decoupling requires that the organisation, in different ways, separates the actual work processes (technical co-ordination processes and structures) from the processes and structures that are directed towards reflecting norms in the institutional environment. Nils Brunsson has developed the concept of decoupling in more detail and specifies four types (Brunsson 1989, Brunsson & Olsen 1993). First, the strategy can be to decouple "policy-producing departments" from operational departments – in other words, legitimising, standardised structures are displayed by certain departments while other departments carry out tangible activities regulated by practical and action-oriented considerations. Second, it is possible to decouple from the environment: the organisation expends energy displaying legitimising myths to certain parts of its environment, while in relation to other parts of its environment the focus is on informal activity. Third, an organisation can decouple over time, so that in some periods it gives priority to displaying institutional norms, while in others it acts informally. Finally, organisations can decouple in relation to subjects, insofar as they use some subjects or themes to display institutional myths, while they approach other subjects in "irrational", informal ways. We give examples of decoupled welfare organisations below.

Another general way in which organisations can deal with recurrent inconsistencies is through what is referred to as the "logic of confidence and good faith" (Meyer & Rowan 1977: 357). With reference to Goffman, the neo-institutionalists stress that both internal members and external parties tend to maintain "good face" and trust in institutionalised organisations, even when their usefulness and effectiveness cannot be proven empirically, and their paradoxical nature becomes obvious. Inconsistency and conflict are avoided by creating decoupled units, and evident paradoxes are typically overlooked and ignored. All involved parties – both internal and external – tend to work together to keep up the organisation's "face" (see the chapter on Goffman in this book). In other words, they contribute to enabling the organisation to present itself as a legitimate, useful and valuable agent, despite the absence of, or lack of clarity in, the documentation of its actual results.

Welfare organisations seen through neo-institutional glasses

Welfare organisations are highly institutionalised organisations insofar as they manifest stable societal and field-specific values that endow them with legitimacy, regardless of what they actually produce. Welfare organisations serve to illustrate the neo-institutionalists' point that an organisation can grow and achieve stability through history, while at the same time failing in the strict production sense (Meyer et al. 1981). Pioneers in neo-institutional organisation theory John Meyer and Richard Scott used educational institutions as their main empirical examples, claiming that the Western world's perception of the objective of schools – to co-ordinate and streamline the activities of providing education – is erroneous. Instead, educational institutions have emerged in order to provide socially standardised and legitimised educational programmes that reflect institutionalised values (Meyer et al. 1981, Levin 1998: 31). If it is to survive, a school must manifest the societal and field-specific myths about what a school is.

The point is, in other words, that for highly institutionalised organisations such as those working in the area of welfare, adaptation to prevalent rationality myths is often more important than the actual "production". This gives structural, technological and procedural devices (especially legal and financial ones) a vital role. The important questions are whether legitimate structures exist, whether the budget is adhered to, whether the right professionals are employed, whether accepted methods and principles are used, and whether capacity is utilised well enough. Such elements are evaluated and controlled to a much greater extent than whether these same elements actually achieve the stated goals. The lack of attention given to welfare organisations' specific results is due to the fact that those organisations express deeply entrenched social values (Levin 1998). It is this relationship that makes institutionalised organisations pervasive and hard to question. "Survival is the major aim of the activity, since they administer societal values. As long as these values have power and permanency, the organisations will live on" (Levin 1998: 34).[1]

What differentiates neo-institutional theory from previous types of institutionalism is that it stresses the fact that organisations consist of cognitive structures. These constitute a kind of lens through which the organisation's members see the world and formulate relevant options for action. Institutionalised norms are installed in the organisation in the shape of formal rules, classification systems and indisputable programmes for action. The particular welfare organisation – say, a social services department – can be seen as a tangible manifestation of societal myths about what a social services department is, the norms to which it should adhere and which functions it performs. Levin describes it as follows:

> "Cultural ideas of what a social services department is, what social work is, and what clients are, become embedded over time in the organisation and turn into 'truths', social facts around which work is organised. The organisation 'installs' these social facts in the physical structure, in systems of rules, in handbooks, in ideas held by managers and staff, in patterns of action, in institutionalised technologies, etc." (Levin 1998: 45).

We can therefore say that welfare organisations observe the world through a specific set of ideas – a filter that permeates the organisation and gives it a specific, limited rationality. It follows that when citizens turn up at a social services office or another welfare organisation, they must be fitted into the categories and programmes for action that are already embedded in the organisation. Scott describes this process as a necessary "symbolic coding" of the material received by the organisation (Scott 1992: 208). This means that it is impossible for the organisation to perceive the citizen as a 'whole' or unique person, because the organisation is only capable of showing interest in (i.e. classifying, investigating and processing) certain characteristics and ways of behaving. For this reason, one may say that welfare organisations actively construct or create clients and their problems in their own image (on this specific point, the neo-institutional perspective resembles Luhmann's systems theory, as described in Chapter 5).

However, the filter through which welfare organisations look at the world is rarely unambiguous and free from contradictions. On the contrary, having to honour several conflicting institutional myths is a particularly pertinent challenge for welfare organisations. Dominant agents within an organisational field may organise, incite and sanction so that conflicting logics become unavoidable guidelines for members of the field, as demonstrated in Reay and Hinings' study of Regional Health Authorities in Alberta (2005). A social services department may be expected, for example, both to process cases in accordance with legal and bureaucratic principles and, at the same time, to do something active about poverty, abuse and the problems faced by young people (Levin 1998: 31). Another example is the appeals system for welfare cases which must, as we will see below, both make decisions that treat people equally under the law while taking the particular individual into account and acting in a financially prudent manner (Jakobsen 2004). The task of balancing multiple conflicting values and demands in modern welfare organisations often takes up considerable energy and resources.

We will now look at two studies that use neo-institutional organisation theory to critically examine welfare institutions. These are the Swedish researcher Claes Levin's study of the reformatory[2] as an institutionalised organisation (Levin 1998, 2002), and Turf Böcker Jakobsen's analysis of dilemmas in the Danish welfare appeals system (Jakobsen 2004).

As we will see, the studies use a broad variety of different methodological approaches. Both of them use historical source material to describe the emergence of certain rationality myths, including legal texts and secondary historical literature. They also both use qualitative interviews with employees in the selected organisations, and Jakobsen includes participant observation. In addition, Levin interviews users, i.e. the young people in the reformatories. This illustrates our point that there is no one particular method that automatically must be used in analyses inspired by neo-institutional organisation theory. Many different methods and types of empirical material can be used – organisations' self-descriptions in text and in speech; documents that present the environment's rationality myths (legal documents, reports, partnership agreements, advice from consultants, audits, reforms, etc.); participant observation; and statistical material, which may be used to, inter alia, document the prevalence of a particular organisational element over time, such as similar job-creation units across municipalities (Gregersen 1996). In terms of methodology, the neo-institutional approach provides a multitude of options.

Case 1: The Reformatory

In the following section, we look at an analysis of the child offenders' reformatory, conducted by Claes Levin and inspired by neo-institutional theory. The study was a PhD project published with the title *Uppfostringsanstalten: Om tvång i föräldrars ställe* (The Reformatory: Coercion in loco parentis) (Levin 1998). Levin's study was based on his surprise upon learning that the treatment of young offenders over the centuries has taken place in the same organisational framework, even though the results have been predominantly negative. The focus is on "the reformatory" or whatever term we may use to refer to placement institutions for young criminals. Levin formulates his problem as a question about how we understand the link between the institutions' ability to survive, their poor rehabilitation results, the ignorance and lack of interest regarding the actual effects they have on those whom they "treat", and the self-evident status the institutions enjoy in society, regardless of the results they achieve (Levin 1998: 21).

Levin uses three methods to examine the problem: 1) A historical and sociological approach to examine the rise of the child care institution. The objective of this approach is to describe the historical genesis of the institutionalised myths that these institutions reflect today. 2) Studies of the practical work in the child care institutions. The main objective of this effort is to examine the impact of the external institutional environment on staff members' definitions and perceptions of the children with whom they work. 3) Interviews with the young people who have previously received treatment in an institution, in order to identify their perceptions of the "treatment" and the procedures to which they had been submitted.

Our study primarily considers Levin's work on point 1 – uncovering the institutional myths that the reformatory has to reflect and balance. In the historical part of the study, Levin looks all the way back to the late Middle Ages, when the reformatory emerged as a completely new type of organisation in Europe. He describes how, particularly in the 18th and 19th centuries, a series of different sources of inspiration, of a philanthropic, disciplinary and humanistic nature, informed the model for care of "wicked" young offenders that was adopted in Sweden and in many other European countries. The model combined incarceration with forced labour, care and providing a proper upbringing. This combination of punishment and rehabilitation through care and learning endowed these institutions with a contradictory character that is retained to this day.

As such, care institutions for children were not only there to punish. Levin stresses how, in Norway, Denmark and Sweden around 1900, children were moved out of the mainstream prison system and the general legal system. Part of the reason for this was to further the pedagogic and humanistic principles of saving children and guaranteeing them a better future, but Levin points out that it was also a way for the middle class to protect itself against the threat posed by poor and unruly children. As a result, a local government institution with powers of forcible confinement was created – outside of normal legal regulation – to deal with both offenders and young people who had gone astray in other ways (Levin 1998: 73).

Levin's analysis gives a thorough description of the treatment ideology that was established in childcare in Western Europe, and especially in the Scandinavian countries. According to Levin, this ideology consists of three perceptions of treatment (Levin 1998: 80–5). First, the Enlightenment era's concept of pedagogic treatment – in brief, that systematic care and a proper upbringing in an institution would reform and civilise an individual's undesirable traits. The care and upbringing was to take place in isolation, away from home and the depravity of the cities, and in an institution characterised by order, discipline and morally-uplifting activities. The large institutions for the insane and morally depraved served as a model for this treatment ideal. Isolation was, in itself, considered to be treatment, and work was thought to be morally uplifting.

Next, there was the medical-rational treatment concept, which partly grew out of the above. This was a consequence of the "medicalisation" of children's problems via medical concepts and strategies for treatment. This concept was closely linked to the development of the medical profession and the somatic idea of disease-diagnosis-cure. From about 1900 onwards, this medical discourse was transferred to children's homes, where the causes of unruliness, crime and vagrancy began to be explained in medical terms, and treatments were developed on the basis of medical expertise. This meant that children who stole, played truant, etc. were diagnosed as "psychopathic". After medical examination, the child or young person could be placed in an institution and kept there until a doctor considered the treatment to have been successful. In certain cases, young people could even be sterilised to stop the spread of harmful genes.

Finally, there is the concept of socio-political treatment, which encapsulates the aforementioned pedagogic idea, and its success in becoming an overarching political ideology. The assumption was that living conditions for poor and marginalised people could be improved through socio-political reforms to reduce and prevent the occurrence of social problems. It was a mindset that imagined that social problems can be prevented and eliminated through a long series of welfare measures and services, among which treatment institutions were the most important. Bringing children up in a treatment institution would, therefore, prevent future damage to society as a result of lawlessness. Levin thinks that the socio-political treatment ideal was most clearly expressed in Sweden via the 1902 child welfare legislation. Under these laws (and later amendments), it was not the child or young person's criminal act that was conceived as the cause of forcible confinement. Rather, the young people were, by virtue of their actions, considered to be in need of care and treatment. In this way, the treatment ideal implied a shift from punishing the act of law-breaking to treatment of the young offender as an individual, his or her state of mind, intellectual maturity or psychological deviation. The treatment ideal redefined the object from a delinquent to a child who lacks responsibility.

Levin's analysis of the treatment ideology demonstrates that it has multiple objectives, including a humanist one of saving children from prison and from negligent parents. He also shows that this has to be done by state intervention in loco parentis, either to monitor the child's upbringing or, in worse cases, confine them in a closed institution. This provides us with a picture of the type of institutional norms the institution was forced to span.

The reformatory derives legitimacy from the use of detention, which is an integral form of punishment in a culture that places great value upon individual freedom. However, it also derives legitimacy from its promise of reforming young offenders by means of treatment. According to Levin, the survival of the reformatory depends on its ability to clearly manifest both of these conflicting norms (Levin 1998: 299). Any attempt to be either one (penal institution) or the other (pedagogic institution) will detract from its legitimacy.

One way for the institution to deal with this contradictory situation was to use a very broad and vaguely-defined concept of treatment. This concept contained elements of the Enlightenment pedagogic ideal, of the medical treatment concept (causal diagnosis and cure), the socio-political ideal of prevention and education in place of punishment and the objective of punishing misdemeanours. The ambiguity of the treatment concept allows the environment to infer many different purposes and types of content from the institution's treatment activities. However, as long as the contradictions do not become evident to the outside world, the reformatory lives on as a treatment concept.

In his analysis of the Reformatory, Levin stresses that the conflict between the treatment ideal and society's demand for incarceration and control is constantly present. The conflicting norms are even observable in the reformatory's physical structures and frameworks. The buildings' design and layout clearly echoes the prison: locked doors, systems of sanctions, isolation units and case files. All of this is alien to the pedagogic objectives and activities that are ascribed to the reformatory. The contrast between the punitive elements on the one hand, and the pedagogic and care-related parts on the other, could be an instance of the previously-introduced concept of "decoupling of departments". In this view, the organisation consists of loosely-coupled units, structures and activities that either contradict or directly counteract each other.

Levin's concluding evaluation of the reformatory's work with young people is deeply negative. His empirical data shows that their levels of substance abuse actually increased after their stay in the institution: 70% used drugs after their stay, while 60% did so prior to incarceration. The results for reintegration into society are also disheartening: almost 60% went on to other institutions after their stay (Levin 1998: 307). Levin thinks that the results should lead to the abandonment of the reformatory as an institution in its current form:

> "The logical consequence is that the reformatory cannot be defended on the basis of individual or general preventive arguments, nor on the basis of any professional treatment rationality. It should therefore be abolished in its current form. However, this has been obvious to most people for 150 years, still it has not happened" (Levin 1998: 309).

The explanation of why the reformatory has not been disbanded, despite its obviously poor or even negative results, can be found in neo-institutional organisation theory. Organisations that have adapted to, and display, key societal myths have a surprising capacity for survival. They are not evaluated primarily on the basis of their (unsatisfactory) results, but on how well they manage to adapt to society's expectations and requirements:

> "People-treating organisations can generate poor treatment and rehabilitation results, and despite that survive and prosper because they are not organisations in the technical sense, that is, tools to produce something specific, where success is measured by efficiency. They are organisations which have assumed institutional form, and the criterion for their success lies in how well they adapt to the environment's expectations" (Levin 1998: 298).

The critical potential consists, not least, in that the neo-institutional approach reveals how welfare organisations' success criteria can be somewhat decoupled from any benefit they have to their clients and users. Highly institutionalised welfare organisations must be assumed to suffer from a degree of blindness about the people with whom they come into contact on two counts. First, the organisations are so eager to display and decode the environment's expectations that they may be expected to pay little attention to the individual citizen and his or her particular problems. Second, the installation of what are referred to as cognitive filters means that the organisation's staff can only observe the citizen through the classifications and programmes that permeate the organisation. Levin stresses that the design of his analysis allows him to capture this feature of "people-treating" organisations (Levin 1998: 47). The neo-institutional perspective facilitates a description of the complexity of highly-institutionalised welfare organisations, and therefore also enables a deep and constructive criticism of these organisations' activities and existence.

Case 2: The Danish social appeals system

Our second example is an analysis of the welfare appeals system in Denmark, inspired by a combination of neo-institutional organisation theory and institutional ethnography. Turf Böcker Jakobsen's PhD project was published with the title *Legitimitetens logik: Institutionelle dilemmaer i det sociale klagesystem* (The Logic of Legitimacy: Institutional Dilemmas in the Social Appeals System) (Jakobsen 2004). The analysis seeks, in a neo-institutional manner, to question the axiomatic status of the concept of legal rights. Jakobsen's premise is that there is a common societal conception of the justification for the social appeals system, which exists relatively independently of the appeals body's actual practice. This general idea is embedded in the rationality myth "legal rights". Jakobsen studies the kind of practice that is supported by this concept. His starting point is that the appeals system's production – the appeal rulings – requires more thorough explanation, and an explanation that does not just see the production of rulings as the product of a technical-scientific method, but as "a complicated meaning construction among active social actors" (Jakobsen 2004: 14).[3]

Legitimacy is absolutely central to the construction of meaning in this context. Jakobsen's thesis is that it is crucial for the actors involved in appeals bodies to reinforce the legitimacy of their work and the existence of the appeals system, rather than achieving results sensitive to specific individuals and their fate.

Jakobsen's research design is, as previously mentioned, not solely inspired by neo-institutional organisation theory, but also by Canadian institutional ethnography (for example, Smith 1987). From neo-institutional organisation theory, Jakobsen takes, for example, the point about the fundamental dependence of institutionalised organisations on legitimacy, and the concepts of conflicting rationality myths and decoupling.

From institutional ethnography, he mobilises the concepts of "research-naivety", institutional thinking and multi-locality. Let us look at these in brief. Institutional ethnography allows the researcher to adopt a conscious naivety and basic curiosity in relation to the social structure being studied (Jakobsen 2004: 35). This renders the supposedly familiar and "grey" world consciously exotic – which is particularly relevant when it comes to a truly "unexotic" institution like the social appeals system.

Institutional ethnography furthermore offers a concept of multi-locality, which makes it possible to study meaning structures that transcend different organisational contexts. The starting point is that contemporary social relations are trans-local, i.e. they transcend the distinction between organisation and environment. As a result of this, the analysis has to focus on social structures that link or separate actors across time and space. In relation to the appeals system, the trans-local perspective makes it possible to follow the conflict, i.e. by tracking cases that start in one part of the appeals system and end somewhere else. It also explores the different meanings that are attributed to the same cases in different places in the system, such as in the Social Complaints Board and the Social Appeals Board. In this way, the perspective can be used to question whether it is meaningful to consider the social appeals system as a single administrative entity with an overall rationale (Jakobsen 2004: 36). In Jakobsen's analysis, the appeals system is revealed to be a multi-contextual system in which individual vantage points are essential to generating meaning about the cases processed.

He argues that this coupling between neo-institutional organisation theory and institutional ethnography is scientifically congruent, as neo-institutional organisation theory was specifically inspired by ethnographic research and cultural theory – particularly, studies of culturally-produced norms and classifications that appear objective to the individual actors. Moreover, Jakobsen argues that most neo-institutional organisation studies typically neglect giving attention to the specific actors' practice, but that this weakness can be remedied by incorporating institutional ethnography (Jakobsen 2004: 42).

His extensive empirical study deals with the meaning of social appeals in several contexts – at the level of municipal social services department, and in the complaints boards, the local family law offices and the Social Appeals Board. Through qualitative interviews and participant observation, Jakobsen studies a municipal social services department, where the complaints arise, a social board that acts as the first appeals body, and the Social Appeals Board, which deals with matters of principle, or of general significance, as the ultimate appeal body (Jakobsen 2004: 13). A key objective was to produce a description of the system's decision-making activities as an exotic and multi-sited cultural practice.

The social appeals system likes to describe itself as a system that, by employing principles and methodologies rooted in legal positivism, is always able to find correct answers to specific legal problems. However, Jakobsen's (2004: 289, 320–2) analysis shows that several institutional requirements coexist in addition to legal positivism's principle of protection of individual rights. This principle is countered by the requirement for administrative efficiency, which pulls in the opposite direction. He points out that the requirement for administrative efficiency did not arise out of efforts to streamline the public sector, but has always been an important consideration in the social appeals system. This applies, for example, to the complaints boards, where it has always been possible to refuse to conduct a full review of discretionary decisions, including for reasons of maintaining the autonomy of local authorities. The Social Appeals Board also rejects the majority of cases submitted to it because it only considers exemplary cases, or "test cases". This requirement for administrative efficiency is not particularly compatible with the principle of ensuring individual rights by means of an in-depth analysis of the particular case under review. On the other hand, it is compatible with another institutional consideration, i.e. uniformity before the law. This consideration has traditionally been central to the appeals system's production of meaning, as the system, like any legal institution, refers to the concept of precedents – i.e. certain cases can reasonably be regarded as identical, and so are considered to be covered by the same legal precedents.

However, uniformity before the law is challenged by a fourth institutional consideration – the holistic evaluation of social work. This consideration is a result of the fact that the social appeals system also has to consider the way in which a decision will impact on the specific person's overall situation. This holistic evaluation is secured, inter alia, through the involvement of lay judges. However, in practice they play a minimal role, and it has never been clear how much weight should be attributed to such holistic evaluations.

Furthermore, Jakobsen points out that uniformity before the law does not sit perfectly with a social-work evaluation of what is best for the individual concerned (Jakobsen 2004: 320). This presents an institutional dilemma between conflicting, possibly incompatible, institutional requirements for organisational practice. The empirical analysis demonstrates how the actors in the appeals system struggle to accommodate and balance the different considerations. However, this can be viewed as a legitimising activity, one that has little to do with the individual citizen's needs and situation.

These findings illustrate a key neo-institutional point – that highly institutionalised welfare organisations often expend so much energy legitimising their work and existence that their focus on individuals is minimised or completely subsumed. In neo-institutional terms, it might be said that legal rights are the central rationality myth that confers legitimacy upon all of the organisations in the appeals system. This rationality myth is underpinned by the adoption of the principle of legal rights that characterises the ordinary courts. The myth of the appeals system as a legal rights institution can be maintained through decoupling formal structural elements from actual practice. The formal concepts and principles of social legal rights do not provide an adequate representation of social practice, which, in the appeal bodies studied, appeared to be guided by conflicting legitimisation considerations. Legal rights therefore become a highly effective rationality myth.

Overall, this study shows how key institutional norms in the welfare state are established and subverted in the practices of the social appeals system. The conflict is, in fact, not with the citizen (who in many cases has been encouraged to appeal) – rather, it is about reaching consensus within the social appeals system itself. Jakobsen writes: "When the actors in the social appeals system process the actual case and make decisions about a wide range of human fates, this work is not about the individual citizen concerned, but about generating institutional legitimacy" (Jakobsen 2004: 47). Jakobsen considers the assurances in recent years in the Danish context of a closer focus on legal rights as the activation of a rationality myth designed to assure us all that the welfare state is based on clear legal guarantees. However, insofar as we are able, at the same time, to discern an increased emphasis on several of the conflicting considerations, including the recently-increased focus on administrative efficiency, the difficulties involved in balancing considerations and retaining legitimacy will most likely be exacerbated in the future.

Conclusion

Neo-institutional organisation theory is an effective tool for questioning axiomatic or "hyped-up" models, structures and technologies in the welfare sector. As a perspective, it does not generate abstract criticism, but relies on a very tangible, empirical basis for problematisation and criticism. The theory's strength lies not least in its many concrete means of conducting organisational analyses. Neo-institutional organisation theory provides an approach that sees welfare organisations as extremely open to their environments and dependent upon sharing resources with them. This makes it possible to study how certain organisational elements manage to diffuse across specific areas of welfare production, and how the desire to maintain organisational legitimacy drives this process.

A key aspect of neo-institutional organisation theory, in relation to welfare organisations, is that it highlights the crucial importance of legitimacy for the organisations' work and survival. It affords us an opportunity to look at welfare agencies as a type of organisation whose existence depends fundamentally on institutional legitimacy, and not merely on the efficiency of their actual services. Typically, for organisations that supply products that are difficult to quantify, such as treatment, detoxification, rehabilitation or punishment, it is crucial to ensure that the organisation lives up to institutionally-entrenched norms for good organisation, structure and technology. The neo-institutional perspective makes it possible to discuss the extent to which an organisation, or a particular type of organisation, is subject to institutional pressure. The perspective also makes it possible to conduct detailed studies of the specific types of environmental pressure to which an organisation is subject, and which likely create isomorphism – whether through coercive, mimetic or normative isomorphic pressure.

Neo-institutional organisation theory also makes it possible to study whether different types of decoupling exist in welfare organisations – i.e. whether departments are loosely coupled to each other, since some are maintained by legitimacy considerations, while others provide an actual product or service. Although the theory does not directly focus on the citizen's encounters with the welfare state, the processes and mechanisms it describes have a decisive influence on this encounter. Particularly pertinent is the assumption that institutionalised welfare organisations are only able to observe the citizen through a filter of the ideas, classifications and treatment programmes that the organisation has installed. The neo-institutional perspective sets the stage for studying how such filters determine how the individual citizen – or aspects of the individual concerned – can be made visible in the welfare organisations. This attention is crucial in that these culturally-produced filters achieve a status as objective to the actors concerned.

Finally, the neo-institutional approach encourages studying the complexity that arises by virtue of the presence of multiple institutional norms. Welfare agencies are a type of organisation that is particularly subject to strong and conflicting institutional norms – as we saw above, the activities of reformatories and social appeals bodies are indeed subject to irreconcilable requirements. The ability to carefully demonstrate how welfare organisations in practice "solve" or balance such institutional paradoxes (for example, punishing and providing care at the same time) is a quality that makes neo-institutional organisational analyses potentially very relevant.

7 Risk theory: Normality, deviation and neo-liberalism

Risk theory: Ulrich Beck's *Risk Society: Towards a New Modernity* (1992) analyses Western society, focusing on the many risks posed by globalisation, including technological development. Beck centres in particular on the environment, and shows how local actions in one part of the world have global (negative) consequences in other parts. Mary Douglas' *Risk and Blame: Essays in Cultural Theory* (1994) focuses, to a greater extent than Beck, on the cultural and symbolic origins of thinking about risk. In *Risk and Blame*, the reader is presented with concepts that aim to provide tools with which to analyse the relationships between culture (values), individuals (type) and institutions in a risk perspective. Aaron Doyle and Richard Ericson's anthology *Risk and Morality* (2003) and Lupton's anthology *Risk and Socio-cultural Theory: New Directions and Perspectives* (1999) contain a series of contributions that explicitly link risk with neo-liberalism. The two anthologies concentrate on risk as a significant governance technology in the present day. Good, short introductions to theories of risk are Lupton's (2005) *Risk (Key Ideas)* and Arnoldi's (2009) recent book *Risk (Key Concepts)*.

KEY CONCEPTS: risk, morality, politics, neo-liberal governance, normality/deviance.

This chapter differs from most of the others in this book, as literature on risk does not constitute a coherent theoretical literature. In our short introduction above we present four key works that exemplify the three branches of sociological research of risk. These are: 1) theory that provides a general description of society as a risk society (Beck); 2) theory that focuses on culture and symbols in risk analysis (Douglas); and 3) theory that emphasises the governmentality-based approach to the analysis of risk (Doyle & Ericson, Lupton). Obviously, this distinction is an analytical one – in the actual risk literature, no sharp distinction is made between the three branches.[1] This chapter is organised around the common questions raised by all three on the subject of the citizen's encounter with the state.[2] We therefore draw on discussions in risk literature that relate to the constitution of the citizen as a risk object. In this context, we have chosen to pay particular attention to

Douglas' cultural theory (Douglas 1994, Douglas & Wildavsky 1997) and the governmentality-inspired analyses of risk and morals (e.g. Lupton 1999: 59–85, Dean 1999a). These two approaches – despite their differences – complement each other in their analysis of how Western/neo-liberal societies present risk in a particular way and, as such, place certain conditions on the encounter between citizen and state. First, however, we will provide more detailed descriptions of the three branches of sociological risk literature.

Since the 1980s, a number of prominent sociologists have analysed Western societies, focusing on the links between globalisation, risk and modernity (e.g. Beck 1992, Giddens 2002, Bauman 2000). This literature typically relates to Beck's ground-breaking book *The Risk Society*, published (in English) for the first time in 1992, which generated considerable interest in analysing Western society as a risk society.[3] The literature focuses on how globalisation is not just an economic phenomenon, but also a political, technological and cultural phenomenon (Giddens 2002: 10). The literature on globalisation argues that we increasingly feel as if we are living in a single world and that this condition creates a new situation for the individual's life and self-perception. Globalisation is not just about what we want or hope to accomplish, it is also about what happens to us all (Bauman 2000). The globalisation concept paves the way for an understanding of social relationships that extend beyond the nation state, and risk calculations are assumed to play a crucial role in this context (e.g. Beck 1992).

The thesis is that modern science and technology have created a risk society, both globally and locally (environmental disasters and epidemics like AIDS know no borders, new technology leads to mass redundancies etc.). Past "industrial" and "class" societies, which focused on manufacturing and distribution, have been replaced by a risk society that focuses on security. As a result of this, the welfare state becomes a "risk-management system", which "is designed to protect against hazards that were once treated as at the disposition of gods – sickness, disablement, job loss and old age" (Giddens 2002: 24). In general, this literature provides an analysis of society, through the concepts of globalisation, risk and modernity, which aims to capture the changing conditions under which modern (and postmodern) people live.

This literature is largely concerned with describing the processes that Western societies undergo – and, in the case of Beck's work, with an understanding of risk that is at times almost realistic. In this chapter, however, we draw on an understanding of risk that is in line with Douglas' (1994, Douglas & Widavsky 1997: 6) work – with the dual concepts of risk and culture – as well as on governmentality-inspired risk literature, which emphasises that risks should be seen as social constructions: "Nothing is a risk in itself; there is no risk in reality. But on the other hand, anything *can* be a risk; it all depends on how one analyses the danger, considers the event", as Ewald writes (Ewald 1991: 199 – italics in original). In this context, we examine how neo-liberal values interact with the formation of specific risk groups and help to define certain groups in society, such as people in need of treatment. In other words, we are interested in how power relates to the definition process in relation to deciding what are considered – for example – risky (deviant) actions.

In the first chapter of *Risk and Blame* (1994), Douglas explains that her work on risk and culture in Western society was inspired by her colleague Aaron Wildavsky's sarcastic assertions that anthropological work on classification systems was only suitable for commenting on history, not the present (see Douglas' *Purity and Danger* (1988), first published in 1966). According to Douglas (1994: 10), "he touched the sore point: is pollution behaviour really different in tribal society? Are we [Westerners] above all that sort of thing?" This criticism led to her developing a more abstract statement of "purity" and "danger" in the organisational structure of any society (Douglas 1994: 10). The particularly unique aspect of Douglas' work on risk is therefore her starting point: she develops a theory of organisation in Western societies through knowledge of tribal communities' (different) forms of social organisation, which results in a theory of how classification systems relate to different cultural forms of organisation.

This approach brings into focus conditions that previously have been considered so obvious and natural that they have escaped the critical gaze of research. Inspired by her work on how "the other", "danger" and "pollution" are linked in non-Western cultures, Douglas shows that we have a similar concept in the West for everything that is dangerous – the risk concept – which, just as in tribal societies, is inextricably linked with political and moral processes. She focuses explicitly on the cultural and symbolic ideas of risk, proposing the concept of risk culture rather than risk society (see Beck 1992), in order to make explicit the fact that risk is unequivocally a social phenomenon. She uses the concept to point out that risk is not a neutral, context-independent concept, but a way of thinking (see Fleck's (1979) concept of "thought style") that is created and influenced by different cultural communities. She also argues that danger should replace risk in political debate, as risk in this context is always equated with (future) unwanted and dangerous situations. These dangerous situations are shaped by a dominant way of thinking in the cultural communities, which is (or should be) the object of the researcher's interest (Douglas 1994: 46).

We have, as previously mentioned, chosen to complement Douglas' work with a governmentality-inspired analysis, since this branch of risk research, even more explicitly than Douglas and Beck, links risk with the characteristics of a neo-liberal or advanced liberal political current present in Western societies. The governmentality-inspired risk literature has an explicit focus on how risk perceptions are used as governing technologies in contemporary neo-liberal Western society.

Asserting that contemporary Western society can be described as risk-controlled, as Beck, Douglas and the governmentality researchers do, represents a desire to highlight the fact that many social processes are guided by risk perceptions, and that these processes are fundamental to our self-perception.

Another key theme addressed in all three currents in sociology is that what appears as risky today will not necessarily be so in another time or place. For example, fears of an obesity epidemic in Western society can be considered a risk. We know that some overweight people develop illnesses due to their weight, so all overweight people are therefore assumed to be at potential risk of contracting the same illnesses. The process we are describing here is based on risk perceptions – i.e. incomplete knowledge. The point is that this type of incomplete knowledge process is fundamental to our society. The peculiar characteristic of a risk perception is that it is a type of knowledge that is different from more common perceptions of knowledge in that it is not only by definition incomplete, but it is morally rooted and also (usually) involves an idea of danger (Beck 1992, Douglas 1994).

The very fact that risk perceptions are based on incomplete knowledge raises a key question about how to act in relation to incomplete knowledge. The literature on risk identifies morals and politics as two concepts that are absolutely key to understanding and analysing the individual's actions, specifically with regard to knowledge of risk (Beck 1992, Douglas 1994, Doyle & Ericson 2003). The fact is that risk perceptions must necessarily be rooted in moral and political considerations, as the drawing up of possible scenarios – e.g. an obesity epidemic – demands that we take up a moral position on which scenarios we choose to define (and act upon). In other words, we live in a moralised and politicised world that generates specific narratives about how people define and explain accidents (Douglas 1994: 5). "Risk analysis that tries to exclude moral ideas and politics from its calculations is putting professional integrity before sense [...] The political question is always about acceptable risk", as Douglas (1994: 44) states.

Risks: objective and neutral or an expression of morals and politics?

Of course, anthropological studies of tribal societies' rituals and classification systems, like the one Douglas conducted in *Purity and Danger*, improve understanding of the organisation and cohesiveness of the society in question. However, knowledge of how tribal societies organise themselves – for example, focusing on what is considered to be sinful and taboo in the particular society – also constitutes a tool that enables us to look critically at the way Western societies are organised. The concepts of "sinful" and "taboo" in the West, according to Douglas, have been replaced by the neutral term "risk". Her point is that even though sin, taboo and risk do not, of course, represent quite the same processes, all of these concepts are related to a hypothetical, dangerous situation (Douglas 1994: 26–8). Apart from the fact that sin and taboo relate to a backward-oriented process, and derive importance from religious discourse, while risk relates to future dangers and is linked to a scientific discourse (albeit shrouded in politics and morals), sin and taboo are also linked to protection of the community, whereas risk is formulated as protection of the individual (Douglas 1994: 28). As a result, Western societies' focus on risk says something significant about their dominant values, e.g. prioritisation of the individual, science and the desire to control the future. Precisely because the focus on risk is relatively new in the West, our era is characterised by a major preoccupation with providing information about significant cultural changes in society. The perils of the past – which scientific discourse now presents as "risks" – can therefore indicate more fundamental changes in society made visible by the emphasis on concepts of individuality and personal responsibility.

But what, then, determines whether something is proclaimed risky (and therefore problematic)? According to Douglas (1994: 140ff), the starting point has to be that a particular culture – whether hierarchical, individualist or sectarian – produces its own understanding of what is dangerous and should therefore be assigned to the category of risk: "The choice of risk to worry about depends on the social forms selected. The choice of risk and the choice of how to live are taken together. Each form of social life has its own typical risk portfolio. Common values lead to common fears" (Douglas & Wildavsky 1997: 8). The purpose of a cultural approach like the one espoused by Douglas is to explain how different types of collective actions, or culture, relate to different logical bases and the role that risk plays in this context (Douglas 1994: 136f). Since cultural stability is short-lived and often not visible to those that are part of the culture (ibid.: 25), we are in constant danger of developing a "cultural blindness" that prevents us from looking critically at the organisational principles and collective norms and actions that define the underlying aspects of cultures and hence also define certain actions as risk actions (ibid.: 64f).

According to Douglas, this means that we need an approach where we can put the isolated risk into a context of a larger system: "Instead of isolating the risk as a technical problem, we should formulate it so as to include, however crudely, its moral and political implications" (Douglas 1994: 51). In Western society, dominated as it is by an individualistic culture, this type of study begins and ends by looking at, inter alia, "the good of individuals" (Douglas 1994: 53). The ideal citizen in a market society is an individual who is a "rational agent [...] sovereign in control of his own choices, decisive and consistent enough to give clear signals to partners" (Douglas 1994: 142). Via the concept of "the constrained dialogue" (Douglas 1994: 135) and Fleck's (1979) concept of "thought style", Douglas (1986, 1994) develops a theory of how culture – which in Western society places the individual at the centre (for example, through exchange- and market mechanisms) – restricts dialogue in public space, thus resulting in certain types of thinking. The idea of the unitary self in the West, according to Douglas (1994: 217), concords very well with both the legal and economic institutions within Western civilisation that require individuals to take personal responsibility for their actions. There is, of course, also the idea of the multiple self, which, despite its prevalence in many other cultures, is totally unacceptable in the West exactly because responsibility must not be diffused (ibid.).

As she highlights, the legal system, which is a fundamental institution in Western society, dictates that individuals can be held accountable for their actions, and responsibility is therefore something absolute – for instance, it is not possible to be granted an exemption from liability by claiming that you were possessed by evil spirits or demons etc. The idea that the self is an autonomous and unique entity reflects the West's juridical and economic institutions and becomes a distinctive "thought style" (Douglas 1994: 217). However, according to Douglas, parallel with this "forensic model" of the self, there is also a therapeutic model in Western countries, which treats people whose self-perception differs from the one presented (Douglas 1994: 229). This therapeutic model captures people who are seen as irresponsible in some manner, so that society is obliged to prescribe treatment for them. To remain passive in response to a problematic situation (e.g. if the individual does not think that their problem is self-inflicted) clashes with the prevailing belief in the West that we should take responsibility for our actions and actively relate to them. An individual's passivity makes them suitable for a therapeutic approach that seeks to install responsibility and commitment. The point here is that a society is home to both types (as well as many more, of course) of institutions that relate to associated cultures and dominant "thought styles" (e.g. legal/economic and therapeutic), and which operate with different basic conceptions of the self. This is only possible because the two types of institutions are sharply differentiated, and because one of them (legal) defines the person as an "independent agent", which in turn creates the need for the other institution (therapeutic) and its "passive patient/victim" (Douglas 1994: 230).

Risk identities and exclusion mechanisms

Interest in exclusion mechanisms is central to a great deal of risk literature, although the analytical approach, as mentioned previously, does vary. Bauman (2000, 2004) also analyses and describes classification processes in Western societies, among other things, modernity's "wasted lives" – the "outcasts" and "vagabonds" of our time. In this contemporary analysis, the vagabond is in motion, like a tourist travelling around the world, but their limited resources make them a failed consumer at the bottom of society. Bauman's point is that, in a modern consumer society, only a fine line separates the normal (tourist) from the outcast (vagabond), and it is this "abominable likeness which makes it so hard to decide at which point the portrait becomes a caricature and the proper and healthy specimen of the species turns into a mutant and a monster" (Bauman 2000: 96). In this sense, that which makes tourists "shudder" and "tremble" (ibid.: 97) is not the perception of what the vagabond is, but of what the tourist might become, as Bauman so aptly states, 'It is in other words what separates the normal from the deviant that are in focus'. If we take the growing deviant and high degree risk profile group of overweight people in Western society as an example, the problem identity for the general public might not only be related to their large size, but might also be caused by the fact that, when confronted with the sight of them, thinner people are constantly reminded of what they could develop into – a thought process excacerbated by the range of possible lifestyle diseases that are constantly discussed in the media and in political discourse. In relation to the cases in this chapter, the social morality that excludes individuals at risk is strengthened because of the continuous focus on potential ailments and future illnesses – for example, overweight individuals are thought to face more problems than just the ones related to weight, and pregnant women, through various medical tests, are also transformed into patients in the medical system. This in turn, confirms the belief held by the majority that their own way of life is desirable and complete.

In both cultural theory of risk and governmentality-inspired analyses, deviation is closely linked to the dominant medical discourse in Western society (e.g. Lupton 1999: 59–85). In Douglas' analyses, the exclusion mechanisms whereby some groups in society become "peripheralized", are related to culturally based perceptions of health and hygiene, which are assumed to be established, on a very basic level, in the citizens' "consciousness" (Douglas 1994: 108–10). As our aim is to analyse exclusion mechanisms, with a particular focus on how prevailing neo-liberal values in Western society relate to the establishment of risk groups, we will now turn our attention to governmentality-inspired risk literature.

Novas and Rose (2000) point out that risk discourse leads to the emergence of a new type of person: "the somatic individual". This individual is primarily constructed on the basis of the body, which is currently understood as the setting for a potentially unlimited number of risks (in this case, it is the genetically risky individual that is in focus) (Novas & Rose 2000: 487). Despite a clean bill of health, the body is understood as potentially ill, so is always in need of care. As a result, individuals who are perceived to be at risk of falling ill are the modern-day deviants. Rose (2001: 18) argues that selfhood in the 21st century has become "intrinsically somatic", which makes the body the primary focus of work on the self. Rose also links personhood in contemporary Western culture with the current devotion to producing risk profiles and identifying our future possibilities: "Individuals seem to have acquired a kind of biological citizenship [...] We have become the kinds of people who think of our present and our future in terms of the quality of our individual biological lives and those with whom we identify" (Rose 2001: 21–2). The individual is identified on the basis of a risk profile – the range of factors to which the body can be said to be exposed. However, Rose (2003: 3) points out that the increased attention paid to the body and its condition does not represent a resurrection of essentialist and reductionist thinking, as there is still room for autonomy, choice, individuality and responsibility (see also Novas & Rose 2000).

Even though Douglas argues that a favoured paradigm in Western countries is the "paradigm of individual rational choice" (Douglas 1994: 11), she – like Goffman – operates with a non-universal concept of rationality. The individual's actions must always be interpreted in the context of the political and moral conditions from which the actions arise and are reproduced. In a neo-liberal discourse, a lack of effort to minimise risk is seen as irrational or incompetent behaviour. The point is that risk can be equated with that which is dangerous in a culture – actions that invite danger are by definition problematic and pose a threat, which in turn necessitates governance by a range of state institutions (Garland 2003). Risk is absolutely something to be avoided: "To be designated 'at high risk' compared with others is to be singled out as requiring expert advice, surveillance and self-regulation" (Lupton 1999: 61).

Within this governmentality-inspired risk approach, it is argued that a greater knowledge of diseases etc., does not serve to liberate the individual, but in fact has a controlling effect on his/her potential due to the many concerns to which risk perceptions invariably give rise (Rose 2001). Since today's "normal" citizen is a person who is potentially ill, the distinction between normalisation and treatment becomes more and more blurred, resulting in the expansion of what it takes to be defined as deviant. It is precisely the relation between the normal and the deviant that we, from a risk perspective, find particularly relevant in the analysis of the citizen's encounter with the welfare state. However, before we look at some real-life examples of the relationship between risk and deviation, we will look more closely at the state and power concept that pervades risk literature, and in particular, governmentality-inspired risk sociology.

State, power and risk

As we wrote by way of introduction, society has always been preoccupied with risk perceptions (Rose 2001), irrespective of whether these have been defined using concepts such as taboo or risk. For example, it can be argued that the welfare state's justification is all about risk, since the primary task of this type of state has been to redistribute, via a public-sector insurance system, the risks associated with problematic situations that may arise in any citizen's life. The purpose of the welfare state was to collectivise risks and problems so that they became the responsibility of society rather than of the individual citizen in need. Governmentality-inspired researchers point out, however, that the current way in which society is organised – with a number of private initiatives that aim to alleviate pressure on the public sector – suggests that the collective welfare philosophy is gradually being replaced by another, more individual-focused governing technology that gives the individual far more responsibility for his or her situation than previously. Using Douglas' concepts, it can be argued that there has been a shift in the predominant "thought styles" that we can actually localise – e.g. in political debates about the welfare state's areas of responsibility.

Like Douglas, governmentality-inspired researchers wish to show that a prevailing ideology (or culture) of individuality, responsibility and rationality etc. is rooted in the individual's self-perception. The neo-liberal state emphasises individual responsibility, willpower and activity (see Rose 1996b, Dean 1999b). The neo-liberal state differentiates itself from, say, the 1970s welfare state by focusing on what individuals can do to improve their situation (e.g. in relation to health and work), rather than on redistributing risk by means of a public insurance system that places less of an emphasis on the individual citizen's personal responsibility for a problematic life situation. According to Ericson, Barry and Doyle (2000: 533), neo-liberalism is based on the following three principles: risk, governance and responsibility – and is a model of society that goes beyond the traditional domain of the welfare state. In this context, the neo-liberal form of government is a state that also uses "indirect techniques for leading and controlling individuals without at the same time being responsible for them" (Lemke 2001: 201). Although it might be argued that neo-liberal society has reduced the level of intervention by the welfare state, this is only the case if you focus on direct state intervention. If, on the other hand, you look at the actors through which the state governs (see also the discussions about governing "at a distance" in Rose & Miller 1992: 181) – for example, private insurance companies, private schools, private hospitals etc., all of which are subjected to central legislation – it can be argued that the state in a neo-liberal society still governs its citizens, but it does so by using more indirect techniques than previously.

Ericson, Barry and Doyle (2000) identify private insurance companies as the institutions that have most directly taken over areas that have traditionally been key responsibilities of the welfare state. Private insurance companies function by assigning citizens to selective risk categories. In other words, this type of institution develops administrative and policy-supporting technologies in order to manage today's risk groups. In doing so, insurance companies categorise the population just as welfare offices did before them. Both types of institutions are governing "at a distance", in which monitoring and power are embedded in risk profiles and categories etc. (Rose & Miller 1992: 181, Ericson et al. 2000: 550). Similar procedures are found in private schools for example, where parents attend "admission interviews" at which the school assesses the student's aptitude (or "risk profile", in risk sociology's parlance) in relation to the category of "difficult pupils". All of the privatisation processes that Western societies are currently implementing are taking place at the same time as the neo-liberal state is trying to divest itself of some of its obligations by treating its citizens as "an active partner in the drive for health, accepting their responsibility for securing their own well-being", as Rose (2001: 6), among others, puts it.

The state administration and welfare institutions that develop strategies – to promote health, for instance – can therefore be seen as actors who offer advice and treatment or implement prevention measures on behalf of the active, free citizen so that he or she is able to make choices that reduce the risk(s) he or she faces (Lupton 2005: 100). These processes occur both in traditional welfare institutions and in the private sector, which is increasingly encroaching on the welfare sphere. If, for example, we look at the many technologies that are currently being developed in both the public and private sectors in the West to address the weight issue, it could be argued – based on a risk-oriented perspective with a focus on dominant "thought styles", and the translation of these into various control and management mechanisms – that overweight people have been particularly visible in recent years. This is because this group represents a challenge on neo-liberal values, such as the ability to exercise self-restraint, willpower, responsibility and self-control. As a result, overweight people are referred to therapeutic institutions for treatment, where they are either normalised (lose weight) or conditioned to accept the role of victim (see Mik-Meyer (2010a) and Douglas (1994) and her thesis on the special place of "the victim" in Western society). Morally embedded criteria for the ideal citizen (e.g. self-restraint, self-control and willpower etc.) are formulated in neo-liberal discourse such as in health policy and the media etc. where the overweight are told to lose weight, or at least consider their weight to be a problem. This is a dual process, which, through the construction of a "normal" identity, positions the overweight person as being in a risky situation, which in turn confirms that he/she is abnormal. It becomes impossible to distinguish the concept of risk from the concept of normalisation, as risk identities are developed and confirmed in relation to prevailing perceptions of the normal (and ideal) citizen. As Lupton (1999: 4) notes, normalisation is a fundamental aspect of liberal governance, in which a biomedically defined health status has assumed central importance.

Greco (2004) has also focused on the body in contemporary society and on how, for example, obesity can be seen as a part of what she calls "the politics of indeterminacy" – in other words, the impure and dangerous, who fall between the categories (Douglas 1988). By using the concept of indeterminacy, she wishes also to stress that health is interwoven with societal values and is, by definition, an area regulated by social and moral values (Greco 2004: 4–9). Health policy is often discussed as if health has a determinate value "that can be identified with a set of objective evidences" (Greco 2004: 6), which is typically based on extensive calculations of probability. The constructivist perspective – or a perspective that explicitly links perceptions of risk identities with morality and politics – allows us to reject the notion of such "evidence". As Foucault's studies have also shown, the body can be seen as a site for power struggles, which explains why certain bodies at certain times in history are defined as "normal", others as "abnormal" (Blaikie et al. 2004). And if health can be considered a "meta-value" in today's society, as Greco (2004: 1) argues, there is – and will remain – a significant need for critical research that examines the relationship between (unhealthy) risk identities and the prevailing societal politics and morality.

Some researchers have studied how risk perceptions affect the strengthening of unequal power structures created by growth of experts in today's society. For example, Beck (1992) argues that knowledge of risk is produced and quantified by experts, which means that, in a risk-focused society, every citizen becomes increasingly dependent on expert knowledge. Tulloch and Lupton (2005) consider the implications of experts' risk perceptions for lay people's everyday life. The public do not see risk in the same way as the experts (Douglas 1994: 11). Even if risk perceptions are perceived and interpreted differently in different cultures/segments of society, as indicated by risk theory, not everybody's risk perceptions are elevated to the status of "objective" truths that are "natural" and so necessitate action. Rather, it is the experts' risk perceptions that form the basis for political initiatives and subsequently affect the lay person's life (if he/she is trapped in a risk group). "Being categorised as 'at risk' from a medical problem means that one is placed in a liminal category of wellness: neither actually ill (yet) nor fully well", as Lupton (2006: 17) writes. In line with Rose and Novas, her point is that people in risk groups will constantly seek to clarify their precarious situation through diagnostic testing etc. As a result, the risk society has, by making space for a potential sick person, created a dependency – in this case, on experts in the health system – even though the individuals concerned do not yet have a disease; all they have is a higher risk profile for developing a disease.

Risk literature works with an understanding of power that seeks to expose the processes in society that produce responsible citizens. These processes have in common the fact that they appear to be so natural and obvious that even those whom they categorise as deviants will help to reproduce the "natural" categories that have created their deviant identities. This is a Foucauldian concept of power, focusing on its productive nature – and as we wrote earlier, power relates to risk, as the definition of risk factors depends precisely on, and reflects a prevalent norm in, the society/culture being analysed. The relationship between normality and deviance is thus a highly relevant area for researchers or students inspired by risk literature's perspectives to focus on. If we agree with the risk sociologists that the norm nowadays is largely defined by the language and techniques of risk discourse, it is precisely this context that will determine who is normal and, therefore, who is marginalised as deviant. Novas and Rose show that the risk discourse is highly dominant in contemporary Western society, and that the modern human being is somatic as a result of the endless examinations to which individuals are exposed, and which may, at any time, place any individual in a risk group. The normal citizen who is not (yet) linked to a risk group must therefore primarily reflect an ideal state, since nobody's body – in theory – is able to exempt itself from the wide range of risks increasingly identified by the medical gaze (see Rose & Novas 2005, Rose 2003, 2004).

Case 1: Risk and weight

As previously mentioned, risk sociologists (and many other sociologists) stress the individualisation process that modern Western society has been undergoing. The focus on individual choice and responsibility makes it clear that we are operating in a discourse in which the assumption is that the individual is capable of deciding his or her own fate through free choice. This discourse is particularly dominant when we look at the weight issue. Our first case is taken from Mik-Meyer's analyses of the overweight issue viewed from a risk perspective (e.g. Mik-Meyer 2009, 2010a). In her research, we see that many of the interviews with clients and professionals alike revolve around the ability of the former to act responsibly, exercise self-control and change what is perceived as their problematic risk situation. Below, we present an excerpt from an interview with an overweight woman, Lisa, who talks about the prejudices to which her risk identity gave rise:

LISA: My doctor has kind of the attitude that if it's self-inflicted, he doesn't pay so much attention to it. So, his only comment is, well, you gotta just lose weight [...]

INTERVIEWER: How do you think other people look at individuals who're overweight?

LISA: I think people think they're lazy and can't be bothered, cos you so often hear: 'Why don't you just do something about it?', But it isn't like it's that easy, they make it sound as if you just do this and that and voilà! It's just cos you're lazy and can't be bothered.

INTERVIEWER: So overweight people are lazy and can't be bothered. What other prejudices get an airing?

LISA: Like you just lie at home on the couch and eat all the time, that you can't get a grip, that you've no self-control. And I think that's a major problem for overweight people, cos you just need some self-control, just get a grip of yourself. I think that's a major problem.

There's no doubt for many – such as the doctor referred to in the quote above – that lifestyle risks are linked with problematic individual choices and the individual's lacking an ability to act responsibly. Lifestyle risks become something that the individual should address, as the woman's responses show. Similar descriptions of the many problems associated with the increased knowledge of an overweight person's own risk profile often emerge when they embark on weight-loss programmes that involve measuring BMI and body-fat levels. On these state-initiated programmes, they are presented with a chart displaying their risk profile. The higher the BMI and body-fat level, the higher the risk. Mik-Meyer's data show that overweight people are often shocked by the new information presented to them, which provides a clear picture of the potential illnesses they face. Since few people actually manage to lose weight during their time on the programme, the risk profile is, in some cases, an additional stress factor to which they have to relate. For this group, greater knowledge about possible illness is counter-productive because it makes them more anxious and nervous than before they were presented with their risk profile. Other overweight individuals feel somewhat alienated from the risk profile, as the interview with Susan (age 27) below illustrates:

SUSAN: I'm, like, fat and I know that people – not wanting to hurt my feelings – say 'Gee you're just big or you're just a bit overweight'. But you're fat when you weigh 60 kilograms too much. You really are fat.

INTERVIEWER: So you're fat – is that an alternative definition I don't know about … ?

SUSAN: No, but there's like a table. If you have a BMI over 30/35, you're fat and so on.

INTERVIEWER: What does 'risk class three' mean?

SUSAN: It means you're even more prone to side effects.

INTERVIEWER: Which are what exactly?

SUSAN: Well like heart problems, diabetes and all that.

INTERVIEWER: Is that something that worries you?

SUSAN: Not really, but it probably should. Sometimes I'm afraid of dying, cos my heart's too big due to my size. It, like, has to work harder, so it's also become larger, like other muscles. So sometimes, when I get a tightness in my chest, I get a bit worried, because I'm only 27. Otherwise, not so much in everyday life.

Analysing interviews with individuals who have an increased risk of developing diseases – such as overweight people – reveals that they draw on a variety of rationales, or "thought styles" (cf. Douglas 1986, 1994) to describe their personal situations. These "thought styles" can be far removed from a medical way of thinking, which basically assumes that the majority of people want to make choices that will improve the chances of a long and healthy life. Susan is concerned, she is sometimes afraid of dying and she has considerable knowledge of the risk of falling ill (as also demonstrated by other excerpts that are not included here), but she still does nothing active to lose weight and says that in everyday life she is not particularly worried. This is exactly the plurality that emerges when a culturally based risk perspective is applied to risk and health (see the next case, below). It is clear that some cultures – or dominant discourses, as they are also referred to – are more prevalent than others. For example, in terms of risk, weight problems are primarily addressed in a biomedical universe, which in this particular instance is part of a neo-liberal society that emphasises the individual's ability to make choices and act responsibly etc. However, Mik-Meyer's interviews with overweight people show that risk perceptions are produced in various competing cultures that have different rationales for handling different risk scenarios. The starting point for a risk analysis will therefore always be a study of the values – or the "package" of cultural values (Douglas 1994: 168) – dominant within a given discourse, culture or setting. In this context, Douglas advocates concentrating on how different institutional forms relate to different societal values, which result in certain "thought styles" (Douglas 1986).

Case 2: Risk and pregnancy

Our second case is from Deborah Lupton's analysis of first-time mothers in Australia (Lupton 1999: 59). Her study of pregnancy is greatly inspired by governmentality and risk, as revealed by the following quote, in which she defines her theoretical framework:

> "The centrality of risk discourse in relation to pregnancy can be linked to apparatuses of 'biopolitics' in relation to neo-liberal societies, efforts on the part of the state and other agencies to discipline and normalise citizens, to render them docile and productive bodies. One of these apparatuses, that of normalization, involves gathering information about populations and subpopulations and subjecting it to statistical analysis. Through normalisation, individuals may be compared to others, their attributes assessed according to whether they fall within the norm or outside it. If found to fall outside the norm, people are routinely encouraged (or sometimes coerced) to engage in practices that bring them closer to the norm. Risk is a pivotal discourse in strategies of normalisation, used to gloss over the potential for deviations from the norm" (Lupton 1999: 61).

Lupton analyses how pregnant women tackle the many risks currently linked to pregnancy and shows how the pregnant body "is constructed and experienced through the discourses, knowledges and strategies of risk" (Lupton 1999: 61). She highlights the scientific basis for defining risk in pregnancy, including clinical and epidemiological risk elements. Both types of risk attribute a central role to experts in relation to the expectant parents' assessment of the viability of the foetus. Both types of risk transform pregnancy into a "calculated and governable" practice (Lupton 1999: 63).

The pregnant body is exposed to a variety of medical tests designed to quantify – and control – the increased risk of disease in the foetus. The risks are then recorded on "a card, which the pregnant woman takes with her to each visit. This card becomes the repository of the woman's risk factors, designating her as being 'high' or 'low risk'", as Lupton (1999: 65) writes. This practice emphasises the need for the pregnant woman constantly to seek – and receive advice from – experts who are able to guide her in relation to a responsible way of life (Lupton 1999: 66). More wide-ranging research also reveals no lack of good advice in popular literature about how to minimise the risk of disease in the foetus during pregnancy. Handbooks advise on how proper food intake, proper emotional involvement during pregnancy, controlled stress levels and proper handling of hazards (e.g. bacteria) reduce the enhanced risk that the pregnant woman is automatically assumed to face (Lupton 1999: 64–5). The pregnant woman is very much aware of both expert and lay understandings of risk behaviour and pregnancy – and, as in the previous case, she is not considered to be a passive object in the relationship: "These women are reflexive, actively seeking out knowledge about risk and acting upon it. They do so voluntarily, as autonomous, self-regulating citizens attempting to achieve peace of mind about the viability of their pregnancy" (Lupton 1999: 76).

The major focus on risk during pregnancy means that a pregnant woman has to make a series of choices in order to achieve the best conditions for giving birth to a healthy, normal child. A key problem in the literature Lupton discusses (and which, like Lupton, problematises the "medicalisation" of the pregnant body) is that, in cases where the woman refuses to undergo extensive examinations and receive advice, she is made responsible for the possibility that she will bring an unhealthy and abnormal child into the world. One woman explains:

> "I was hoping that I'd never have to make this choice, to become responsible for choosing the kind of baby I'd get, the kind of baby we'd accepted [...] And they all told me I'd feel more in control. But in some ways, I feel less in control. Oh, it's still my baby, but only if it's good enough to be our baby, if you see what I mean" (Quoted in Rapp, in Lupton 1999: 69).

Drawing on another quote from Beck-Gernsheim (1996: 140), Lupton writes that, in our age of risk, life is "in many respects more open and malleable. But it also means that new demands, controls and obligations are placed upon the individual [...] Because people are now viewed as having more responsibility for life outcomes, negative events come to be seen as their fault" (Lupton 1999: 67). The technological developments that continuously produce new options for examinations mean that the individual has to make more choices. As in the case example cited above, this can lead to citizens feeling that they have lost control of their situation. And it is exactly the choices that risk discourse produces for the individual, that cause the problems. For example, these two women talk about the choice of abortion in relation to the various tests that had shown signs of Down's syndrome in their foetuses:

"WOMAN 1: It was the hardest thing I've ever done [...] I kept trying to make excuses, I didn't want to go through with it. But even though I knew I had to do it, it was still harder in the actual doing than I had expected [...] Let's not gloss over it. I killed my baby.

WOMAN 2: Whatever the decision, we would feel some guilt [...] If we terminated we'd feel guilty about not giving him a chance because he was less than perfect" (Both quoted in Eccleston 1999, in Lupton 1999: 70).

Lupton's conclusion is consistent with governmentality-inspired risk-literature:

> "The introduction of new technologies for determining the 'normality' of foetuses has resulted in pregnant women being forced to deal with risk statistics in making decisions about whether or not to have a test and what to do should the test suggest a foetal abnormality [...] The more such tests are introduced, the more intensified the discourses of risk that surround the pregnant woman and the more choices she is faced with making" (Lupton 1999: 68–9).

These choices are not always easy to make and – as our discussions in this chapter have also underlined – they are also socioculturally based and therefore difficult to predict: "The meanings of 'normality' and 'disability' vary depending on the sociocultural context and the meaning of the pregnancy in a woman's life" (Lupton 1999: 71). Again, we see a risk analysis that places weight upon a concrete study of how risk is negotiated and visible in everyday life when the citizen meets the state. It is hence a study that includes interactions between people, policy papers etc.

Conclusion

The risk perspective, with its explicit focus on dominant discourses/cultures and their influence on people's perceptions of themselves and their environment, constitutes a good starting point for the analysis of the relationship between the citizen and the state. To be "at risk" is to be "located within a network of factors drawn from observations of others" (Lupton 2005: 93) making submission processes an obvious focus point in a sociological risk analysis of the encounter between the state and citizen. We have shown that risk is not an objective, quantifiable entity, so it is pointless to study perceptions of risk without systematically taking into account cultural conditions (Douglas 1994: 32). Culture – Lupton's "network of factors" and Douglas' collective "thought styles" – therefore becomes crucial in the analysis of risk and deviation. Our analysis of two common risk areas in neo-liberal society (pregnancy and overweight) shows that these "grotesque" bodies (see Lupton 1999: 78) fall between existing categories, so the individuals in question are expected to apply to themselves concepts defined by biomedical discourse – and a morally rooted discourse, at that. The first case concerns detailed knowledge of potential illnesses for people with a high BMI. The second case is about how a wrong lifestyle (or the wrong genes/age) can increase the risk of giving birth to an abnormal child.

Despite the fact that the overweight or pregnant woman does not always want to look at her situation from the medically embedded point of view that is offered to her, both cases highlighted that the encounter with the state's experts means that these institutions' concepts and techniques – their "thought styles" – form the basis for these two women's self-evaluation. The very fact that the state's technologies govern the relationship between citizen and state is an important point in risk literature. For example, even if the pregnant woman chose to refuse all of the proposed examinations, she would still be defined by a medically influenced perception of risk because her act of rejection would be recorded in her medical history. Similarly, even though the overweight woman, Susan, chooses a perception of her situation other than the one offered by the specific health programme, her participation in it will be evaluated in the light of the programme's understanding of her situation (in this case, through the series of exercises in which she will participate, and which harmonise with the programme's concept of health and being overweight).

No matter how much people try to avoid a risk-dominated health discourse, each time the individual comes into contact with state institutions such as schools, universities, public-sector workplaces or hospitals, he or she is transformed and perceived through the language of the risk discourse. We can choose not to use the gym, buy the healthy lunch or participate in the annual cycling competition, and instead continue to smoke, eat fatty foods etc. – but all of these choices will be perceived by others as irresponsible, the actions of out-of-control people. This process takes place in all public spaces – not only in well-established welfare institutions such as those mentioned above, but also in all the spaces that we enter as soon as we step out of the private sphere. When we make the "wrong" choice (and thus represent a heightened risk profile) we help to affirm (in relation to the risk literature) that we are abnormal, that we are acting irresponsibly and incompetently, and that we are in need of care/guidance/advice from one of the state's many therapeutic institutions.

In this chapter, we have also tried to focus on the fact that there is nothing that does not constitute a risk per se (Ewald 1991: 199). Risk is, in the words of Garland (2003: 69), "always a risk *of* something *for* someone [...] 'risk' is a thoroughly social, thoroughly cultural, thoroughly psychological phenomenon". Risk is therefore a pervasive social and cultural phenomenon. We have dealt with the risk literature that stresses the relative nature of the risk concept: it is created and re-created in the social world between human beings and is therefore rooted in morals. We have also focused sharply on the effects that a strong risk discourse in society has on citizens with a visible risk profile, who therefore – by virtue of their very existence – attract negative attention from the others. Groups with a high and even self-created risk, such as the overweight, are obvious targets for treatment. And this fits precisely with the developments we are now witnessing: there has been a very clear focus on overweight people in recent years, both in the private and public sector (and especially in the media).

We have tried to draw attention to a new, fascinating area of research into the relationship between risk, normality and deviance. If the risk society makes us all somatic individuals – potentially sick people – what are the consequences of this for the concept of normality, since normality seems so clearly associated with the healthy, fit body? We have tentatively outlined a relationship between normality and the ideal, suggesting that normality no longer represents an achievable state but merely a desirable ideal state. In social work and in health care that strives to improve clients'/patients' life situations, it must be assumed that, if normality is an ideal state, then people whose lives are under constant evaluation and assessment will, by definition, never attain normality. In other words, clients/patients are assessed and evaluated according to parameters that reflect the unattainable. This must have profound significance for the encounter between citizens (as clients and patients) and the state's institutions, as the client's/patient's position within this perspective would automatically be that of the deviant. There would appear to be an opportunity to forge exciting new links between more traditional micro-sociological studies of social work and health care work and normality, and literature that diagnoses and analyses today's society as a risk society, since all three approaches explore the governance and control mechanisms used in the state's encounter with the citizen.

8 Integrating the approaches

There are many different critical approaches to the state's encounter with the citizen. Certain social scientists have focused on generating greater respect for cultural diversity in an era of multiculturalism and fragmentation (Isin & Turner 2002, Young 1990), others advocate greater recognition of the individual in user-oriented social services (Juul 2009) while other factions reflect upon how universal welfare principles can be maintained under post-modern conditions (Fraser 1997). Despite their differences, what these approaches have in common is that they are based on certain ideals against which practice, including the encounter between the state and its citizen, is weighed. These theories offer a "normative critique" that often leads to social practices and institutions being considered inadequate in relation to the ideal. The strength of this kind of critique is its foundation in normative ideals that provide the critic with a clear direction and specify certain model solutions.

In this book, we have presented a range of approaches that are capable of providing "analytical critique". However, empirical work is indispensable before any such critique is possible. The task is to study the historical roots of discourses, the way institutions legitimise their practices, or the logics according to which agents orient themselves in specific fields. Essentially, it is a type of critical activity that consists of "showing, rather than telling". In this regard, we are inspired by Foucault's ideas about how to avoid exercising critique that tells people what to think and do – what he in a lecture in 1978 calls an "imperative discourse" (Foucault 2007: 3). There, Foucault (2007) stresses that it is difficult – even in scientific practice – to completely eradicate implicit imperatives, or, we might add, to avoid the exercise of power-related effects in our own discourse. However, he does not wish to tell people how to fight or what they must fight for, but rather he outlines, through careful analysis, the obstacles and possible points of support that participants must take into consideration if they choose to engage in struggle within a particular field. Foucault puts it like this:

> "So, since there has to be an imperative, I would like the one underpinning the theoretical analysis we are attempting to be quite simply a conditional imperative of the kind: If you want to struggle, here are

> some key points, here are some lines of force, here are some constrictions and blockages. In other words, I would like these imperatives to be no more than tactical pointers" (Foucault 2007: 3).

With regard to exercising critique, Foucault's position is not intended to serve as an overarching framework for the other approaches. While there are obvious differences in terms of how and to what degree the approaches in this book are based on an ideal of analytical critique, what all them share is that they contrast with the tendency of normative critique to deploy abstract argumentation at the expense of empirical studies of how specific institutions emerged historically and function in practice. Our critical input regarding welfare institutions is, therefore, not anchored in a critique that immediately points towards a normative ideal or propagates a theory of optimal welfare provision. Rather, we want to draw attention to a series of analytical concepts that can be used by practitioners, students and researchers to study power in its specific forms.

We accept the hypothesis that power is always at stake in the citizen's encounters with welfare institutions. However, for the researcher to be able to discern and problematise the complex forms of power at play in those encounters, he or she needs precise analytical concepts with which to describe power. In this book, we have presented a catalogue of different analytical approaches for exploring the many dimensions of these encounters – historical, institutional, interactionist, field-specific, systemic and risk-focused. The tools that we present are also diagnostic, in that they facilitate descriptions of the current forms of power and its paradoxes and therefore seek to trigger critical reflection among professionals and commentators. In this chapter, we highlight the particular strengths and identify the weaknesses and "blind spots" of the different analytical approaches of the book. We will also make some suggestions for integrating and combining of the approaches.

From Foucault to Goffman

In the chapter on Foucault, we stressed how nuanced his definitions of the forms that power takes in modern society were. In his description of the liberal welfare state, Foucault highlights how the subject of government appears as a double-sided figure. On the one hand, this subject is a juridical category with inviolable rights, and, on the other hand, the subject is a living being that is submitted to an extensive pastoral care. The rise of the modern state thus implies the development of an extensive apparatus of institutions and experts in pastoral care. They seek to care for, educate, discipline, rehabilitate, empower and "self-actualise" the citizen, in many cases by working on his or her own self-understanding and morality. However, as the chapter made clear, we must avoid understanding this apparent paradox as an expression of a coherent program for social control, in which control mechanisms extend their reach under the guise of a liberal music that celebrates individual freedom. Rather than looking at the exercise of power by welfare institutions as repressive control, Foucault's analytics focus on the productive nature of modern power and the fact that the exercise of power typically seeks to enhance individuals' capacities rather than just impose restrictions. Modern power takes free individuals as its object, and its effects are conditional on making individuals into – or rather getting individuals to make themselves into – particular types of subjects. Although such productive exercises of power invariably reflect a particular strategy, they are also characterised by a certain openness, indeterminacy and reversibility. At the same time, Foucault's analytics avoid identifying specific individuals – experts or therapists – as "the governors", and therefore as the legitimate addressees of critique and demands. Instead, Foucault's approach shows how both the "governors" (such as social workers) and the "governed" (such as clients) are subjected to power strategies that seek to shape them as subjects with particular self-relations.

Foucault's analytics show us that liberal governance is based on a paradoxical dual concept of the objects it governs, in that it is envisioned as both natural reality and social creation at one and the same time. From this it follows that interventions must rest upon knowledge of the natural qualities of the object, or domain, in question. Therefore, to govern an individual or a community that is viewed as essentially autonomous and self-governing, "truths" need to be established about the inherent nature of such objects of government. One prolific way of resolving this duality of nature/creation is when welfare institutions or practitioners work with reference to an idea of "realising" the client's own will, "rediscovering" inner potential or even "awakening" repressed humanity. In the face of such naturalised, universal concepts, Foucault's critical ambition is, in brief, to open up and destabilise discourse that has sedimented itself in self-evident conceptions of what it means to be a human being. This constant problematisation and thinking "on the boundaries" of our categories obviously constitutes potential critical input to welfare professional's self-reflection.

However, we would point out two weaknesses of Foucauldian analytics: first, the tendency towards "discourse determinism" and second, the question of the analytics' "timeliness" in the current context. Regarding the first objection, Foucault does indeed provide compelling and provocative analyses of how various discourses in the human sciences arose in close connection with political strategies for the administration and utilisation of individuals and whole populations. However, what he failed to study is how individuals use these discursive categories in practice, and especially how they become a dynamic component of institutions' work and way of functioning. As such, a commonplace objection to Foucault and his followers, is that their analytics are inadequate for studying how programmes and categories are enacted in practice – that is, how they are negotiated, contested or transformed by, for example, professionals and users. This recurring critique concerns Foucauldians' alleged adoption of a deterministic view, "in which discourses are represented as subjugating human agency with little scope for resistance or acknowledgement of the lived experience of the body" (Lupton 1997: 101). In this light, Foucault's assertions that "power is at play in micro-relationships" and "power comes from everywhere", although highly convincing, remain merely theoretical proposals for a concept of modern power. In short, the perspective neglects to comprehend how discursive categories interact, are exercised in practice and might possibly be modified in dynamic social relations and institutional practices. It is, however, noticeable that Foucault himself had no ambition of conducting such ethnographic and sociological analyses.

The second objection to Foucault (and later governmentality literature) concerns the question of the effects of Foucauldian critique in a contemporary context. It has been argued from several sides that contemporary power-holders (in our case, the welfare system and its professionals) have begun to speak in terms that have an unmistakable resemblance to the language developed by Foucault himself and post-structuralism in general. The claim is that modernity's hierarchical and institutionally entrenched forms of power are being superseded by ways of governing that are more flexible and which transcend institutional boundaries (Deleuze 1997). As part of this process, the professionals have begun to employ a "power critique" in the form of demands to break down hierarchies, dissolve boundaries between sectors and create space for creative self-fashioning. As such, the language now used by those who wield power has, as its central frame of reference, concepts familiar to post-structural critique such as cultural difference, diversity, differentiation, context and respect for the individual etc. (Hardt & Negri 2001). This objection to Foucauldian analytics stems from the fact that there is a troubling compatibility between the languages of critique and of power. It is our opinion that this objection is difficult to reject because it refers to Foucault's own ambition to exercise a critical practice, relevant to its time, that takes stock of the truth claims that are most in need of a particularly critical vigilance. One response would be to avoid simply mechanically repeating Foucault's insights, and instead accept the more demanding task of developing analytics that take into account contemporary transformations and challenges.

However, our main concern in this context is to deal with the first point of critique – discursive determinism and its "neglect of human agency". This problem in Foucault's work is more directly analytical and methodological than the other problem of contemporary critique we just described. We believe that the problem with the impression of a frozen discursive structure in Foucauldian analyses can be countered by incorporating Goffman's interactionism into Foucault's analytical framework. While Foucault's work primarily analysed the historical discursive transformations that enabled the emergence of key institutions in Western societies, Goffman developed a strategy to analyse the inner life of such institutions. As mentioned previously, Goffman's aim was to observe how certain roles are reproduced in actual face-to-face interactions, and how certain ideas of normality and deviance inscribe themselves in actors' self-presentations and self-perceptions. At the same time, Goffman showed how the actors, qua their actions, can shift and modify the concepts of normality by means of which they are categorised. We suggest that Goffman and Foucault are broadly reconcilable in that they attempt to break with conventional (modern) social sciences on three key aspects: a) the unitary subject; b) human sciences as benevolent, progressive and objective; and c) society as a totality or meaningful unity regulated by "the state" (Battershill 1990). Goffman and Foucault also share a "bracketing" of the question of the truthfulness of human knowledge. Instead, they speak about the "social effects" or "tactical function" of *claims* for true knowledge in particular contexts. In brief, they pay attention to the procedures for speaking the truth rather than seeking to assert the validity of the truth claims.

In principle, Foucault's thinking displays a recognition that scientific and administrative categories might be modified when they encounter practice, such as when governing fails or produces unintended results. Yet, he does not analyse such dynamic reverberations. By comparison, Goffman offers a critical study of "total institutions", which is an approach to studying how individuals are shaped by scientific-administrative classification. However, he also directed attention to how classified individuals can defy these categories, twist them for their own purposes and influence them in return. Goffman showed how total institutions like psychiatric institutions, prisons or boarding schools change individuals, but not always in the desired direction.

Famously, Foucault asserts that the term "subject" designates a dual process, namely how an individual becomes "subject to someone else by control and dependence, and tied to his own identity by conscience or self-knowledge" (Foucault 1982: 212). It is obvious that there need not be – and probably in practice there is not – a perfect correspondence between the external demands and expectations directed towards the subject and the subject's own self-identity. It is precisely this tension-filled relationship that Goffman's approach is able to capture in great detail. People placed in "total institutions" can, for example, exercise strategies to preserve their understanding of themselves as players of a role, under pressure from the institution's staff, who are trying to influence the inmates to take on the institution's version of the inmate's character and history.

Goffman's micro-sociological approach can, therefore, be particularly helpful with identifying how institutional roles are actively exercised, challenged or negotiated. Goffman makes a distinction between "the person, individual, or player and the role, capacity, or function" (Branaman 2001: li). The point of this distinction is to clarify that both the person (with their experiences etc.) and the actions of the individual (in the specific situation) are dependent on the social definition. With reference to *Encounters* (p. 52), Branaman (2001: li–lii) writes: "The individual's expressions of a self behind a role are as much subject to role analysis as the roles themselves [...] person-role formulas are socially, not individually, determined". Even when people refer to an "authentic" self – i.e. who they "really are" – this reference is made using culturally received symbols of authentic and unique character. Another way of displaying character is by exercising distance to the role one is playing, and different situations may call for different degrees of role distance. This means that resistance to a subject position, as in Foucault, does not arise from something inherent in the subject/person, but rather arises by virtue of the power relations that are installed by different scripts or situations. This resistance must not be theorised, but it can be observed tangibly in forms of self-presentation (with all their meticulous gestures, equipment etc.) by which actors may occasionally distance themselves or resist the gallery of roles in, for example, institutionalised encounters between citizens and professionals.

The kinship between Goffman and Foucault has been noted by several commentators. Jenkins formulates the similarity between them by focusing on the relationship between power and form. For Goffman, "[p]ower and form are intimately connected. Power is a matter of a taken-for-granted, 'normal' everyday order of interaction, which enables and constrains efficacy and capacity. Hence, the theoretical homology, such as it may be, with Foucault" (Jenkins 2008: 164). Hacking suggests a more analytical comparison and integration of the two when he reformulates Goffman's concept of "looping effects" in an attempt to bridge "abstract discourse and face-to-face interaction" (Hacking 2004: 78). Hacking's position is rooted in the fundamental difference between the natural and social sciences – the former's object of study (cells, for example) is not influenced by being categorised, unlike the latter's object of study, human actors. When people are categorised in scientific-administrative discourse (for example, diagnosis of mental disorder or evaluation of capacity to work), it often affects those who are categorised, as they begin to change their behaviour and how they see themselves. It may be necessary to modify the categories, as some of the people to which they were applied have changed. Hacking (1999: 11) suggests the term "matrix" to capture how the categories are embedded in a web of relationships that decisively shape how individuals are able to construct themselves and others. In the matrix, contingent categories influence classified selves, who interact with other classified material and with material artefacts, all of which have social significance and real effects. This results in a concept similar to Foucault's "technology", except that it points more exclusively towards interactions.

From Goffman to Bourdieu

The strength of Goffman's interactional approach is its eye for the situation-specific dynamics in social interaction between people. Micro-interaction is a good choice of focus if the objective is to analyse the situational and dynamic elements of the exercise of power as it is played out in the citizen's encounter with welfare institutions. Although the concept of power is largely absent in Goffman's work, we agree with Jenkins that "Goffman's body of work offers many insights into what power is and how it actually works" (Jenkins 2008: 157). Jenkins proposes that Goffman should be considered a "significant theorist of power" (ibid.), since he offers an understanding of power that highlights the "mundane matter of everyday relationships between ends, on the one hand, and ways and means, on the other" (Jenkins 2008: 159). It is a perception of power that directs our attention towards actors' routine micro-relationships, in which they assist each other by maintaining the roles assigned in the specific context.

An interactional approach can describe how a given situation or institutional context requires the exercise of a particular repertoire of symbolically valorised actions, statements and gestures. It can therefore uncover the painstaking rituals for performance that apply in the different contexts and institutional settings in which citizens encounter the expertise of organised welfare. When an actor (such as a social worker or a client) performs a ritual, this then restricts the other actor's scope for action, since she or he is forced to respond within a clearly defined range of ritualised actions in order to maintain a credible self-presentation, as Goffman notes in *Asylums* (1974a). In this book, he demonstrates the reproduction of roles and expectations of roles and, in doing so, makes clear how both professionals and inmates "help" and sanction each other in order to reproduce frames and maintain roles and self-identity. Goffman's concept of the frame has to be considered ambiguous, because it refers both to the interaction (which, in principle, is unpredictable) and to the formal structures, which means that the concept's function is both to classify the actors' actions based on their experiences, perceptions and statements etc., and yet relate this classification to a realistic description of reality as constituted by formal structures. The situation consists of both of these dimensions (Crook & Taylor 1980).

Basically, for Goffman, the potential for action and recognition is created through credible self-presentation in the situation. The actor adopts a kind of dual perspective in the interaction – he or she relates to the structures and the symbols in the setting and at the same time relates to the "front stage" actions performed in relation to the structure and symbols of the setting. As shown in the chapter on Goffman, clients, patients and other users of welfare institutions indulge in specific forms of impression management in order to appear as credible and legitimate clients with a right to benefits. The symbolic interactionist approach thus offers significant empirically based, critical potential. Using this approach we can demonstrate how specific settings are governed by certain scripts that may, in some cases, be disadvantageous, but which the actors reproduce nevertheless, as deviations from the script might lead to loss of status and scope for action.

The points revealed by Goffman's analyses about the self as processual and dynamic phenomena can be used as an implicit critique of a dominant reasoning in welfare institutions. From Goffman's vantage point, the self becomes a modern myth that the individual is forced to exercise, rather than a fixed entity. Actors do not have a permanent self or an identity – rather, this is something that actors ascribe to themselves on an ongoing basis, and which others attribute to them, in the specific interaction. However, this picture of the non-essential self under continuous creation and transformation fits uncomfortably with the idea of individuality, on the basis of which most welfare institutions approach their encounters with the citizen. In this context, the starting point is not that there is an inevitable situation-specific negotiation of identity, but rather that the client or patient has a fixed (problematic) identity that needs to be addressed. The contrast between welfare professionals (who tend to maintain a particular client identity with a particular problem history and future prospects) and citizens (who adapt to different institutional settings in their own self-presentation) is therefore an obvious area for further analyses.

The interactionist approach does, of course, have its weaknesses. One critique is that this type of analysis neither develops nor relates to concepts of society or the state, since the focus is narrowly on the interaction and its immediate frameworks (such as the specific institutional context). As such, although there is an emphasis on norms in the interaction/institution, these are not normally linked with more general societal norms, for example with a particular type of welfare state, or with other historical factors that may be important to the analysed interaction (see the discussion of this critique in Maines 2003). However, since Goffman did not wish to (or claim to be able to) develop an overarching social theory, this particular critique may be somewhat misplaced. Books have been written about his contribution as a theorist, in the broadest understanding of the concept (including Drew & Wootton 1988), but it must be remembered that this was not Goffman's own ambition. He did not describe himself as a "social theorist", preferring the more modest description "student of society" (Smith 1989). That his work has subsequently been seen by others as a contribution to a theory of human interaction is hardly something for which Goffman can be blamed.

A second, related objection concerns the range of his oeuvre as a whole and the nature of the institutional critique to which a Goffman-inspired analysis may give rise. This critique concentrates on the inner life of a total institution, and exhibits the gallery of roles that the inmates adopt or into which they are forced, and therefore typically restricts its focus to the specific institutions. Out of this can easily arise a kind of demonisation of the staff, who have a range of power resources at their disposal, such as breaking down and then reconstituting people, see *Asylums* (1974a). As we have pointed out, the richness of detail in the interactionist analysis overshadows the question of what type of society it is, and the broader structures and mechanisms that facilitate and legitimise such institutions.

A final critique concerns the status Goffman assigned to his own analysis. Was it to be considered a theory capable of reflecting an individual's social existence in a more adequate and objective manner, primarily concentrating on structural conditions? Or was it, with its allusions to theatre and drama, rather an exercise in metaphor, which provided surprising and provocative re-descriptions of human action, but which were to be considered as analytical experiments, and therefore did not claim a higher truth status? Denzin and Keller (1981: 52) formulate a critique with reference to whether Goffman should be read on the basis of a "structural perspective" with emphasis on objective description, or whether he is more representative of the symbolic interactionist tradition, which stresses the interpretive approach (ibid.).

In the article, *Frame Analysis Reconsidered*, they argue that Goffman's main contribution is to a structural-based analysis, and that his work has only peripheral relevance to the analysis of everyday life (Denzin & Keller 1981: 53). *Frame Analysis* is cited as an illustration of this, but they think that their critique applies to his work more broadly. Goffman is presented as a classical Aristotelian-inspired thinker who:

> "Begins with objects and then dissects them into classes. Interpretive scientific method concerns itself, instead, not with objects, but with the 'how' of processes […] *Goffman's frame analysis is very much preoccupied with the classification of frames that are responsible for telling persons what it is that is going on here.* In Mead's terms, we get the nature of the object first (the frame), and the experiences which follow are defined in terms of the frame's basic dimensions" (Denzin & Keller 1981: 56 – italics in original).

We do not agree with this fundamental critique that Goffman's work was not of significance for the "interpretive social sciences" (and incidentally, this critique has also been effectively refuted by the series of sociological and anthropological studies that, drawing inspiration from Goffman, use a symbolic interactionist approach). Nevertheless, the critique relates to the lack of clarity found in Goffman's many works with regard to his distinction between the situational and the situated – that which is "inherent in the procedural form" and that which is "a matter of contingent conduct" (Jenkins 2008: 165). In response to Denzin and Keller's critique, Goffman states that:

> "Certainly individuals bring something of what they are and know to each of their social encounters, but there are rules of etiquette and reference for guiding this importation, and when these norms are threatened or breached it is in some moment's interaction that this will occur and have to be managed" (Goffman 1981: 68).

Goffman does not therefore accept the foundation for Denzin and Keller's critique, which rests on a structuralist reading of his work. It may well be in his point regarding the dynamic interdependency between structure and actor that Goffman's work – like Bourdieu's – has had major significance in social science. Nevertheless, the relationship between human actions and the institutional environment can rightly be criticised for being described and discussed in a somewhat ambiguous manner by Goffman.

In addition to being coupled with Foucault, Goffman's approach can also be combined with both Bourdieu and the risk sociologists. A coupling with Bourdieu would emphasise the class-specific markers in the scripts and institutions studied (Jenkins 2008). This coupling would also bring to the research design a greater emphasis on the relational construction of meaning, in which the social is perceived as a system of differences. A symbolic interactional approach could also benefit from a broader social theory that highlights the role, in terms of power, played by the state and economics. Goffman's favoured object of study, "the situation", could then be inserted in social fields where symbolic interaction can show how, for example, the value of certain symbolic representations is minutely negotiated in the field. Similarly, a coupling with risk sociology facilitates analyses based on a diagnosis of society as increasingly organised according to ideas of risk. In this combination, symbolic interaction can show how that which is claimed to represent risk is negotiated in a range of institutional contexts – and, in addition, such studies can be used to differentiate between risk conceptions across different institutional settings (Mik-Meyer 2010b).

The chapter on Bourdieu makes it clear how his approach differs from Goffman, in that field theory also enables the researcher to analyse structures (in terms of games of recognition, illusio and symbolic violence) that the agents themselves find difficult to approach and to make the object of their analysis. Rather than being informed by the problems, conflicts and paradoxes formulated by the practitioners or clients themselves, this field approach, via its strong focus on objective structural conditions, reveals hierarchical positioning and status differences etc., even when they are not recognised by the agents.

In the Bourdieu chapter, we stressed how his conceptual apparatus is both well suited to analyse the interaction between individuals (his practice theory) and at the same time can be used to document how objective structures influence – or even, to a significant degree "determine" – individuals' actions (King 2000). The objective of this sociological approach is both to describe the objective structures in society and to maintain that the individual is an agent who actively contributes to reproduce the structures, even when they seem disadvantageous and restrictive to him or her. In this context, Bourdieu stresses the state's role, since state institutions – schools, hospitals etc. – train the actor in perception categories, that is, the dominant principles for categorisation ("vision" and "division"). The state and its institutions enforce a contingent (cultural) order that assumes an objective status for the participants. This is done through the reproduction of "structures" in the broadest sense, including through language, educational curricula, the selection of specific social groups for particular professions and symbols of creation etc. Bourdieu explains reproduction, amongst other things, with reference to the existence of a general trend towards correspondence between the agent's mental structures and a given society's objective structures. For Bourdieu, therefore, the state has a dual effect – objectively, in the form of specific structures, and subjectively, in the form of mental structures. In other words, the state shapes how the world is perceived and understood.

With the concept of symbolic violence, Bourdieu wishes, in particular, to draw attention to the exercise of power, inter alia, symbolic violence. It follows that symbolic violence is closely related to a field's "truths" (doxa) – conditions that the agents perceive as so "natural" that they subordinate themselves to them quite voluntarily, exposing themselves to a symbolic violence in which the domination is perceived as natural and proper.

Uncovering the governing but hidden structures that fundamentally shape agents' scope for action is therefore central to Bourdieu's sociology. An important point in this context is that any (oppressive) hierarchical order can only be maintained as long as the agents perceive it as legitimate. As a result, an analysis of power that seeks to exhibit a given hierarchical order within a specific field will focus on how the agents bring different forms of capital and their symbolic effect into play in their struggle to define a field's truths (doxa). Field theory is in this sense a "more or less coherent approach in the social sciences, whose essence is the explanation of regularities in individual action by recourse to position vis-á-vis others [...] Field theory offers social scientists a combination of analytical insight and attention to the concrete" (Martin 2003: 1).

A field-analytical approach sets certain conditions for analytical work, which can be problematised. One frequent critique is whether Bourdieu actually succeeds in overcoming the duality of subject/object and agency/structure. The question is whether he manages to link structure and agency through his concepts of practice, habitus and field, without the objective structures gaining precedence and therefore determining individuals' actions, with the consequence that this theoretical apparatus suffers from an "inability to cope with subjectivity" (Jenkins 1992: 97). A similar critique is raised by Alexander in his book *The Meanings of Social Life* (2003), in which Bourdieu's sociology is criticised for being "weak", based on the belief that the conceptual apparatus fails to assign culture an autonomous role, but rather produces analyses in which culture and structure (the economy) are inseparable. This interrelatedness between culture and structure means that the approach can easily end up producing structural-deterministic analyses of human behaviour. As such, it is the objective structures' central position in Bourdieuian analysis that comes under attack. Gartman (2007: 399) writes: "If it is true, as Bourdieu asserts, that the products of even autonomous cultural fields are based on class privilege and ultimately appropriated by the dominant to legitimate and reproduce their power, then how can society be criticized and changed?" This leads Gartman (2007: 399) to the conclusion that Bourdieu's "theory of social change is weak, if not nonexistent" (ibid.).

This critique directs attention to Bourdieu's explicit focus on reproduction. If all of the concepts have been developed in order to encapsulate reproduction in society (which, it is noted in parenthesis, is in fact documented by various statistical studies of a number of important social processes, such as the relationship between class and education), then it follows naturally, as Gartman points out, that this theoretical perspective is not as suitable for studying and understanding processes of change in society or institutions. In other words, the theoretical point of departure in field analysis will inevitably direct our attention to the structures that contribute to reproduction, rather than processes of change. This does not mean that field theory marginalises external events and structures (as far as this field is concerned) as irrelevant for the agents but the external events and structures' significance to the agents will always be translated in line with the field's internal logic: "Akin to the principle that the magnet may cause the field, it is the field that has the effects on the iron filings" (Martin 2003: 23).

With regard to other theories discussed in the book, there is an obvious potential in combining field theory with symbolic interactionism. Bourdieu's theory of society as consisting of a number of fields can provide an analytical tool with which to analyse the surrounding or "outer" frameworks for interaction between people. These analyses will be capable of situating specific analyses of the interactions that form this book's theme in a model of society that emphasises objective structures and the state's particularly significant role in this encounter. In addition to the fact that this perspective focuses on how the state's principles for dividing citizens into certain categories comes into play in the encounter between citizen and professional, Bourdieu's concept of habitus could strengthen an interactionist analysis via its interest in what determines agents' positioning in the social space. The concept of habitus denotes the fact that objective structures have a tendency to be internalised physically and shape the agent's scope for action. In addition, since different upbringings create different conditions for internalisation of the objective structures, the agent will be equipped with different forms of capital, which will give him/her different conditions for asserting him/herself in various fields. As previously mentioned, in this context some very specific forms of capital figure as worthy of recognition in welfare institutions – including job-creation projects, services for the homeless, migrant projects – and these constitute the framework for the citizen's encounter with the state.

From Luhmann to Foucault

Luhmann's systems theory provides a perspective that views modern society as consisting of a plurality of social systems that describe and close themselves off in an autonomous and self-referential fashion. Systems theory assumes the existence of a series of parallel systems, each of which refers to its own logic and its own rationality. It has, therefore, a particularly observant eye for the conflicting demands on both citizens and professionals when several different system logics come into play at once. This means that we are able to explore how social problems, needs, welfare, motivation, progress and so on simply become fundamentally different objects depending on the system observing them.

Luhmann's point about the differentiation of society also has analytical potential vis-à-vis the question of how the political system can attempt to manage welfare institutions and staff. With systems theory as our perspective, we assume that political authorities' possibilities for governing and directly impacting on practices in welfare institutions are subject to substantial restrictions. This, however, does not prevent politicians from expressing their views *as if* they were able to exert control at all levels, all the way down to the welfare institutions' practices. From a systems-theory starting point, the means of political control – political programmes, legal provisions and new technologies etc., are in principle received by welfare organisations as a kind of "irritation", dealt with on the basis of the organisations' particular rationality and self-description. Systems theory also allows us to study, conversely, how the welfare organisations produce problems and demands for action that are processed by the political system according to its particular rationality. Furthermore, it allows us to study the structural couplings that are formed between the political system and the welfare organisations so that the complexity generated by one system is made available to another.

The starting point, that systems must reduce complexity, allows the questions surrounding welfare institutions' encounters with citizens to emerge in a very particular way. We recall that systems theory refuses to take individuals with intentions as its starting point. Instead, we are offered an observation of how welfare organisations communicate roles and role-expectations, and in this way construct various "actor fictions". Within the systems-theory perspective, a welfare organisation cannot observe clients, users or patients in their full complexity, it can only observe its self-constructed image of these categories. The organisation does this in order to reduce complexity, treating the client by determining his or her problems and needs through the categories and programmes that it has at its disposal (Moe 1998).

Systems theory defines organisations as systems that are characterised by making decisions about who may be included or obtain membership. Since welfare organisations are far from able to help everyone, it is critical to study which criteria are specified for inclusion and exclusion in the organisations and the services they provide. In the chapter on systems theory, we gave an example of an analysis of the specific criteria for participation in programmes used by public and voluntary organisations working with homeless people. However, another option is to study whether there are differing inclusion criteria within the same welfare organisation, as studied by Højlund (2009).

It should be stressed that, in this book, we have only discussed how Luhmann's systems theory can be applied to (welfare) organisations. The theory offers a wide range of concepts that hold potential for future studies of the encounter between the citizen and organised welfare, such as the concept of interaction systems, system differentiation or historical semantic analysis (for a comprehensive introduction to the different analytical strategies in systems theory, see Andersen 2003a).

Luhmann distinguishes himself from other perspectives in this book by not subscribing to any explicit critical function in his work. Indeed, Luhmann has been accused of operating with a "barren" and technocratic theoretical apparatus, which offers no proper critique of the societal conditions and implicit power relations being described. In several places, Luhmann himself has contributed to such an assessment, including a negative characterisation of the social scientists who champion "normative commitment or social-political engagement" (Luhmann 1982b: 70). He has also been criticised for providing a theoretical apparatus that is apparently capable of serving any purpose, as it is decidedly cleansed of any criteria for defining what is progressive and what is regressive. In terms of interventions, systems theory allows us to observe the difficulties a given system faces in reproducing itself due – for example – to urgent, internal paradoxes. We can make observations of these problems, which can then be made available for the system and its internal processes. We can also identify possible functional equivalents to existing systems or programmes, as we saw in Chapter 5's discussion of the systems theorists who pondered the functional contribution of social work to modern society. However, if the contribution of systems theory is fundamentally functional, the role of technocrat seems to be open. In principle, the theory seems able to contribute to all types of social systems, including, perhaps, those of an autocratic and fascist nature.

As a consequence of this, Luhmann has been criticised for completely writing out of his theory the question of values, since the locus of meaning is reduced to nothing more than a communicative fiction (Habermas 1987). A more analytical critique has argued that the theory confuses a theoretical assumption about systems' autopoiesis with an empirically observable societal differentiation. On the one hand, systems theorists champion a vague realism, since the theory is presented as merely an outline of a theory for modern society. The world can be viewed as consisting of autopoietic systems, but the persuasiveness of the analysis must be evaluated by actual observers. On the other hand, when justifying the theory's adequacy, systems theorists fall back on empirical references, such as the idea that there was a historical process of functional differentiation (Münch 1992). The abstract theory precludes contradiction by empirical data but nevertheless makes justifying reference to empirical reality.

Notwithstanding these objections, it can be argued that the empirical applications of Luhmann, especially in recent years, have demonstrated rich possible applications for critical social analyses (Scherr 1999, Andersen 2008, Højlund 2009, Villadsen 2011a). Systems theory provides a framework for unsentimental, and precise, descriptions of how different social systems observe, but it does not allow us to determine how clients "actually" are, or to make claims regarding what good social work, integration or medical care ought to be. Yet, the fact that we do not have access to the actual social relations that lie beneath the veil of ideology does not prevent us from putting systems-theoretical concepts to work in relation to specific social political problems.

One obvious possible combination with the other perspectives covered in the book is with Foucault. In recent years, several researchers have sought to develop this combination theoretically (see Andersen 2003a, Pottage 1998, Borch 2005), so here we merely outline some potential analytical benefits. Foucault works with a complex conceptual framework for the analysis of power, but he offers no concept of the organisation. The incorporation of systems theory would introduce concepts for the specific study of the forms of communication-logic and rationality that dominate in various welfare organisations. It offers us the opportunity to analyse power as a question of how organisations close themselves off, and how, by stabilising recursive forms of communication, they develop resistance to their environment and reduce complexity in ways that are functional for their own reproduction but neither naturally given, nor necessarily desirable. In this way, both thinkers display, each in their particular way, the disturbing contingency of discourse. In terms of analytical design, Luhmann's relentless search for binary guiding distinctions brings an analytical precision and "tightness" to Foucault-inspired analyses.

Despite the similarities between the two, Luhmann's aim of developing a universal social theory immediately contrasts with Foucault's empirical, specific and problem-driven approach. Luhmann's barren conceptual apparatus consists of strictly formal concepts (such as system/environment) that can be used to describe virtually any empirical material. They are, by virtue of their purely formal definitions, freed of any substance or critical connotation and this quality may help produce empirical surprises. What is critical or problematic for systems theory is therefore in no sense derived a priori. On the contrary, Foucault's concepts were developed as part of specific critical engagements in which he was involved at a certain point in time and in a particular intellectual and political context. In this sense, the analyst risks importing a critique via specific concepts of Foucault's that may not be strictly pertinent to the case concerned, or which may have very different effects when used in a completely different context.

From neo-institutional organisation theory to Bourdieu

In the chapter on neo-institutional organisation theory, we showed how this approach can be used to analyse citizens' encounters with the state by problematising "institutions" (in the broadest sense of the term) that have obtained a taken-for-granted status. The theory creates an awareness of how certain ideas, organisational forms and technologies can spread and be reproduced, in spite of lacking evidence that they meet the stated objectives. These myth-like organisational methods are assumed to ensure efficiency, justice, welfare, client development etc. However, institutionalised organisations often spend more time showing that they are using the "legitimate" structures, processes and technologies than on evaluating the actual usefulness and appropriateness of such "organisational elements". Neo-institutional organisation theory provides explanations for the striking similarity of institutionalised organisations by taking as its starting point the relationship between the organisation and its immediate surroundings – its environment. In this way, the theory explicitly cultivates the inter-organisational level in its analysis, and in doing so differs from the other approaches in this book.

Compared to the other approaches, neo-institutional organisation theory gives particular privilege to the inter-organisational relations. By contrast, Luhmann inserts the organisation in a broader theory about the modern, differentiated society. Moreover, systems theory sees organisations as being far more self-contained and self-creating than neo-institutional organisation theory, which works with a concept of organisations as open systems. Foucault was interested in the historical origins and transformation of discourses, technologies and institutions, but he did not develop a specific concept of the organisation. Similarly, risk literature is concerned with showing how a dominant discourse on risk creates special conditions for individual and collective action, as well as the constitution of society, without placing particular emphasis on organisations. Goffman's interactionism operates on the level of individuals' interactions, and this perspective dissolves or decentres the organisation into practices and micro-games around the construction of persons. It therefore lacks a concept with which to analyse specific organisations and their relationships to each other. Bourdieu's approach is apparently the one that comes closest to neo-institutional organisation theory, as he is also interested in how agents seek to achieve recognition in a field by presenting the symbolism that gains recognition in the field (symbolic capital). Parts of neo-institutional organisation theory indeed took inspiration from Bourdieu's field concept, but have developed a more specified conceptual framework for analysing the strategic actions of organisations. In particular, the addition of the neo-institutional concept of conflicting myths of rationality allows for an analysis of the complexity faced by many modern welfare organisations. The neo-institutional organisation theory focuses sharply on modern organisations' orientation towards their environment and their need to constantly maintain their legitimacy.

We remember that the neo-institutional approach is particularly well suited to analysing public (or private/voluntary) welfare organisations, whose "product" is difficult to quantify. These organisations both have the substantial task of providing welfare for their users and the symbolic task of displaying the myths that prevail in the surrounding environment and in the wider community. In the chapter on neo-institutional organisation theory, we gave an example of how institutions for criminals and juvenile delinquents should provide care and training for the children at the same time as they were to punish them and gratify society's sense of justice. The example showed how it was crucial that a reformatory perpetuates institutionalised norms and technologies for child care and punishment, even though their historical origins had been forgotten and their actual effects on children were widely documented as ineffective or even harmful. Nevertheless they survive, and a specific model of child custody is carried on because it manifests socially and institutionally embedded norms.

Objections can, however, be raised about neo-institutional organisation theory and its explanations. First and foremost, it adopts an analytical view that searches for homogenisation – in other words, it may be objected that its view is biased, as it consistently seeks to find "the same". This follows from the assumption that modern organisations install elements from the environment, and that these elements will have homogenising or "isomorphic" effects in the organisations that assimilate them. One example of this could be the assertion that voluntary organisations that employ professionally trained staff will automatically gravitate towards a bureaucratic and instrumental rationality. Hence, it has been argued that the concepts of "conformity" and "isomorphism" in neo-institutional organisation theory is vague, since the criteria for concluding the existence of isomorphism are not well-defined: "[E]mpirical studies of isomorphism usually examine only one organisational characteristic that provides a narrow and potentially biased view of the extent of conformity. We argue that a much more comprehensive assessment of organisational change is required to test claims of isomorphism" (Ashworth et al. 2009: 166).

The neo-institutional perspective that seeks homogenisation has difficulty encapsulating the complex processes that arise when, for example, specific technologies are installed in a welfare institution that is characterised by particular professional codes and historically evolved self-understandings. In this instance, the neo-institutional organisation concept of decoupling does not seem to be subtle enough in analytical terms. One way of countering this problem, however, could be to theoretically permit that organisations, in certain contexts and at certain times, may be able to maintain a high degree of closure and self-reference.

Another weakness is that neo-institutional organisation theory lacks concepts with which to more closely study the historical emergence of the myths of rationality at stake (even though, in principle, the theory stresses the importance of analysing origins). This is another context in which Foucault could be used to hone the institutional analysis by means of his concepts of genealogical lines and his attention to re-articulations of historical, discursive or technological elements. Similarly, integrating risk sociology with neo-institutionalism would show how risk management in modern organisations is linked to a much wider risk discourse. It can also be argued that neo-institutional organisation theory lacks concepts for how individuals are formed and exercise self-government by means of certain technologies. Again, Foucault and risk sociology could clearly expand the analytical potentials here. Finally, as regards the possibility of combining with

Bourdieu, at least two of his assumptions would be highly combinable: first, that the production of meaning depends on symbols which achieve their signification strictly in relation to other symbols, and second, that hierarchical categories and symbols are non-essential, but socially constructed. Both points might be used to specify how rationality myths about welfare diffuse across organisations.

It can also be added, briefly, that much neo-institutional organisation theory operates with an implicitly positive valorisation of organisational and normative pluralism, which would appear to be rooted in an American liberal-pluralist tradition. By virtue of this "political and cultural anchoring", plural and diverse forms of organisation are seemingly always preferable to homogeneity, and therefore the theory tends to have a negative bias against initiatives that promote or enforce uniformity in services across organisations and sectors. However, the question is whether plurality is to be preferred in all circumstances, since societies and welfare areas may be identified where securing uniformity and universality could certainly be deemed as a positive approach.

From risk theory to Foucault and Goffman

In the chapter on risk theory we introduced sociological literature in which it is argued that modern Western societies are increasingly governed with reference to risk. As shown in the chapter, literature on the concept of risk is wide-ranging and varied (e.g. Beck 1992, Douglas 1994, Doyle & Ericson 2003, Lupton 1999). We presented discussions from the literature concerning the constitution of the citizen as a risk object. In general, this literature – despite mutual, sometimes great, differences – claims that most social processes today are influenced by risk perceptions, and that these processes are fundamental to how we understand ourselves. A central tenet of this literature is that risk perceptions are based on incomplete knowledge, and that morals and politics therefore have a crucial impact on which factors are identified as risky, and which are not (Douglas 1994). The aspect of the risk literature that we have used as our starting point is that risk, by definition, is assumed to be problematic (or "dangerous", cf. Douglas 1994) and so requires action. This makes it imperative to study which risks are determined to be acceptable or unacceptable in political terms.

In the chapter, we focused on the risk literature that either has a culture theory foundation (Douglas 1994) or is rooted in the governmentality tradition's focus on knowledge, including knowledge about risk and how this knowledge shapes political government (Arnoldi 2009: 55). Common to both streams is their constructivist basis, which means that risk is not conceived as an objective phenomenon, but rather should be viewed as created socially. Many of the risk analyses inspired by the governmentality tradition in sociology focus on how the individual manages the risk profile they are ascribed through socially constructed discourses that emphasise personal responsibility and autonomy etc. (O'Malley 1996). In addition, several of the empirically based risk analyses are also interested in the body and the demarcation between what is defined as disease and what is defined as healthy, both change over time and in relation to powerful organisations and their interests (e.g. Rose 2006). Focus on the body as a risk object is linked to the fact that a neo-liberal focus on personal responsibility, self-realisation and autonomy, logically implies a critical attention to "at-risk bodies" (Lupton 1999, Rose 2007: 125).

In the chapter on risk, we showed how a risk group like overweight people is linked to a dominant perception of today's normal citizen as someone who acts in a controlled and responsible manner. Since the body in contemporary Western society has become a place where an unlimited number of risk factors can be assembled (there are no limits to the range of possible diseases that people in the modern world may have, or acquire), Rose argues that selfhood in the 21st century has become "intrinsically somatic" (2001: 18). As a result, the body has been turned into the primary focus of work on the self. This "somatic individual" (Novas & Rose 2000) is an individual who, in spite of his or her immediate healthy state, is assumed to be potentially ill. Those individuals who are currently regarded as belonging to a risk group (and so require state intervention) can, through the looking glass of the risk literature, be considered the deviants of our time.

Constructivist-inspired risk analyses study the consequences for the citizen's encounter with welfare services and what they see as a gradual modification of a philosophy of collective welfare towards more and more individual-focused technologies of government. Douglas' concept heralds a shift in the prevailing "thought styles" that are assumed to set the terms for welfare institutions' encounter with citizens (Douglas 1994). In broad terms the neo-liberal state differs from the 1970s welfare state because of its focus on what individuals can do themselves to improve their situation, rather than on redistributing the risks to which citizens are exposed by means of national health and insurance schemes. In this context, it is particularly important to study the power base for the definition process when it comes to deciding what are considered as risky and deviant acts. In this context, risk sociologists identify morally coloured indicators (self-restraint, self-governance and willpower etc.) as particularly significant study objects when it comes to defining what is presently meant by normality.

In relation to the citizen's encounter with the state, several constructivist-inspired risk sociologists demonstrate how the growing range of experts aggravates the inequality of power that characterises the relation between the citizen and welfare institutions (qua the expert). The point is that, even though risk is perceived and interpreted differently in different cultures and segments of society, as the literature indicates, not all risk perceptions are raised to the level of "objective" truths that call for intervention. Rather, it is the (biomedical) experts' risk perceptions that form the basis for political initiatives, with the effect that certain citizens end up being labelled as individuals at risk and in need of treatment (Lupton 1999). In this sense, the governmentality inspired risk literature also echoed a Foucauldian concept of power that captures the productive nature of modern power. Power intertwines with risk, since the definition of risk factors is structured by a dominant discourse embedded in the prevailing power relations of society.

Of course, a risk-focused analysis also has its limitations. A crucial prerequisite (which at the same time constitutes a restriction) is that the researcher needs to accept the risk diagnosis. It must therefore be accepted that the most dominant discourse in contemporary Western societies is a risk discourse, which is assumed to have profound consequences for all processes in modern society, spanning policy making, public welfare arrangements and the individual's practices of self-creation (Dean 1999b). The risk discourse is assumed to fundamentally influence the state's priorities, technologies, programmes etc., and therefore also the encounter between citizen and the forms of expertise that are authorised or regulated by the state (Lupton 1999). No matter how much citizens try to escape a risk-dominated discourse, the thesis is that when they enter into contact with the key institutions of modern society – schools, hospitals, social services etc. – they are transformed and understood through the language of risk. Another limitation of constructivist-inspired risk analyses is found in their constructivist basis. A thorny question is thus whether all risk can be reduced to culture (Douglas 1994). And does a governmentality approach preclude other important analyses because of its exclusive interest in risk perceptions and their consequences in social life, instead of focusing on "real", substantial risks and how they are perceived (Arnoldi 2009: 46, 55)? Another weakness is the fact that governmentality-inspired risk analyses are primarily interested in the role that risk plays in relations of government (internally in institutions and between actors), and therefore ignores "how proliferation of technology has radically changed society" (Arnoldi 2009: 60).

Governmentality-inspired risk sociology is largely inspired by Foucault's work – it conceives of risk in modern society as a major technology of government that makes new forms of control of individuals and groups possible. There remains potential for utilising Foucault's insights further for studies of risk, and therefore to combine risk literature even more closely with Foucault's work than is the case at present. Taking into account the focus of this book – citizens' encounters with welfare institutions – an obvious path would be to combine risk literature with Goffman's interactionist approach. Risk literature provides an overarching societal diagnosis – and concepts – that could contribute by focusing on a specific theme in micro-encounters between citizens and professionals in particular institutional settings. Finally, both symbolic interactionism and risk literature take a special interest in the relationship between normality and deviation in a control and governing perspective, so there would appear to be scope for future studies of how deviation and normality are negotiated in specific situations when the interaction studied revolves around, and embodies, a societal diagnosis of risk.

Notes

Chapter 3

1 Goffman's theatrical metaphors are most clearly presented in *The Presentation of Self in Everyday Life* (1990a); his game- and strategy metaphors in *Strategic Interaction* (1970), and his ritual metaphors in *Interaction Ritual* (1967) and *Relations in Public* (1971).

2 Several writers, including Branaman (2001: xlvii), have pointed out that Goffman operates with two contradictory perceptions of the self: one is a purely social product, the other an individual capable of manipulating strategically in relation to the social order and other actors. We have chosen to present both approaches but with the emphasis on the structured interpretation, in which the self is regarded to a greater extent as a social product. We do so first because this understanding of the self is more widespread in Goffman's work and second because it best addresses the problem posed in this book.

Chapter 4

1 The French welfare state differs from other welfare states in a number of areas. However, we will not be able to discuss further the particularity of the French welfare state in this chapter.

Chapter 5

1 The case analysis stems from a more extensive empirical study of homeless shelters in two Danish jurisdictions, Odense council, and the city council of Copenhagen. Qualitative interviews were made with 25 persons from public and voluntary shelters, i.e. leaders and employees/volunteers, who were asked about their working principles, their professional values and their practical methods. Results from the study were published in English in Villadsen (2008a, 2011a).

Chapter 6

1 The citations from Levin (1998) are translated from Swedish by the authors.

2 The "Uppfostringsanstalten" is a specifically Swedish institution. It is a cross between a children's home and a young offenders' institution for which there is no direct equivalent in English-speaking countries. We use the term "reformatory".

3 The citations from Jakobsen (2004) are translated from Danish by the authors.

Chapter 7

1 See Lupton (2005, 2006) for in-depth discussion of the three currents.

2 A great deal of very varied literature discusses risk in terms of international politics, business etc. However, this chapter refers to sociological risk literature.

3 A great deal of criticism has been directed at Beck's book, e.g. that he pragmatically alternates between a realist and a constructivist approach to the analysis of risk, and that he has a very pessimistic view of the directions in which science and technology are moving. Nevertheless, it is difficult to find sociological texts on risk that do not refer to him.

Bibliography

Alexander, J.C. (2003) *The Meanings of Social Life: A cultural sociology*, New York, NY: Oxford University Press.

Andersen, N.Å. (2003a) *Discursive Analytical Strategies*, Bristol: The Policy Press.

——(2003b) 'Polyphonic Organisations', in T. Bakken and T. Hernes (eds) *Autopoietic Organization Theory: Drawing on Niklas Luhmann's social systems perspective*, Oslo: Abstrakt Forlag, 151–82.

——(2003c) 'Organisationen i anden ordens perspektiv: systemteoriens analysestrategiske maskine', in H. Højlund and M. Knudsen (eds) *Organiseret kommunikation*, Frederiksberg: Samfundslitteratur, pp.310–23.

——(2008) 'The World as Will and Adaptation: The interdiscursive coupling of citizens' contracts', *Critical Discourse Studies*, 5(1): 75–89.

Aradau, C. and Munster, R.V. (2008) 'Taming the Future: The dispositif of risk in the war on terror', in L. Amoore and M. de Goede (eds) *Risk and the War on Terror*, London and New York, NY: Routledge, pp.23–40.

Arnoldi, J. (2009) *Risk (Key Concepts)*, Cambridge: Polity Press.

Ashworth, R., Boyne, G. and Delbridge, R. (2009) 'Escape from the Iron Cage? Organizational change and isomorphic pressures in the public sector', *Journal of Public Administration Research*, 19(1): 165–87.

Baecker, D. (1994) 'Soziale Hilfe als Funktionssystem der Gesellschaft', *Zeitschrift für Soziologie*, 23(2): 93–110.

Bärens, J.H. (1811) *Penia eller Blade for Skole-, Industri-, Medicinal-og Fattigvæsen*, Sjette Aargang, no. 22, Kiøbenhavn.

Battershill, C.D. (1990) 'Erving Goffman as Precursor Post-modern Sociology', in S.H. Riggins (ed.) *Beyond Goffman: Studies on communication, institution, and social interaction*, New York, NY: Mouton de Gruyter, pp.163–86.

Bauman, Z. (1992) *Intimations of Postmodernity*, London: Routledge.

——(2000) *Globalisation: The Human Consequences*, Oxford: Polity Press.

——(2004) *Wasted Lives: Modernity and its outcasts*, Cambridge: Polity Press.

Beck, U. (1992 (1986)) *Risk Society: Towards a new modernity*, New Delhi: Sage.

Berger, P. and Luckmann, T. (1966) *The Social Construction of Reality: A treatise in the sociology of knowledge*, New York, NY: Anchor Books.

Besley, T. (2002) *Counseling Youth: Foucault, power, and the ethics of subjectivity*, Westport: Besley Greenwood Publishing Group.

Blaikie, A., Hepworth, M., Holmes, M., Howson, A., Inglis, D. and Sartain, S. (2004) 'General Introduction. The Sociology of the Body: Genesis, development and futures', in A. Blaikie, M. Hepworth M. Holmes and A. Howson (Editor,

Introduction), D. Inglis and S. Sartain (eds) *The Body: Critical concepts in sociology*, London: Routledge, pp.1–23.

Blumer, H. (1969) *Symbolic Interactionism: Perspective and method*, Berkeley: University of California Press.

Borch, C. (2005) 'Systemic Power: Luhmann, Foucault, and analytics of power', *Acta Sociologica*, 48(2): 155–67.

——(2011) *Niklas Luhmann: Key sociologists*, London and New York, NY: Routledge.

Bourdieu, P. (1987 (1979)) *Distinction: A social critique of the judgement of taste*, Cambridge, MA: Harvard University Press.

——(1988 (1984)) *Homo Academicus*, Cambridge: Polity Press.

——(1998a (1989)) *The State Nobility: Elite schools in the field of power*, Cambridge: Polity Press.

——(1998b (1994)) *Practical Reason: On the theory of action*, Stanford, CA: Stanford University Press.

——(1999 (1980)) *The Logic of Practice*, Cambridge: Polity Press.

——(2000a (1977)) *Outline of a Theory of Practice*, Cambridge: Cambridge University Press.

——(2000b (1997)) *Pascalian Meditations*, Cambridge: Polity Press.

——(2005) 'The Political Field, the Social Science Field, and Journalistic Field', in R. Benson and E. Neveu (eds) *Bourdieu and the Journalistic Field*, Cambridge: Polity Press, pp.29–47.

Bourdieu, P. and Passeron, J.C. (1990 (1970)) *Reproduction in Education, Society and Culture*, London: Sage.

Bourdieu, P. and Wacquant, L.J.D. (1996 (1992)) *An invitation to Reflexive Sociology*, Cambridge: Polity Press.

Branaman, A. (2001) 'Goffman's Social Theory', in C. Lemert and A. Branaman (eds) *The Goffman Reader*, Oxford: Blackwell Publishers Ltd, pp.xlv–lxxxii.

Bröckling, U., Krasmann, S. and Lemke, T. (2011) *Governmentality: Current issues and future challenges*, New York, NY: Routledge.

Brunsson, N. (1989) *The Organization of Hypocrisy: Talk, decisions and actions in organizations*, Chichester: John Wiley & Sons.

Brunsson, N. and Olsen, J.P. (1993) *The Reforming Organization*, London and New York, NY: Routledge.

Burns, T. (1992) *Erving Goffman*, London: Routledge.

Chamberlin, C. and Chamberlin, L. (1993) 'Alternative Schools as Critique of Traditional Schools: The Tvind Schools in Denmark', *Canadian Social Studies*, 27(3): 115–20.

Clarke, J. and Newman, J. (1997) *The Managerial State: Power, politics and ideology in the remaking of social welfare*, London: Sage.

Collier, S. (2010) 'Topologies of Power: Foucault's analysis of political government beyond 'governmentality'', *Theory Culture Society*, 26(6): 78–108.

Contandriopoulos, D. and Brousselle, A. (2010) 'Reliable in their Failure: An analysis of healthcare reform policies in public systems, *Health Policy*, 95(2): 144–52.

Cooney, K. (2007) 'Fields, Organizations, and Agency: Toward a Multilevel Theory of Institutionalization in Action', *Administration & Society*, 39(6): 687–718.

Coveney, J. (1998) 'The Government and Ethics of Health Promotion: The importance of Michel Foucault', *Health Education Research*, 13(3): 459–68.

Crook, S. and Taylor, L. (1980) 'Goffman's Version of Reality', in J. Ditton (ed.) *The View from Goffman*, London: Macmillan, pp.233–51.

Cruikshank, B. (1999) *The Will to Empower: Democratic citizens and other subjects*, Ithaca, NY: Cornell University Press.

Dean, M. (1991) *The Constitution of Poverty*, London: Routledge.

——(1995) 'Governing the Unemployed Self in an Active Society', *Economy and Society* 24(4): 559–83

——(1998) 'Administering Ascetism: Reworking the life of the unemployed citizen', in M. Dean and B. Hindess (eds) *Governing Australia: Studies of contemporary government*, Melbourne: Cambridge University Press, pp.87–109.

——(1999a) *Governmentality: Power and rule in modern society*, London: Sage Publications.

——(1999b) 'Risk, Calculable and Incalculable', in D. Lupton (ed.) *Risk and Socio-cultural Theory: New directions and perspectives*, Cambridge: Cambridge University Press, pp.131–59.

——(2002) 'Liberal Government and Authoritarianism', *Economy and Society*, 31(1): 37–61.

Deleuze, G. (1992) 'What is a Dispositif?', in T.J. Amstrong, (ed.) *Michel Foucault: Philosopher*, London: Harvester Wheatsheaf, pp.159–68

——(1997) 'Postscript on Control Societies', in G. Deleuze (ed.) *Negotiations 1972–1990*, New York, NY: Columbia University Press, pp.177–82.

Denzin, N.K and Keller, C.M. (1981) 'Frame Analysis Reconsidered', *Contemporary Sociology*, 10(1): 52–60.

DiMaggio, P.J. and Powell, W.W. (1983) 'The Iron Cage Revisited: Institutional isomorphism and collective rationality in organizational fields', *American Sociological Review*, 48(2): 147–60.

DiMaggio, P.J. and Powell, W.W. (eds) (1991a) *The New Institutionalism in Organizational Analysis*, Chicago: University of Chicago Press.

DiMaggio, P.J. and Powell, W.W. (1991b) 'Introduction', in P.J. DiMaggio and W.W. Powell (eds) *The New Institutionalism in Organizational Analysis*, Chicago: University of Chicago Press, pp.1–38.

Donzelot, J. (1979) *The Policing of Families*, New York, NY: Pantheon Books.

Douglas, M. (1986) *How Institutions Think*, Syracuse: Syracuse University Press.

——(1988 (1966)) *Purity and Danger: An analysis of the concepts of pollution and taboo*, New York, NY: Routledge & Kegan Paul Inc.

——(1994) *Risk and Blame: Essays in cultural theory*, London: Routledge.

Douglas, M. and Wildavsky A. (1997) *Risk and Culture: An essay on the selection of technological and environmental dangers*, California: University of California Press.

Doyle, A. and Ericson, R.V. (eds) (2003) *Risk and Morality*, Toronto: University of Toronto Press.

Drew, P. and Wootton, A. (1988) *Erving Goffman: Exploring the interaction order*, Oxford: Polity Press.

Epstein, L., Chambon, A. and Irving, A. (1999) *Reading Foucault for Social Work*, New York, NY: Columbia University Press.

Ericson, R., Barry, D. and Doyle, A. (2000) 'The Moral Hazards of Neo-Liberalism: Lessons from the private insurance industry', *Economy and Society*, 29(4): 532–58.

Ewald, F. (1991) 'Insurance and Risk', in G. Burchell, C. Gordon and P. Miller (eds) *The Foucault Effect: Studies in governmentality*, Hemel Hempstead: Harvester Wheatsheaf, pp.197–210.

Fleck, L. (1979) *Genesis and Development of a Scientific Fact*, Chicago: Chicago University Press.

Foucault, M. (1977) *Discipline and Punish: The birth of the prison*, London: Allen Lane.

——(1979) *Discipline and Punish*, New York, NY: Vintage Books.

——(1982) 'The Subject and Power', in H. Dreyfus and P. Rabinow (eds) *Michel Foucault: Beyond structuralism and hermeneutics*, New York, NY: Harvester Wheatsheaf, pp.208–26.

——(1990) *The History of Sexuality, Vol. I: An Introduction*, New York, NY: Vintage Books.

——(1994) *The Order of Things: An archaeology of the human sciences*, New York, NY: Vintage Books.

——(2000a) 'Omnes et Singulatim: Toward a critique of political reason', in M. Foucault and J.D. Faubion (ed.) *Power: Essential works of Foucault 1954–1984*, New York, NY: The New Press, pp.298–325.

——(2000b (1978)) 'About the Concept of the 'Dangerous Individual' in 19th-Century Legal Psychiatry', in J.D. Faubion (ed.) *Power: The essential works of Foucault*. New York, NY: The New Press, pp.176–200.

——(2003) *Society Must Be Defended: Lectures at the Collège de France, 1975–1976*, New York, NY: Picador.

——(2007) *Security, Territory, Population*, New York, NY: Palgrave Macmillan.

Fox, K.J. (2001) 'Self-Change and Resistance in Prison', in J.F. Gubrium and J.A. Holstein (eds) *Institutional Selves: Troubled identities in a postmodern world*, Oxford: Oxford University Press, pp.176–92.

Fraser, N. (1997) *Justice Interruptus: Critical reflections on the 'postsocialist' condition*, New York, NY: Routledge.

Garland, D. (2003) 'The Rise of Risk', in A. Doyle and R. Ericson (eds) *Risk and Morality*, Toronto: University of Toronto Press, pp.48–86.

Gartman, D. (2007) 'The Strength of Weak Programs in Cultural Sociology: A critique of Alexander's critique of Bourdieu', *Theory and Society*, 36(5): 381–413.

Gibson, B., Gregory, J. and Robinson, P.G. (2005) 'The Intersection between Systems Theory and Grounded Theory: The emergence of the grounded observer', *Qualitative Sociology Review*, 1(2): 3–21.

Giddens, A. (1991) *Modernity and Self-Identity*, Cambridge: Polity Press.

——(2002) *Runaway World: How globalization is reshaping our lives*, London: Profile Books Ltd.

Goffman, E. (1967) *Interactional Ritual: Essays on face-to-face behavior*, New York, NY: Anchor Books.

——(1970) *Strategic Interaction*, Oxford: Basil Blackwell.

——(1971) *Relations in Public: Microstudies of the public order*, Middlesex: Penguin Books.

——(1972 (1961)) *Encounters: Two studies in the sociology of interaction*, Harmondsworth: Penguin Books.

——(1974a (1961)) *Asylums: Essays on the social situation of mental patients and other inmates*, Middlesex, England: Penguin books.

——(1974b) *Frame Analysis: An essay on the organization of experience*, New York, NY: Harper and Row.

——(1981) 'A Reply to Denzin and Keller', *Contemporary Sociology*, 10(1): 60–8.

——(1983) 'The Interaction Order', *American Sociological Review*, 48(1): 1–17.

——(1990a (1959)) *The Presentation of Self in Everyday Life*, London: Penguin Books.

——(1990b (1963)) *Stigma: Notes on the management of spoiled identity*, Englewood Cliffs, NJ: Prentice-Hall.

Gordon, C. (1991) 'Governmental Rationality: An introduction', in G. Burchell, C. Gordon and P. Miller (eds) *The Foucault Effect: Studies in governmentality*, London: Harvester/Wheatsheaf, pp.1–51.

Greco, M. (1993) 'Psychosomatic Subjects and the 'Duty to be Well': Personal Agency within Medical Rationality', *Economy and Society*, 22(3): 352–72.

——(2004) 'The Politics of Indeterminacy and the Right to Health', *Theory, Culture & Society*, 21(6): 1–22.

Gregersen, O. (1996) *Forandring i socialforvaltningernes organisering*, Ph.D., Copenhagen Business School.

Grenfell, M. (2008) *Pierre Bourdieu: Key Concepts*, Durham: Acumen Publishing.

Gubrium, J.F. (1997 (1975)) *Living and Dying at Murray Manor*. London: University Press of Virginia.

Gubrium, J.F. and Holstein, J.A. (eds) (2001) *Institutional Selves: Troubled Identities in a Postmodern World*, Oxford: Oxford University Press.

Gutting, G. (2005) *Foucault: A Very Short Introduction*, Oxford: Oxford University Press.

Habermas, J. (1987) 'Excursus on Luhmann's appropriation of the philosophy of the subject through systems theory', in J. Habermas (ed.) *The Philosophical Discourse of Modernity*, Cambridge, MA: MIT Press, pp.368–85.

Hacking, I. (1999) *The Social Construction of What?* Cambridge, MA: Harvard University Press.

——(2004) 'Between Michel Foucault and Erving Goffman: Between discourse in the abstract and face-to-face interaction', *Economy and Society*, 33(3): 277–302.

Hardt, M. and Negri, A. (2001) *Empire*, Boston: Harvard University Press.

Heede, T.D. (2011) *Samtalekunst & ledelsesdisciplin*, Ph.D.,Copenhagen: Department of Management, Politics and Philosophy, Copenhagen Business School.

Hoff, V.J. (1881) *Hjemmet*, Copenhagen: Karl Schønbergs Forlag.

Højlund, H. (2009) 'Hybrid Inclusion: The New Consumerism of Danish Welfare Services', *Journal of European Social Policy*, 19(5): 421–31.

Howe, D. (1996) 'Surface and Depth in Social-work Practice', in N. Parton (ed.) *Social Theory, Social Change and Social Work*, London: Routledge, pp.77–97.

Isin, E.F. and Turner, B.S. (2002) *Handbook of Citizenship Studies*, London: Thousand Oaks.

Jakobsen, T.B. (2004) *Legitimitetens logik: Institutionelle dilemmaer i det sociale klagesystem*, Ph.D., Department of Sociology, University of Copenhagen.

Järvinen, M. and Mik-Meyer, N. (2005) 'Observationer i en interaktionistisk begrebsramme', in M. Järvinen and N. Mik-Meyer (eds) *Kvalitative metoder i et interaktionistisk perspektiv*, Copenhagen: Hans Reitzel Publishers.

Jenkins, R. (1992) *Pierre Bourdieu*, London : Routledge.

——(2002) *Pierre Bourdieu (Key Sociologists)*, London: Routledge.

——(2008) 'Erving Goffman: A major theorist of power?', Journal of Power, 1(2): 157–68.

Johansen, K. (1883) *Om Opdragelsen og dens særlige Forhold til Filantropi og Hygiejne*, Kjøbenhavn: Karl Schønbergs Forlag.

Juul, S. (2009) 'Recognition and Judgement in Social Work', *European Journal of Social Work*, 12(4): 403–17.

Karlsen, M.P. and Villadsen, K. (2008) 'Who Should Do the Talking? The proliferation of dialogue as governmental technology', *Culture and Organization*, 14(4): 345–63.

King, A. (2000) 'Thinking with Bourdieu Against Bourdieu: A "Practical" Critique of the Habitus', *Sociological Theory*, 18(3): 418–33.

Kneer, G. and Nassehi, A. (1993) *Luhmann's Theory of Social Systems NIC-read: An introduction*, Munich: Finch.

Lemert, C. and Branaman, A. (2001) *The Goffman Reader*, Oxford: Blackwell Publishers Inc.

Lemke, T. (2001) 'The Birth of Biopolitics: Michel Foucault's lecture at the Collège de France on neo-liberal governmentality', *Economy and Society*, 30(2): 190–207.

Lessenich, S. (2011) 'Constructing the Socialized Self: Mobilization and control in the active society', in U. Bröckling et al. (eds) *Governmentality: Current issues and future challenges*, London: Routledge, pp.304–20.

Levin, C. (1998) *Uppfostringsanstalten: Om tvång i föräldrars ställe*, Lund: Arkiv förlag.

——(2002) *Special Supervisory Homes in Sweden: Paper presented September 12th at the 7th EUSARF Congress 2002 in Trondheim: Revitalising Residential and Foster Care*, Trondheim.

Loseke, D.R. (1999) *Thinking About Social Problems. An introduction to constructionist perspectives*, New York, NY: Aldine de Gruyter.

——(2001) 'Lived Realities and Formula Stories of "Battered Women"', in J.F. Gubrium and J.A. Holstein (eds) *Institutional Selves: Troubled identities in a postmodern world*, Oxford: Oxford University Press, pp.107–26.

Luhmann, N. (1982a (1977)) 'The Differentiation of Society', in N. Luhmann (ed.) *The Differentiation of Society*, New York, NY: Columbia University Press, pp.229–55.

——(1982b (1977)) 'Interaction, Organization and Society', in N. Luhmann (ed.) *The Differentiation of Society*, New York, NY: Columbia University Press, pp. 69–90.

——(1992) 'The Coding of the Legal System', in G. Teubner and A. Febbrajo (eds) *State, Law and Economy as Autopoietic Systems*, Milano: Dott. A. Gufré Editore, pp.145–85.

——(1997) *Die Gesellschaft der Gesellschaft*, Frankfurt am Main: Suhrkamp.

——(1995) *Social Systems*, Stanford: Stanford University Press.

Lupton, D. (1997) 'Foucault and the Medicalisation Critique', in A. Petersen and R. Bunton (eds) *Foucault, Health and Medicine*, New York, NY: Routledge, pp.59–87.

——(1999) (ed.) *Risk and Sociocultural Theory: New directions and perspectives*, Cambridge: Cambridge University Press.

——(2005) *Risk*, London: Routledge.

——(2006) 'Sociology and Risk', in G. Mythen and S. Walklate (eds) *Beyond the Risk Society: Critical reflections on risk and human security*, London: Open University Press, pp.11–24.

Lützen, K. (1998) *Byen tæmmes: Kernefamilie, sociale reformer og velgørenhed i 1800-tallets København*, Copenhagen: Hans Reitzel Publishers.

Maines, D.R. (2003) 'Interactionism's Place', *Symbolic Interaction*, 26(1): 5–18.

March, J.G. and Olsen, J.P. (1989) *Rediscovering Institutions: The organizational basis of politics*, New York: The Free Press.

Martin, J.L. (2003) 'What Is Field Theory?', *American Journal of Sociology*, 109(1): 1–49.

Maturana, H.R. (1981) 'Autopoiesis', in M. Zeleny (ed.) *Autopoiesis: A theory of living organization*, New York, NY: North Holland, pp.21–47.

Mead, G.H. (1967 (1934)) *Mind, Self, & Society from the Standpoint of a Social Behaviorist.* Edited and with an introduction by Charles W. Morris, Chicago: University of Chicago Press.

Merten, R. (ed.) (2000) *Systemtheorien Sozialer Arbeit. Neue Ansätze und veränderte Perspektiven*, Opladen: Leske & Budrich.

Meyer, J.W. and Rowan, B. (1977) 'Institutionalized Organizations: Formal structure as myth and ceremony', *The American Journal of Sociology*, 83(2): 340–63.

Meyer, J.W. and Scott, R. (1983) *Organizational Environments: Ritual and rationality*, Beverly Hills: Sage.

Meyer, J.W., Scott, R. and Deal, T. (1981) 'Institutional and Technical Sources of Organizational Structure: Explaining the structure of educational organizations', in H.D. Stein (ed.) *Organization and the Human Services*, Philadelphia: Temple University Press, pp. 151–79.

Michailakis, D. and Schirmer, W. (2010) 'Agents of Their Health? How the Swedish welfare state introduces expectations of individual responsibility', *Sociology of Health and Illness*, 32(6): 930–47.

Mik-Meyer, N. (2004) *Dømt til personlig udvikling: Identitetsarbejde i revalidering*, Copenhagen: Hans Reitzel Publishers.

——(2006) 'Identities and Organizations. Evaluating the personality traits of clients in two Danish rehabilitation organizations', *Critical Social Studies*, 8(1): 32–48.

——(2007) 'Interpersonal Relations or Jokes of Social Structures? Laughter in social work', *Qualitative Social Work*, 6(1): 9–26.

——(2009) 'Managing Fat Bodies: Identity work between public and private domains', *Critical Social Studies*, 10(2): 20–35.

——(2010a) 'Putting the Right Face on a Wrong Body: An initial interpretation of fat identities in social work organizations', *Qualitative Social Work*, 9(3): 385–405.

——(2010b) 'An Illness of One's Own: Power and the negotiation of identity among social workers, doctors and patients without a bio-medical diagnosis', *Journal of Power*, 3(2): 171–86.

——(2011) 'On Being Credibly Ill: Class and gender in illness', *Health Sociology Review*, 20(1): 28–40.

Mik-Meyer, N. and Obling, A. R. (2012) 'The Negotiation of the Sick Role: General practitioners' classification of patients with medically unexplained symptoms', *Sociology of Health & Illness*, 34(7): 1025–38.

Miller, G. (2001) 'Changing the Subject: Self-construction in brief therapy', in J.F. Gubrium and J.A. Holstein (eds) *Institutional Selves: Troubled identities in a postmodern world*, Oxford: Oxford University Press, pp. 64–83.

Miller, P. and Rose, N. (1992) 'Political Power Beyond the State: Problematics of government', *British Journal of Sociology*, 43(2): 173–206.

Moe, S. (1998) *Den moderne hjelpens sociologi: Velferd i systemteoretisk perspektiv*, Sandness: Apeiros Forlag.

Münch, R. (1992) 'Autopoiesis by Definition', *Cardozo Law Review*, 13(5): 1463–72.

Nassehi, A. (2002) 'Exclusion Individuality or Individualization by Inclusion?', *Soziale Systeme*, 8(1): 124–35.

Novas, C. and Rose, N. (2000) 'Genetic Risk and the Birth of the Somatic Individual', *Economy and Society*, 29(4): 485–513.

O'Malley, P. (1996) 'Risk and Responsibility', in A. Barry, T. Osborne and N. Rose (eds) *Foucault and Political Reason: Liberalism, neo-liberalism and rationalities of government*, London: University College of London Press, pp.189–208.

Philp, M. (1979) 'Notes on the Form of Knowledge in Social Work', *Sociological Review*, 27(1): 83–111.

Pottage, A. (1998) 'Power as an Art of Contingency: Luhmann, Deleuze, Foucault', *Economy and Society*, 27(1): 1–27.

Procacci, G. (1989) 'Sociology and its Poor', *Politics and Society*, 17(2): 163–87.

——(1991) 'Social Economy and the Government of Poverty', in G. Burchell, C. Gordon and P. Miller (eds) *The Foucault Effect*, Chicago: University of Chicago Press, pp.151–68.

Qvortrup, L. (2003) *The Hypercomplex Society*, New York, NY: Peter Lang.

Raffnsøe, S., Gudmand-Høyer, M. and Thaning, M.S. (2010) *Foucault: Studienhandbuch*, Munich: Wilhelm Fink Verlag.

Reay, T. and Hinings, C.R. (2005) 'The Recomposition of an Organizational Field: Health care in Alberta', *Organization Studies*, 26(3): 351–84.

Rose, N. (1996a) 'Governing "Advanced" Liberal Democracies', in A. Barry, T. Osborne and N. Rose (eds.) *Foucault and Political Reason*, London: UCL Press.

——(1996b) 'The Death of the Social?', *Economy and Society*, 25(3): 327–56.

——(1999) *Governing the Soul. The shaping of the private self*, London: Free Association Books.

——(2001) 'The Politics of Life Itself', *Theory, Culture & Society*, 18(6): 1–30.

——(2003) 'The Neurochemical Self and its Anomalies', in A. Doyle and R.V. Ericson (eds) *Risk and Morality*, Toronto: University of Toronto Press, pp.407–37.

——(2004) 'Becoming Neurochemical Selves', in N. Stehr (ed.) *Biotechnology Between Commerce and Civil Society*, New Brunswick, NJ: Transaction Publishers, pp.89–126.

——(2006) 'Disorders Without Borders? The Expanding Scope of Psychiatric Practice', *BioSocieties*, 1: 465–84.

——(2007) *The Politics of Life Itself. Biopower, power, and subjectivity in the twenty-first century*, Princeton: Princeton University Press.

Rose, N. and Miller, P. (1992) 'Political Power beyond the State: Problematics of government', *British Journal of Sociology*, 43(2): 173–205.

Rose, N. and Novas, C. (2005) 'Biological Citizenship', in A. Ong and S. Collier (eds) *Global Assemblages: Technology, politics and ethics as anthropological problems*, Oxford: Blackwell, pp. 439–63.

Saussure, F. (1974 (1916)) *Course in General Linguistics*, London: Fontana.

Scherr, A. (1999) 'Transformations in Social Work: From help towards social inclusion to the management of exclusion', *European Journal of Social Work*, 2(1): 15–25.

Schimank, U. (1996) *Theorien gesellschaftlicher Differenzierung*, Opladen: Leske & Budrich.

Schmidt, L.H. and Kristensen, J.E. (1986) *Lys, luft og renlighed: Den moderne socialhygiejnes fødsel*, Copenhagen: Akademisk Forlag.

Scott, R. (1992) *Organizations: Rational, natural and open systems*, 3rd edn, Englewood Cliffs: Prentice Hall.

Scott, R.W. (2000) *Institutional Change and Healthcare Organizations: From professional dominance to managed care*, Chicago: University of Chicago Press.

Scott, W.R. (2001) *Institutions and Organizations*, Thousand Oaks, CA: Sage.

Seidl, D. and Becker, K.H. (2006) 'Organizations as Distinction Generating and Processing Systems: Niklas Luhmann's contribution to organization studies', *Organization*, 13 (1): 9–35.

——(2005) *Niklas Luhmann and Organization Studies*, Copenhagen: Copenhagen Business School Press.

Smith, D. (1987) *The Everyday World as Problematic: A feministic sociology*, Toronto: University of Toronto Press & Northeastern Press.

Smith, G. (1989) 'Book review of "Erving Goffman: exploring the interactional order"', *Sociological Review*, 37(2): 389–91.

——(2006) *Erving Goffman (Key Sociologists)*, New York, NY: Routledge.

Sosin, M.R. (2009) 'Discretion in Human Service Organizations: Traditional and institutional perspectives', in Y. Hasenfeld (ed.) *Human Service Organizations as Complex Organizations*, New York, NY: Sage, pp.381–404.

Spencer, J.W. (2001) 'Self-Presentation and Organizational Processing in a Human Service Agency', in J.F. Gubrium and J.A. Holstein (eds) *Institutional Selves: Troubled identities in a postmodern world*, Oxford: Oxford University Press, pp.158–75.

Spencer-Brown, G. (1969) *Laws of Form*, London: Allen & Unwin.

Teubner, G. and Hutter, M. (2000) 'Homo Oeconomicus and Homo Juridicus: Communicative fictions', in T. Baums, K.J. Hopt and N. Horn (eds) *Corporation, Capital Markets and Business in the Law*, England: Klüwer Law International, pp.569–89.

Thomas, W.I. and Thomas, D.S. (1928) *The Child in America: Behavior problems and programs*, New York, NY: Knopf.

Thyssen, O. (2009) *Business Ethics and Organizational Values: A systems-theoretical analysis*, Basingstoke: Palgrave Macmillan.

Tulloch, J. and Lupton, D. (2005) *Risk and Everyday Life*, London: Sage.

Valverde, M. (1996) '"Despotism" and Ethical Liberal Governance', *Economy and Society*, 25(3): 357–72.

Villadsen, K. (2007) 'The Emergence of "Neo-Philanthropy": A new discursive space in welfare policy?', *Acta Sociologica*, 3(50): 309–23.

——(2008a) '"Polyphonic" Welfare: Luhmann's systems theory applied to modern social work', *International Journal of Social Welfare*, 17(1): 65–73.

——(2008b) 'Freedom as Self-Transgression: Transformations in the "governmentality" of social work', *European Journal of Social Work*, 2(11): 93–104.

——(2008c) 'Doing without the State and Civil Society as Universals: "Dispositifs" of care across the classic sector divide', *Journal of Civil Society*, 4(3): 171–91.

——(2011a) 'Ambiguous Citizenship: "Modern" and "postmodern" welfare at the margins', *Distinktion: Scandinavian Journal of Social Theory*, 12(3): 309–29.

——(2011b) 'Modern Welfare and "Good Old" Philanthropy: A forgotten or a troubling trajectory?', *Public Management Review*, 13(8): 1057–75.

——(2012) 'Paradoxes of Welfare: Universality, truth, and power in modern welfare provision', in R. Laratta (ed.) *Social Welfare*, Rijeka: Intech, pp.63–89.

Villadsen, K. and Karlsen, M.P. (2012) 'Public Policy and Foucaultian Critique: Towards a happy marriage?', *Review of European Studies*, 4(1): 138–47.

Wacquant, L.J.D. (1998) 'Foreword', in P. Bourdieu (ed.) *The State Nobility: Elite schools in the field of power*, Cambridge: Polity Press, pp.ix–xxii.

——(2001) 'The Rise of Advanced Marginality: Notes on its nature and implications', *Acta Sociologica*, 39: 121–39.

——(2010) *Urban Outcasts. A comparative sociology of advanced marginality*, Cambridge: Polity Press.

Weber, M. (1946) 'Science as a Vocation', in H.H. Gerth and C. Wright Mills (eds) *From Max Weber: Essays in sociology*, New York, NY: Oxford University Press, pp.129–56.

——(1947 (1922)) *The Theory of Social and Economic Organization*, New York, NY: Oxford University Press.

——(1968 (1922)) *Economy and Society: An outline of interpretive sociology*, vol. 3, edited by G. Roth & C. Wittich, New York, NY: Bedminster Press.

Willke, H. (1997) *Supervision des Staates*, Frankfurt: Suhrkamp.

Wirth, J.V. (2009) 'The Function of Social Work', *Journal of Social Work*, 9(4): 405–19.

Young, I.M. (1990) *Justice and Politics of Difference*, Princeton: Princeton University Press.

Index

Notes are indicated by suffix 'n' followed by [chapter number] then note number (e.g. "145n[3]1" means page 145, chapter 3 note 1)

adaptation modes 33
advanced liberalism 3–5
"advanced marginality" [Wacquant's term] 62, 65
agency–structure dichotomy 49
agency–structure interrelationship 55
Alexander, J.C. 135
American ghettos: compared with French *banlieues* 62–3, 64–5; factors affecting 64
analytical approaches 7–9; Bourdieu 8, 52–6; Foucault 8, 10–17; Goffman 8, 29–35; Luhmann 68–72
Andersen, N.Å. 15, 68, 71, 72, 74, 75, 80, 138, 139
Aradau, C. 15
Arnoldi, J. 107, 142, 144
Ashworth, R. 94, 141
Australian unemployment insurance system: reforms 23–7
autopoesis concept 69, 71

Baecker, D. 67
banlieues 62, 64–5; *see also* ghetto(s)
Bärens, J.H. 18
Barry, D. 115
Battershill, C.D. 129
Bauman, Z. 4, 108, 112, 113
Beck, U. 107, 108, 109, 110, 117, 142, 146n[7]3
Beck-Gernsheim, E. 121
Becker, K.H. 67, 73
Berger, P. 90
Besley, T. 14
binary codes 71, 73
biopolitics 10, 115
Blaikie, A. 117
Blumer, H. 30
Borch, C. 67, 139
Bourdieu, Pierre 48–66; analytical concepts 52–6; "capital" concept 53–4; cited 48, 49, 50, 51, 52, 53, 54, 55, 57, 62; compared with Foucault 49; compared with Goffman 49, 134; "doxa" concept 8, 55, 57, 59, 65, 135; on education 48–9, 50; example cases 56–65; "field" theory 52–3, 135, 140; "habitus" concept 51, 54–5, 58, 136; health policy case 56–61; and neo-institutional theory 140; poverty studies in USA and France 62–5; on power and governance in institutions 49–52; on reproduction processes 48; "symbolic violence" concept 8, 51, 55–6, 58–61, 65, 66
Boyne, G. 94
Branaman, A. 29, 31, 34, 129, 145n[3]2
Bröckling, U. 10
Brousselle, A. 87
Brunsson, N. 95
Burns, T. 29

"capital" [Bourdieu's concept] 53–4
central government: conflict of interest with local institutions 2, 5–7
Chamberlin, C. 91
Chamberlin, L. 91
Chicago ghetto studies 62
Chicago School [of sociology] 30
Clarke, J. 2, 5
clinical interview 20, 21
coercive isomorphism 92–3

Collier, S. 16
communicative differentiation: Luhmann's theory 70
communicative systems 71, 72; welfare organisations as 72–4
"confession" 20–1
"constrained dialogue" 111
constructivist-inspired risk analysis 108, 117, 142, 144
Contandriopoulos, D. 87
Cooney, K. 87
Coveney: J. 14
Crook, S. 131
Cruikshank, B. 4
cultural capital [Bourdieu] 53
cultural theory of risk [Douglas] 108, 111; and exclusion mechanisms 113; linked with governmentality-inspired analysis 108, 109

Danish philanthropists [19th C.] 22
Deal, T. 96
Dean, M. 1, 3, 10, 15, 17, 19, 23, 24, 25, 26, 27, 108, 115, 144
decoupling [neo-institutional concept] 95–6, 141; in welfare organisations 101, 104, 105
"definition of the situation" [Goffman's concept] 35
Delbridge, R. 94
Deleuze, G. 17, 128
Denmark: health policy as tool of state ideology 56–61; homeless shelters and housing support 76–82; rehabilitation centres 42–5; social welfare appeals system 102–5
Denzin, N.K. 133
differentiation of society 68, 70–2, 137
DiMaggio, P.J. 87, 89, 92, 93
discipline: as technology of power 16, 27
discursive determinism 127, 128
domination 49–50, 55; state-initiated 58, 64, 66
Donzelot, J. 15, 19, 21, 22
Douglas, M. 107, 108, 109, 110, 111, 112, 113, 114, 116, 117, 119, 120, 123, 142, 143, 144
Down's syndrome: choices during pregnancy 122
"doxa" [Bourdieu's concept] 8, 55, 135; in health case 57, 59, 65
Doyle, A. 107, 110, 115, 142
Drew, P. 132

Eccleston, R. 122
economic capital [Bourdieu] 53
education system: Bourdieu on 48–9, 50
enunciation regimes 17
Epstein, L. 14
Ericson, R. 115, 116
Ericson, R.V. 107, 110, 142
ethnographic institutional analysis: nursing home 39–42; social appeals system 102–3
Ewald, F. 15, 108, 124
exclusion management 84; social work as 85
exclusion mechanisms 112–13

"face-work" [Goffman's concept] 35, 95
"field" [Bourdieu's concept] 52
field analysis 52–3, 136; health field 58
field theory [Bourdieu] 52–3, 135, 140; criticisms 135–6
fieldwork: in Bourdieu-inspired analyses 63, 64; Goffman's and Gubrium's use 39, 40
Fleck, L. 109, 111
"forming analysis" 74–5
Foucault, Michel 10–28; advantages of [his] analytics 28; cited 7, 10, 11, 12, 13, 16, 24, 125, 126, 129; compared with Bourdieu 49; compared with Goffman 128–30; compared with Luhmann 139; on discipline 16; example cases 17–27; on genealogy 14–15, 140; on "imperative discourse" 125–6; on modern forms of power 12–14; and neo-institutional theory 140, 141; philanthropy examples 17–23; on power–knowledge connection 13–14, 28; on power in liberal state 10–12, 126–7; on power technologies 8, 15–17; on problematisations 24–5, 127; self-government of unemployed people case 23–7; weaknesses of [his] analytics 127–8
Fox, K.J. 6, 39
frame analysis concept [Goffman] 8, 30, 133
Fraser, N. 125
French welfare state 145n[4]1
function system(s) 71, 72; social work as 83–4

Garland, D. 114, 124
Gartman, D. 135

genealogical analysis 15–17;
philanthropy as power technology 17–23
genealogy 14–15
ghetto(s): American compared with French 62–3, 64–5; Wacquant on 63; *see also banlieues*
Gibson, B. 68, 71
Giddens, A. 4, 108
Goffman, Erving 29–47; cited 29, 30, 31, 32, 33, 34, 35, 36, 37, 38, 39, 40, 44, 46, 131, 132, 133, 145n[3]1; compared with Bourdieu 49, 134; compared with Foucault 128–30; compared with neo-institutional theory 140; criticisms 132–4; example cases 38–9, 39–45; interactional approach 29–35, 45, 130, 140; "looping effects" concept 130; nursing home case 38–9, 39–42; on power and control in institutions 33, 35–9; rehabilitation centre case 39, 42–5; ritual metaphor 34–5, 131; on social interactions 29–35, 45; theatrical metaphors 33–4, 131, 145n[3]1
"good face" [Goffman's concept] 35, 37, 95
Gordon, C. 6
governmental–ethical practices 24
governmentality 10–11; example case 23–7
governmentality-inspired risk analysis 108, 113–14, 142, 143, 144; linked with cultural approach 108, 109; pregnancy study 120–2
Greco, M. 57, 114, 117
Gregersen, O. 94, 98
Grenfell, M. 48
Gubrium, J.F. 2, 3, 6, 38, 39, 40, 41, 42
Gutting, G. 10

Habermas, J. 138
"habitus" [Bourdieu's concept] 51, 54–5, 136; in health field 58
Hacking, I. 130
Hardt, M. 128
health field: state power and 56–7
Heede, T.D. 20
help programmes: interventionist distinction and 73–4
Hinings, C.R. 97
historiography: genealogical approach 14–15
Hoff, V.J. 22
Højlund, H. 68, 137, 138
holistic evaluation of social work: in social appeals system 104
Holstein, J.A. 2, 3, 6, 39
home visits [in philanthropic poor relief] 19, 20
homeless people: description in action plans 80–2; systems theory to describe social work 76–82, 137
homeless shelters [in Denmark] 77, 145n[5]1; relationship with municipal housing support units 80–1; self-descriptions 77–8, 79–80, 82; staff 77–8, 79–80
Howe, D. 3, 4, 5
Hutter, M. 70

identity/identification [role] 34
"illusio" [Bourdieu's term] 93, 134
"imperative discourse" [Foucault] 125–6
incomplete knowledge: risk perceptions based on 110
indeterminacy concept 117
individualising processes/techniques 4, 11–12, 111, 118
individuals: accountability for actions 111, 112
industrialisation [late 19th C.]: social predicaments 18–19
institutional environments: compared with technical environments 91
institutional ethnography 102; coupled with neo-institutional organisation theory 102, 103; in nursing home case 39–42; in social appeals system case 102–3
institutionalisation: Meyer and Rowan's definition 90–1; of organisational norms 88
insurance companies 115–16
interaction: as analytical strategy 29–35, 45
interaction order 35
interactional approach [Goffman] 29–35, 130–2; weaknesses 132–4
interactionist studies 30, 35, 38, 47
"irritations" from environment [in systems theory]: organisational inputs as 70, 72, 76, 137
Isin, E.F. 125
isomorphism 92, 141; types 92–3

Jakobsen, T.B. 97, 102, 103, 104, 105, 145n[6]3
Järvinen, M. 35

Jenkins, R. 48, 130, 131, 133, 134, 135
"job-readiness" [in unemployment system] 26
Johansen, K. 22
judicial communication 71–2
Juul, S. 125

Karlsen, M.P. 1, 6, 12, 15
Keller, C.M. 133
King, A. 134
Kneer, G. 67
knowledge: power and 13–14, 28
Krasmann, S. 10
Kristensen, J.E. 21

law: as technology of power 16, 27
legal positivism 103
legal system: on individuals' accountability 112
legitimacy of organisations: factors affecting 90, 92, 94, 96; importance for their survival 89, 105; reformatory example 100; social appeals system example 102, 105
Lemert, C. 29
Lemke, T. 10, 115
Lessenich, S. 4
Levin, C. 89, 95, 96, 97, 98, 99, 100, 101, 102, 145n[6]1
lifestyle risks 119
Loseke, D.R. 6, 39, 43
Luckmann, T. 90
Luhmann, Niklas 67–86; cited 67, 68, 69, 70, 71, 72, 73, 75, 138; communicative differentiation theory 70; communicative systems 72; compared with Foucault 139; compared with neo-institutional theory 140; criticisms 138; empirical applications 138–9; function systems 71; "structural coupling" concept 73; systems theory 67, 68, 69, 136, 137, 140
Lupton, D. 107, 108, 113, 114, 116, 117, 120, 121, 122, 123, 128, 143, 144, 146n[7]1
Lützen, K. 18

Maines, D.R. 36, 132
March, J.G. 91
Martin, J.L. 135, 136
Marxian analysis: Bourdieu on 49
Maturana, H.R. 69
Mead, G.H. 31
media: Bourdieu on 51–2
"membership rules" for organisations [Luhmann] 75
Merten, R. 69
Meyer, J.W. 87, 90, 91, 93, 95, 96
Michailakis, D. 3, 6, 45
micro–macro dichotomy [in Bourdieuian sociology] 49
Mik-Meyer, N. 2, 3, 4, 5, 6, 7, 8, 35, 37, 39, 42, 43, 45, 56, 58, 59, 116, 118, 119, 120, 134
Miller, G. 4, 39
Miller, P. 25, 28, 115, 116
mimetic isomorphism 93
"misrecognition" [Bourdieu's concept] 55
"misrepresentation": Goffman's use of term 37–8
modern differentiated society 69, 70–2, 83
Moe, S. 73, 74, 137
moral cohesion of society 22
morality: risk perceptions and 110
Münch, R. 138
municipal housing support units [in Denmark] 78–9; relationship with homeless shelters 80–1; self-descriptions 78–9, 82
Munster, R.V. 15

Nassehi, A. 67
Negri, A. 128
neo-institutional organisation theory 87–106; analytical methods used 97–8, 102; background 87–9, 139–40; case studies 97, 98–105; compared with other approaches [Bourdieu/Foucault/Goffman/Luhmann] 140; coupled with institutional ethnography 102, 103; decoupling concept 95–6, 141; reformatory case study 97, 98–102, 140–1; sources of theoretical inspiration 89–92; weaknesses 141; welfare appeals system case 97, 102–5; in welfare organisations 96–8, 101–2, 105–6, 140–1
neo-liberal governance 1, 143; and risk 108, 109; and traditional approach 6
neo-liberalism 3–4; basic principles 115; and power 6
New Public Management (NPM) 2
Newman, J. 2, 5
normalisation concept 116, 124
normality/deviance 112–13, 116, 118, 122, 144

"normative critique" 125
normative isomorphism 93
Novas, C. 57, 113, 114, 118, 143
nursing home: ethnographic institutional study 39–42

objective structures [Bourdieu's terminology] 49; in health field 56, 57, 60, 66
observation: act of 68, 71
official view of institution/organisation 40–1
Olsen, J.P. 91, 95
O'Malley, P. 142
"organisational elements" 88, 140
"organisational fields" 92, 93
organisational isomorphism [DiMaggio and Powell's concept] 92–5
organisations: neo-institutional theory view 89–90
overweight people: in Denmark 56; meeting with health consultant(s) 59–61; risk perspectives 65–6, 110, 113, 118–20, 143; state-initiated domination and 58, 60–1, 66; "thought styles" 119–20

Passeron, J.C. 48, 51
pastoral leadership 11–12
"people-treating" organisations [Levin's term] 101; neo-institutional approach 101–2; *see also* welfare organisations
philanthropy: as power technology 17–23; strategy of power 21–3; strategy of subjectification 20–1; visibility domains 19–20
Philp, M. 21, 84
physical location: impact of various "worlds" 40
politics: risk perceptions and 110
polycontextual society 69, 72
Poor Law Amendment Act [1834, aka "New Poor Law"] 19
poor relief: compared with welfare state 23
Pottage, A. 139
poverty in USA and France: Bourdieu-inspired studies 62–5
Powell, W.W. 87, 89, 92, 93
power: Foucault's approach 8, 10–12, 117, 143; Goffman's approach 36–7; and risk 117–18
power imbalances: in nursing home 41–2
power technologies 8, 15–17
pregnancy: examinations and tests 121, 122; risk and 120–2
presentation of self [Goffman's concept] 37
private insurance companies 115–16
problematisations 24–5, 127
Procacci, G. 19, 20, 22
productiveness of power 11

Qvortrup, L. 72

Raffnsøe, S. 15, 16, 17
rationality myths [in neo-institutional organisation theory] 87–8, 90, 93; "legal rights" as 102
reality-oriented (RO) therapy 41–2, 46
Reay, T. 97
recognition games 93, 134
reformatory: case study 98–102; history 98–9; meaning of term 98, 145n[6]2; medical-rational treatment approach 99; negative results 101; neo-institutional approach 101–2, 140–1; pedagogic approach 99; punishment–rehabilitation combination 99; socio-political approach 99–100
rehabilitation centre: client roles and institutional identities 42–5
reproduction processes: Bourdieu on 48, 134–5
risk analysis: constructivist-inspired 108, 117, 142, 144; limitations 144; starting point for 120
risk culture [Douglas' concept] 109
risk identities 113, 116
risk perceptions 110, 115; experts' 117
risk profiles 116; health and 113–14, 117; overweight people 112–13, 116, 119, 124
risk society: science and technology affecting 108; society as 108
risk technology: reforms of unemployment system as example 23–4
risk theory 107–24; combined with other approaches 141; compared with other approaches 140; culturally based 109, 142, 144; governmentality-inspired 108, 113–14, 142, 143, 144; literature on 107, 142; overweight people case 118–20, 143; pregnancy case 120–2
ritual metaphors 34–5, 131, 145n[3]1

Roelsgaard Obling, A. 5, 8
role play 32
Rose, N. 3, 4, 25, 28, 57, 113, 114, 115, 116, 118, 143
Rowan, B. 90, 91, 93, 95

Saussure, F. 53
Scherr, A. 67, 84, 85, 138
Schimank, U. 70
Schirmer, W. 3, 6, 45
Schmidt, L.H. 21
science and technology: risk society created by 108
Scott, R. 87, 96, 97
Scott, R.W. 87
Scott, W.R. 87
security: as technology of power 16
segmented society 83
Seidl, D. 67, 73
"self": Douglas' views 111–12; Goffman's views 31, 46, 145n[3]2
self-descriptions of organisations 72, 73; homeless shelters 77–8, 79–80, 82; municipal housing support units 78–9, 82
self-government 24; ethical substance and 25, 26; four dimensions 25–7; means of governance and 25, 26–7; mode of subjectification and 25, 27; telos and 25, 27
semantic analysis 75
Smith, D. 102
Smith, G. 29, 132
social appeals system [in Denmark]: analysis 102–5; holistic evaluation of social work 104; requirement for administrative efficiency 103–4; "uniformity before the law" considerations 104
social capital [Bourdieu] 53
social fields [Bourdieu] 52–3, 93
social order [Goffman] 35, 38
social systems [Luhmann]: binary codes and 71; modern society as series of 68, 69; systems theory for observing 71
social work: effect of neo-liberal values 4; as exclusion management 85; as function system 83–4; and individuals' integration into society's function systems 84; role in modern society 82–5, 86
socialisation: factors affecting 51
"somatic individual" [in risk theory] 113, 118, 124, 143
Sosin, M.R. 87
sovereign state power 1–2
Spencer, J.W. 39
Spencer-Brown, G. 69, 71
state: as centre of power 50–1
stigma: Goffman's views 32
"strategic interaction" 37
strategy: socially based 30–1
strategy of power 17; in philanthropy 21–3
strategy of subjectification 17; in philanthropy 20–1
stratified societies 83
structural-based analysis: Goffman's frame analysis as 133–4
"structural coupling" [Luhmann's concept] 73
subjectification 17, 25
symbolic capital [Bourdieu] 53, 93
symbolic interactionism 30, 35, 36, 46, 47, 131
"symbolic violence" [Bourdieu's concept] 51, 55–6, 66, 134, 135; and health 58–61, 65
system/environment analysis 74, 85
systems analysis 74, 77
systems theory 68–9, 136–7; analytical strategies applicable for organisational analysis 74; homeless people case 76–82; role of social work in modern society 82–5; specifying object of analyses 74–5; use in social work 67–8, 76–85; welfare organisations as communicative systems 72–4

Taylor, L. 131
technical environments: compared with institutional environments 91
technologies of power 8, 15–17; analytical approaches 17
telos [ultimate goal] 26, 27
Teubner, G. 70
theatrical metaphors 33–4, 38, 43–4, 46, 131, 145n[3]1
therapeutic establishments: advice/care/guidance from 116, 123
therapeutic model 112
Thomas, D.S. 30
Thomas theorem 30
Thomas, W.I. 30
"thought styles" 111, 112; overweight people 119–20, 123; shift in predominant 115, 116, 143

tribal societies: anthropological studies 110
Tulloch, J. 117
Turner, B.S. 125
Tvind schools 91

unemployed people: self-government of 23–7
"uniformity before the law" considerations [in social appeals system] 104
Uppfostringsanstalten: meaning of term 145n[6]2
"urban outcasts" [Wacquant's term] 62

Valverde, M. 1
Villadsen, K. 1, 2, 3, 4, 5, 6, 7, 8, 12, 14, 15, 17, 19, 20, 21, 25, 45, 68, 75, 76, 77, 138, 145n[5]1
visibility: effect of self-government programmes 26
visibility domains 17; in philanthropy 19–20
"visitor of the poor" 20–1

Wacquant, L.J.D.: "advanced marginality" concept 62, 65; cited 51, 52, 53, 54, 55, 57, 62, 63, 64, 65; "urban outcasts" studies 62–5
Weber, Max 56, 69, 70; cited 70
welfare appeals system [in Denmark] 102–5
welfare organisations: as communicative systems [Luhmann] 72–4; complexity 6–7; neo-institutional approach 96–8, 101–2, 105–6, 140–1; roles of people in communication 75–6, 77
welfare state: compared with [19th C.] poor relief 23; contrast with neo-liberal state 143; as risk-management system 108, 115
Wildavsky, A. 108, 111
Willke, H. 69
Wirth, J.V. 67, 83, 84
Wootton, A. 132
"wrong face" [Goffman's concept] 35, 37, 38

Young, I.M. 125

20938452R00099

Printed in Great Britain
by Amazon